The reduction of working time

Scope and implications in industrialised market economies

ROLANDE CUVILLIER

International Labour Office   Geneva

ISBN 92-2-102702-3 (limp cover)
ISBN 92-2-103817-3 (hard cover)

First published 1984

Originally published in French under the title: *Vers la réduction du temps de travail? Incidences possibles dans les pays industrialisés à économie de marché* (ISBN 92-2-202702-7)

Printed in the United Kingdom

2273638

CONTENTS

INTRODUCTION

1

This study deals with the economic and social effects of a possible reduction in working time in the industrialised market economy countries, where this subject is at present widely discussed. The labour movement is calling for a reduction in working time to be achieved by a variety of means: a higher leaving age for compulsory schooling; shorter normal working time without loss of earnings; reduction in, and control of, overtime; longer paid annual leave; more paid leave for the purposes of education, training, retraining and trade union activities; and a lower normal retirement age without reduction in pension. The 35-hour working week is a central objective of many workers' organisations, although the relative priority or importance attached to it varies according to national attitudes and to the trade union movements concerned.[1]

For reasons of space, this book deals only with the possible effects of measures taken to reduce working time in the following ways: reduction in normal and maximum working time (including overtime), extension of paid annual leave, and shortening of working life by lowering the normal retirement age; the measures taken to achieve these aims may be of a legislative, administrative, contractual or other nature. The other ways of reducing working time already mentioned — raising the leaving age for compulsory schooling and extension of paid educational leave — should not be lost from sight and will be mentioned, but only in passing since they raise issues that are largely distinct from the central problems of reducing working time. To analyse them here would have meant raising such far-reaching and complex issues as the co-ordination of policy regarding education, training and employment. Moreover, they do not really have a prominent place in current discussions about reducing working time.

The above-mentioned calls for a reduction in working time have several objectives: wider opportunities for rest and relaxation, with all the beneficial effects these may have on the physical and mental health, personal satisfaction and well-being of workers in various respects, including in relation to their job; increase in leisure, enabling workers to participate more fully in family life and in recreational, educational and cultural activities, and to play a more active role in their trade unions and in society in general; workers' participation in the fruits of technical and economic progress; and finally, with the emphasis

1

varying as between national trade union programmes, a contribution to the absorption of unemployment. With regard to this last point, major importance is attached to the division or redistribution of work among a larger number of workers, not only as a means of countering the effects of the current depression and the adverse present and future effects of technological developments on employment, but also in the context of continuing economic growth; the reduction of working time is expected to contribute in various ways to stimulating the economy and employment. With regard to lowering "retirement age", the issue really concerns lowering the age at which a worker is entitled to retire on full pension. In this sense, the "retirement age" does not necessarily coincide with cessation of employment, if the pensioner wishes to go on working. In this connection, such expressions as "active retirement" or "optional employment" after retirement are more and more frequently heard.

The above-mentioned demands have created a number of misunderstandings and given rise to a great deal of controversy. Among employers, there has been particularly clear-cut hostility to some of them, most specifically to a reduction in the normal weekly hours of work. Studies carried out on behalf of employers have sought to show that if these demands were met the effects would be counter-productive.[2] Studies of the question by specialists are being published in increasing numbers, and interest in it is constantly growing. Governments have adopted a generally cautious attitude, either individually or within the framework of the European Communities:[3] they are considering whether it is desirable to give first priority in social policy to such a far-reaching reform at a time when there are serious economic difficulties, and wondering what the economic and social effects would be if they did so. Clearly, the stakes are high if the aims to be achieved through these reforms comprise a reduction in unemployment, since there are already millions of unemployed in the industrialised countries concerned and it is to be feared that the situation will continue to worsen in future. In this connection the Parliamentary Assembly of the Council of Europe has set out the principle that States should undertake —

to give consideration, where possible, in the context of a policy for leisure and cultural development, to reducing the number of those seeking work by increasing the length of the annual holiday entitlement, and reducing the length of the working day and the working week.[4]

In the ILO a reduction in working time has long been recognised as a factor in social progress. Under the International Programme for the Improvement of Working Conditions and Environment (PIACT) particular weight is attached to the excessive hours of work in certain sectors and to the need for protection of specific categories of workers, and provides that the various aspects of reduction of hours of work, whose beneficial nature from the social point of view is obvious, must also be studied from the point of view of employment creation.[5] In 1976 the International Labour Conference recalled that the improvement of working conditions and environment must be pursued in times of economic recession as well as in times of economic upturn.[6]

More recently, in 1979, the Third European Regional Conference of the ILO underlined that the progressive reduction of working time should continue to be considered as an important objective in national policies and collective bargaining.[7] In addition, the Conference recognised the need to eliminate any adverse effects on employment arising from the application of new technologies, and therefore called for the adoption of appropriate measures, taking into account such possibilities as the reduction of working time in all its different forms and the improvement of retraining facilities and of income maintenance during the period of retraining. It also called for the ratification and implementation of the Employment Policy Convention, 1964 (No. 122), and the application of the Employment Policy Recommendation, 1964 (No. 122).[8] It may be recalled that the latter instrument (Part III, Paragraph 20 (2) (*a*), (*b*), and (*c*)), includes, among the selective methods to be used to deal with employment problems, reduction of hours of work without a decrease in wages, longer paid holidays and later entry into the labour force, combined with more advanced education and training.

The Council of Europe,[9] the Commission of the European Communities[10] and the ILO[11] are also all in favour of granting older workers the triple possibility of voluntary early retirement with the assurance of as satisfactory remuneration as possible; a gradual transition from ordinary working life to retirement or optional employment; and the maintenance of rights already acquired or in course of acquisition if the pensioner continues in paid employment. At its 66th Session the International Labour Conference adopted the Older Workers Recommendation, 1980. This instrument sets out a selective policy on behalf of older workers, including measures in the field of working time and annual leave, and provisions facilitating gradual transition from working life to retirement.[12]

As has always happened when the question of reducing working time has been raised in the past, the possibility of reductions accompanied by lowering of earnings is still brought up in discussion. However, it should not be forgotten that, historically, the aim of reducing working time as defined in international labour standards implies no reduction in earnings. Thus, the Forty-Hour Week Convention, 1935 (No. 47), states in Article 1 (*a*) that the principle of reduction in working time is to be applied in such a manner that the standard of living is not reduced in consequence. This is reiterated in the Reduction of Hours of Work Recommendation, 1962 (No. 116), which provided in Part I, Paragraphs 4 and 5, as a social standard to be attained, that hours of work should be progressively reduced, where appropriate, without any reduction in the wages of the workers as at the time hours of work are reduced. Similarly, as has been already noted, the Employment Policy Recommendation, 1964 (No. 122), calls for reduction of hours of work without a decrease in wages. The principle of non-reduction of wages means that when the normal weekly hours of work are reduced the weekly wage or, for hourly-paid workers, the previous normal weekly earnings, should not be reduced. Most of the reductions in working time proposed at present would bring weekly hours to under 40. However, it should not be forgotten that a standard is nothing more than a minimum level of protection. It lays down a minimum number of weekly or daily hours of work that should not normally be exceeded or a minimum number of days of annual leave to be granted. In principle, such a standard should not stand in the way of provisions that are more favourable than the minimum protection it provides.

The proposal to lower the normal retirement age does not necessarily mean there would be no reduction in living standards, because a retirement pension usually represents only a fraction of previous earnings. But the idea underlying many proposals in this regard is the same as with reduction in working time. It is proposed that the pension entitlement at full rate at a certain age should be acquired at a lower age, without decrease in the amount. This is not the same as early retirement, which implies an actuarial reduction in the pension.

Reduction in working time accompanied by a reduction in wages raises quite different problems from the social objective of reduction in working time as such, and it falls outside the scope of the present study. Such reduced hours of work correspond to partial unemployment when they are obligatory and to part-time employment when they are voluntary. This is how they are shown in employment and unemployment statistics, when such information can be distinguished — which is rarely the case. (Division of one job into two is also left out of account here, since it is merely a matter of combining two half-time jobs.) The fact that these two kinds of employment are not considered here should not be taken as meaning that they are not worthy of examination, for their own sake and in their effects: on the contrary. At present they are used as methods to regulate the labour market and make it more flexible. Partial unemployment has saved hundreds of thousands of workers from total unemployment in the countries dealt with here, and is still doing so, while part-time employment is apparently growing as a result of spontaneous demand. These issues will be mentioned later in connection with current controversies and the various options envisaged in the discussions now going on.

The examination of possible effects of a reduction in working time, which is the central theme of the present study, must necessarily be of a rather theoretical nature, for various reasons. In the first place, before considering possible or probable effects, we need to know what kind of reductions are being proposed: what form would they take and what would be their scope? Over how long a period would they be introduced? What other measures would accompany them? What would be the economic policy framework in which they would operate? Secondly, past experience is not necessarily a sure guide. History does not repeat itself, and the economic, social and political context has greatly changed during the past few decades. Working time is not as long as it was in the past, average living standards are noticeably higher and social transfers have increased in scale in the countries concerned. Thirdly, it is not feasible to examine the effects of a possible reduction in working time without taking into account the general economic context, which it is difficult to forecast, particularly as regards the possible consequences of the cut-throat competition among industrialised countries and between them and the developing countries, and also the effects of technological developments taking place at increasing speed and in unforeseen ways. Moreover, economic thinking is somewhat at a loss today in the face of the current depression and the prospect of even worse unemployment, and many previously accepted economic theories are increasingly being called in question. Finally, it is difficult to make generalisations, because the point of departure differs from one country to another and national characteristics are not the same. Thus on many issues the present study will put forward more questions than answers.

In the remainder of this book, Chapter 2 deals with the size of the reductions in working time that are being asked for. Claims in this regard are compared with what exists, so as to give an idea of the scope of the reductions that would take place if these claims were met. Chapter 3 concerns the objectives aimed at and the results expected by people who favour reductions in working time. Chapter 4 summarises the discussions and controversies to which reduction in working time has recently given rise, with a backward look at the controversies that took place on the same subject at an earlier stage. The next three chapters review the possible effects of various means of reducing working time, on the basis of research already carried out or in progress at the time of writing of the French original (end of the 1970s), together with other information then available. These surveys relate to three levels: the individual (Chapter 5); the undertaking (Chapter 6); and the community (Chapter 7). By progressively widening the approach, it is intended to give as complete a picture as possible of the effects to be expected, without paying too much attention to the conventional distinction between "economic" and "social" effects. The same effect can be economic or social, depending on the point of view from which it is considered. Changes in individual behaviour and ways of life that may derive from reductions in working time may have repercussions on income, production, consumption and other economic variables, while economic factors are affected by possible reductions in working time in ways that may be either advantageous or disadvantageous to society. The last chapter will put forward certain conclusions.

The author wishes to express her thanks to all her colleagues who have helped her with their comments.

Notes

[1] See European Trade Union Confederation (ETUC): *Supplement to report on activities, 1976-1978*, 3rd Statutory Congress, Munich, 1979 (Brussels, ETUC, n.d.), "Programme of the European Trade Union Confederation regarding the reduction of working hours", p. 48; idem: *Action programme, general resolution and specific resolutions, 1979-1982*, approved by the 3rd Statutory Congress, Munich, 1979 (Brussels, ETUC, n.d.), I: "Full employment planning", p. 8, and IV: "Programme for the improvement of working conditions", p. 18; European Trade Union Institute: *La réduction du temps de travail en Europe occidentale*, première partie: *Analyse des conséquences économiques et sociales* (May, 1980) (Brussels, Euro-Inst.); International Confederation of Free Trade Unions (ICFTU): *The right to a job: Trade union policies in a changing world*, Agenda item 9, Twelfth World Congress, Madrid, 19-23 November, 1979, mimeographed document 12/GA/9 prepared at the request of the ICFTU Executive Board and submitted to the Congress, para. 26.

[2] See, for example, the description of the attitude of the Union of Industries of the European Community by its President, J. J. Oechslin: "Les réserves du patronat européen sur une réduction de la durée du travail", in *Intersocial* (Paris, Bureau des liaisons sociales), No. 48, Apr. 1979, pp. 29-30; Comité de liaison d'employeurs (CLE, Brussels): *La répartition du travail: position du comité de liaison d'employeurs* (6 Apr. 1978); Union internationale chrétienne des dirigeants d'entreprise (UNIAPAC): *Réduire le temps de travail?* Opinions of European managers and parliamentarians expressed at a symposium in March 1980 (Brussels, UNIAPAC-Europe, 1980). See also: "Suicide à la française: durée du travail et compétitivité", in *Inventaires* (Paris, Union des industries métallurgiques et minières), No. 5, June 1979, pp. 4-5; "Shorter working in Europe: More jobs or more problems?", in *Information Bulletin* (Geneva, International Organisation of Employers), Sep. 1979; "Non la réduction de la durée du travail", in *Fabrimétal* (Brussels, Fédération de l'industrie des fabrications métallurgiques, mécaniques, électriques et de la transformation des matières plastiques), Feb. 1978, pp. 11-13; "Employer's statement on short working hours" (Sweden), in *Social and Labour Bulletin* (Geneva, ILO), 1/79, pp. 33-34; "Le 'catalogue des tabous' du patronat allemand", in *Intersocial*, No. 46, Feb. 1979, pp. 25-27; Heinz Allenspach: "Quelques réflexions sur

la réduction du temps de travail", in *Le mois économique et financier* (Basle, Société de Banque Suisse), 1980/3, pp. 10-11; "Durée du travail en Europe", in *Journal des associations patronales* (Zurich), No. 19-20, 8 May 1980; Confederation of Australian Industry, National Employers' Industrial Council: *Will a reduction in hours of work bring back full employment? We say No!* (information leaflet).

[3] See, among more recent publications, Commission of the European Communities: *Communication from the Commission to the Council on Work-sharing*, doc. COM (79) 188 final (Brussels, 7 May 1979); *Bulletin of European Communities* (Brussels), 1979, No. 5, paras. 2.1.48-2.1.53, pp. 45-46; ibid., 1979, No. 11, "Reorganisation of working time", para. 2-1-41, pp. 42-43. The question has also been studied by the Organisation for Economic Co-operation and Development; see Organisation de Coordination et de Développement Economiques, Comité de la main-d'œuvre et des affaires sociales: *Le partage du travail: possibilités d'action et d'évaluation* (doc. MAS (79) 30), and idem: *L'évolution de l'offre de main-d'œuvre, les contraintes de la croissance et le partage du travail* (doc. MAS (80) 10).

[4] "Principles which should appear in a convention on the protection of workers against the effects of unemployment", appendix to Recommendation 804 (1977) on the protection of workers against the effects of unemployment, adopted by the Parliamentary Assembly of the Council of Europe at its 28th Ordinary Session, 24-27 January 1977.

[5] ILO: *International programme for the improvement of working conditions and environment*, Governing Body, 200th Session, May-June 1976, doc. GB.200/PFA/10/8, para. 55, pp. 10-11. See J. de Givry: "The ILO and the quality of working life. A new international programme: PIACT", in *International Labour Review* (Geneva, ILO), May-June 1978, pp. 261-271.

[6] Resolution (No. XII) on working conditions and environment, adopted on 21 June 1976, second preliminary paragraph.

[7] Record of the *Third European Regional Conference (Geneva, 16-25 October 1979)*, doc. GB.212/2/1, Resolution concerning the improvement of working conditions and the working environment in Europe, para. 11.

[8] Resolution (D) concerning the employment consequences of introduction of new technologies, Paragraphs 1 and 2 (*b*) and (*d*), ibid.

[9] Concerning Resolution (76) No. 32 of the Committee of Ministers, adopted on 26 May 1976, see particularly Franco Marziale: "Resolution of the Council of Europe on social security measures to be taken in favour of pensioners and persons remaining in activity after pensionable age", in *International Social Security Review* (Geneva, International Social Security Association), 1976, No. 3, pp. 284-289.

[10] Commission of the European Communities: *Community guidelines on flexible retirement*, doc. COM (80) 393 final (Brussels, 14 July 1980).

[11] ILO: *Older workers: Work and retirement*, Reports VI (1) and (2), International Labour Conference, 65th Session, Geneva, 1979; and Reports IV (1) and (2), 66th Session, Geneva, 1980.

[12] idem: *Record of Proceedings*, International Labour Conference, 66th Session, Geneva, 1980, No. 28.

NATURE OF THE REDUCTIONS SOUGHT

2

The present chapter is intended to compare the claims made for reductions in working time with the current situation and future trends in the various areas of activity concerned, so as to bring out what changes would have to be made if these claims were met. Would they mean a break with the present state of affairs or are they part of a trend that is already under way? The answers to these questions can throw a certain amount of light on the possible effects of any reduction in working time.

In general it would appear from the trends described below that the situation varies in fact from one country to another, often very considerably. The reductions in "normal" working time that are called for would not always constitute a significant change from the present situation. Besides, the possible ways of reducing working time also differ. The action programme of the European Trade Union Confederation (ETUC)[1] calls for raising the leaving age for compulsory schooling to 16, a 10 per cent reduction in working time without loss of earnings over the coming years, and the right to retirement at 60 without reduction in pension. More detailed aims are: a normal working week of 35 hours, extension of paid annual leave to six weeks, tighter control on overtime, compensation of overtime through paid time off, and extension of paid leave for training and retraining; there should also be a fifth shift where there is continuous working. Within this general framework, trade union claims vary from one country to another, emphasising different kinds of reduction and different ways of achieving them. It is accepted that not all the proposed reductions should come at the same time and that they can be put into practice gradually. The various claims are also to be found in a wider geographical setting, again with variations. The International Confederation of Free Trade Unions has also drawn attention to the desirability of a 10 per cent reduction in working time, the overall objective being the 35-hour week in the industrialised countries. This would be achieved either through legislation or through collective bargaining, the preference as to method depending mainly on the kind of reduction proposed or the country concerned.

In a number of countries national policy has already recognised the need to remove unjustified inequalities, as between workers in different grades or in different branches of economic activity, as regards hours of work or leave. On the other hand there is a tendency for special conditions to be granted to specific categories of workers, particularly those employed on heavy or dangerous work. The age of retirement is sometimes lowered for those having a long period of contributory service or of employment.

HOURS OF WORK AND PAID LEAVE

A normal working week of 35 hours is claimed as a matter of priority by trade union organisations in a number of countries as well as a reduction in the time actually worked, to be achieved by controlling overtime. However, in certain countries the claim is less far-reaching — the 36-hour week is proposed in Belgium, for example — or the emphasis is placed on observance of existing provisions or the limitation of overtime, as is the case in Luxembourg (Confederation of Christian Trade Unions), Norway (LO) and Sweden (LO). In the United States a Bill before Congress proposes a standard 35-hour week, elimination of compulsory overtime and payment for overtime at twice the normal hourly rate in order to discourage it; an information campaign has also been launched.[2] The Canadian Labour Congress is looking for a gradual reduction in the work-week to 32 hours, prohibition of compulsory overtime and payment for overtime at two-and-a-half times the normal rate.[3] In Ireland and Sweden some trade unions see the standard 30-hour week as their medium-term or long-term objective.[4] Some trade unions are claiming an even shorter working week: for example the aim of the British National Union of Bank Employees is the 28-hour week spread over four days, the 35-hour week being already in force in banking in the United Kingdom.[5] Greater reductions in weekly working hours are usually called for on a selective basis in the case of shift work.

Weekly working hours have in fact tended to fall over the long term.[6] The statutory standard is still over 40 hours in some countries, including the Federal Republic of Germany, Greece, Ireland, Italy, the Netherlands, Spain and Switzerland, but it is 40 hours in many others, and sometimes has been for quite a long time. In Belgium the norm was to be reduced to 38 hours in 1980. Normal weekly working hours under 40 are to be found in a growing number of special arrangements or collective agreements at the level of the undertaking, sector or occupation. Thus, in the Federal Republic of Germany, where the 40-hour week was already laid down in collective agreements covering 93 per cent of all workers at the end of 1979, the $37\frac{1}{2}$-hour week was normal in a number of sectors (tobacco, soft drinks, office and street cleaning, refuse collection).[7] At the beginning of 1980 it was reported that in one locality in the United Kingdom 196 employers had granted the 39-hour week, nine collective agreements providing for 38 or $38\frac{1}{2}$, 16 other agreements fixing a 37- or $37\frac{1}{2}$-hour week and 22 giving the 35-hour week; weekly working hours under 40 were to be found in 59 national agreements, with hours under 35 in nine cases.[8] In Belgium the $37\frac{1}{2}$-hour week has been adopted in one undertaking in the metallurgical industry, while a maximum of 38 hours per week is current practice in banks, insurance, department stores and the public sector. Banking and insurance normally have weekly working hours of about 38 in several countries, including Denmark, Italy and Sweden, sometimes with variations according to the time of year.[9]

According to one study carried out in the United States, by 1990 the 32-hour week could become the new standard in economic sectors where unions exist.[10] Reductions of varying importance in working hours and overtime are currently being negotiated between unions and employers in a number of countries, at the level of the undertaking. In many cases these are to be put into effect progressively.

More favourable working hours are in force for more vulnerable groups such as older workers or those employed on heavy work or shift workers. The weekly average is even under 35 hours for some shift workers. In some cases this is due to the fact that workers are given additional days off, rather than to a reduction in daily working hours.

Weekly hours actually worked have also fallen in practice over the long term and have gradually come closer to 40, though this trend has slowed down or come to a halt in recent years in some cases.[11] Hours actually worked are, of course, affected by provisions or arrangements about limitation of overtime. Quite considerable differences from one country to another are reported in this regard. Existing arrangements comprise limitation of authorised overtime per day, per week or per year, or a combination of two or three of such types of limitation, with various sytems of exemption. Excessive working hours are a matter of serious concern in a number of countries, in particular the United Kingdom. In 1979 restrictions on overtime were introduced in a number of industries in the Federal Republic of Germany, while in France maximum weekly hours were lowered. Proposals for stricter limitation of overtime are under consideration in Ireland and Denmark; in the latter country, a compulsory register of overtime actually worked is also envisaged. In addition, compensation for overtime by time off is beginning to find wider acceptance in practice, though only partially, in combination with compensation in cash.

Trends towards less hours actually worked need to be interpreted with caution if valid conclusions are to be drawn, because they may conceal other, more complicated tendencies. For example figures on this subject may be distorted by the inclusion of reduced working hours due to part-time working or partial unemployment, both of which are becoming more prevalent. It would also be useful to have statistics on working hours which show differences according to sex, because working hours tend on the average to be lower for women than for men because women are more likely to take part-time work and women form an increasing proportion of the labour force. The fall in working hours is also due to changes in economic organisation to the detriment of sectors with long working hours, such as agriculture.

In the United States, according to certain studies, average weekly working hours for men employed in non-agricultural undertakings are said to have remained more or less unchanged between 1948 (42.7 hours) and 1977 (42.8 hours); there is a very slight reduction if account is taken of longer annual leave and more paid holidays (41.6 hours in 1948 and 41.3 in 1977). The fractional fall in working hours in 1977 as compared with 1969 (when they were 43.5 without adjustment for longer leave and more holidays and 42 with adjustment) is said to be due to persistent high unemployment.[12] Since May 1968 average weekly working hours for all employees have fallen from 39.1 to 38.4, but for full-time employees only from 43 to 42.6.[13] The percentage of workers covered by collective agreements who have base weekly hours of less than 40 remained practically unchanged between 1956 and 1973, while the proportion of workers covered by agreements providing for more than 40 hours per week is said to have risen slightly over the same period.[14] In November 1979 weekly working hours averaged 38.5 for all employees in all sectors of the economy, but were 42.8 for full-time employees.[15]

In practice many workers, especially manual and service workers, still work long hours. Some have normal hours that are determined on the basis of "equivalence"; this lengthens the time during which they are supposed to be at the employer's disposal. In France the duration of such equivalence was recently reduced. Other employees work overtime, the quantity of which varies from one country to another. In Australia average weekly overtime per worker, in September 1979, was nine hours for all major factories in the private sector (namely almost all undertakings employing at least 100 persons and a large proportion of those employing between 50 and 100)[16] and even reached 12.5 hours in the basic metal industry. A sample survey carried out in 1977 in the member countries of the European Community[17] showed that average weekly hours for male employees exceeded 50 in agriculture in the United Kingdom and 45 in the seven other countries. In industry they exceeded 42 in three countries, one being the United Kingdom.[18] In the service trades they exceeded 43 hours in France and 42 hours in two other countries.

The European Trade Union Confederation (ETUC) has called for limitation of overtime and demanded that all hours worked beyond the statutory or contractual limit should be compensated by paid time off, so as to maintain working hours at their normal level and promote increased employment. Priorities vary from one organisation to another: some call for the maintenance of existing provisions, others for stricter limitations, others for only partial compensation. Altogether, however, strict limitation of overtime is considered to be essential; otherwise the effectiveness of any reduction in normal working hours would be permanently in danger.[19]

Extension of paid annual leave — a fifth or sixth week, depending on the organisation concerned — is a priority for some of the unions affiliated to the ETUC. It is one of the ways of achieving the 10 per cent reduction in working hours which the ETUC fixed as an objective in May 1979. An additional week's holiday would not in itself achieve this reduction: it would mean a reduction of 6.12 per cent where there are three weeks' holiday, 4.16 per cent in the case of four weeks and 2.1 per cent in the case of five weeks.[20] Many trade unions do not propose to go beyond five weeks, at least for the time being, and are simultaneously calling for other forms of reduction in working hours. In Finland, however, annual winter holidays are proposed in addition to five weeks' leave for everyone.

In practice, progress has been made almost everywhere as far as paid annual leave is concerned, with variations from one economic sector to another. By law or collective agreement a standard of four weeks is now usual, while five weeks is becoming more widespread and some collective agreements provide for six weeks' leave. In the Federal Republic of Germany, under the collective agreements for the metal, chemical, printing, coal, textile, clothing, rubber, glass, plastic and paper industries, all workers in those sectors were to be entitled to six weeks' annual leave, to become effective between 1981 and 1984.[21] Five weeks' annual leave is fixed by law in Luxembourg and Sweden, and is becoming the general rule in Denmark by collective agreement. In Sweden there is entitlement to annual leave of five to seven weeks in local administration and six to eight weeks in national public services. In the United States it is mainly the increase in the amount of leave (paid leave, leave for personal reasons, holidays) that is responsible for the reduction in total working hours over the last decades.

Grant of additional leave on account of age or seniority is provided for in law or collective agreements in a number of countries, and means that many workers who qualify already enjoy leave of five weeks or more, in cases where the norm is lower. Thus, entitlement to six weeks' paid leave is laid down in the collective agreements for the chemical industry in the Netherlands, in some undertakings in Switzerland (Swissair, the Swiss radio) and in Finland (with leave divided between winter and summer). In the United States some recent collective agreements provide for five to seven weeks' paid leave, on the basis of seniority.

The number of paid holidays varies from one country to another, between two extremes: five to 14 days. In most countries, when holidays fall on a Sunday or another non-working day, they cannot be replaced by another day off. In France it has been proposed to abandon the practice of compensating for holidays and to fix annual leave at 5.6 weeks and annual working time at 46.4 weeks.[22] In a number of countries progress is being made as regards granting leave on family grounds or other reasons of personal convenience and workers over a certain age or seniority are generally granted longer holidays.

The idea of determining working time on an annual basis is currently being discussed. It has been favourably received among employers, but has met with strong resistance from workers' organisations, which are worried lest the gains they have made with respect to leave and holidays would be subordinated to the needs of the undertaking. However, there are also some people in trade unions who support an annual total of working time, at the worker's choice. It is argued that this might increase job satisfaction since workers would be more free to work or rest according to their own wishes and would probably feel more responsible in their relations with the undertaking. It might facilitate adjustment to technological change.[23]

Legislation and other standards are normally concerned with fractions of the annual total of working time: weekly working hours, annual leave and holidays. Annual working time is only discussed in the case of seasonal occupations (hotel trades, agriculture) where it is possible to work more at certain times of the year and less at others. On an annual basis, with holidays and leave deducted, average working hours in the EEC countries are said to be between 1,600 and 2,000. According to the automobile workers' union in the United States, they were 1,752 in that industry in 1979, or 6 per cent less than in 1967.[24]

In some countries the system of specifying an annual amount of working time has aroused interest. In France the Giraudet report (quoted above)[22] proposed a general rearrangement and reduction of total working time as a possible basis for negotiation between employers and unions. For 1983 it proposed a standard total of 1,816 hours a year (or 40 hours a week), this total being reduced to 1,770 hours (39 hours a week) for certain difficult jobs, less 40 hours per year of additional paid time off in both cases; this time off would be taken in accordance with the requirements of the undertaking. Maximum weekly working hours would be reduced from 50 to 48, with the possibility of averages of 46 hours over 12 weeks (24 weeks for irregular working). Overtime would be subject to an annual maximum, and there would also be a maximum number of "exceptional" hours with a system of compensatory paid time off designed to discourage employers from resorting to this practice. Negotiations on the basis of these proposals are still going on.

A LOWER NORMAL AGE OF RETIREMENT

Lowering the normal age of retirement extends the concept of reduced working time to the entire active life of the individual. This idea, which is often put forward in somewhat ambiguous terms,[25] means in practice lowering the age at which the majority of members of pension schemes may normally be entitled to retire with a pension at full rate. This does not mean that they do not remain free to advance or delay their actual termination of employment, subject to consequential adjustments in the amount of their pension.

Despite certain downward trends, the age of retirement on full pension is still 65 (60 for women, in some cases) in the great majority of the countries under consideration, and is 67 in Denmark and Norway. On the other hand 60 is the normal retirement age in the private sector in Italy. More favourable provisions are applicable under special schemes, particularly those covering public servants, and in certain occupations, particularly those involving heavy work. In addition, workers who have paid contributions for at least 35 years may retire on full pension at 60 in Austria and at 63 in the Federal Republic of Germany. Collective agreements in a number of industries in the United States provide for voluntary early retirement on full pension from the age of 55, or without condition as to age, subject to a minimum number of years of contribution. Some of these agreements allot part of the amounts intended for periodic wage adjustments to the improvement of the early retirement scheme.[26]

During the prosperous years of economic expansion, a large number of arrangements were promoted to encourage early retirement, with actuarial reductions.[27] More recently, with the growth of unemployment, various systems of early retirement have been established either by law or by agreement: the amount of early retirement pension may be the same as the normal pension, or either higher or lower. Systems of progressive retirement combined with reduced working time are in operation in some countries. In Sweden partial retirement with reduced working hours — between 17 and 35 hours per week — is possible from the age of 60 onwards. Progressive retirement exists in various sectors of the economy in the Netherlands and in some undertakings in France, where wage levels are maintained in several cases.[28] In some countries concern about the employment situation has caused special measures to be adopted. Thus, in Belgium, an undertaking is required to take on a young person under 30 for every worker retiring with the statutory early retirement pension;

undertakings facing economic difficulties may be exempted from these provisions, however.

At present the number of possible beneficiaries of an earlier retirement age is lower because of the smaller age groups due to the First World War and its consequences. In future, however, the proportion of older persons is expected to increase considerably in the population of most countries under consideration here: those still in employment will therefore have a very heavy burden to carry.[29] These demographic trends strengthen the case for adopting flexible arrangements and some recent measures are even considered to be reversible, if necessary. In the United States the age limit which undertakings may impose has been raised from 65 to 70, and a small rise in the normal retirement age has been suggested from the year 2005 onwards, until the year 2023.[30]

Trade union proposals to lower the normal retirement age have sometimes been influenced by demographic trends and by the technical and financial problems involved in such a measure: in particular it would mean that a full pension would have to be constituted on the basis of a shorter period of contributions. Thus, some workers' organisations have expressed themselves in favour, for the time being, only of selective measures applicable to workers in hard or dangerous occupations, or of improvements in early retirement benefits, rather than generally applicable provisions relating to the normal retirement age.

One important aspect of current developments, as we have seen, is a decline in the tendency to identify retirement with "inactivity", this assimilation being due to confusion between entitlement to retirement pension and cessation of employment. The traditional notion of "post-retirement" life, with its almost "punitive" effect on the cumulation of pension and earnings, is giving way to a more open-minded approach having greater regard for the general interest and that of the pensioner. In fact, the term "free activity" seems to reflect the situation of many pensioners since retirement has given them the opportunity of carrying on all kinds of activity, some paid, some unpaid.

Notes

[1] See note 1 to Chapter 1.

[2] Draft legislation introduced by the Hon. John Conyers, Jr. (H.R. 1784) in the House of Representatives on 10 February 1979. See *Congressional Record* (Washington, DC), Extensions of remarks, 18 Oct. 1979, pp. E.5132-E.5133.

[3] See "CLC presents brief on redundancies and layoffs", in *Canadian Industrial Relations and Personnel Developments* (Don Mills, Ontario), 13 Dec. 1978, pp. 902-904.

[4] In this connection see "Jobs report turns down 30-hr week", in *Industrial Relations — Europe* (Brussels, Management Centre Europe), May 1979, p. 6, and "Working hours cut 'could boost productivity'", ibid., July 1979, p. 6.

[5] Report submitted to the meeting of the EURO-FIET Trade Section Committee of Bank Workers, London, 6-7 March 1979, in *Social and Labour Bulletin* (Geneva, ILO), 2/79, p. 124. FIET is the International Federation of Commercial, Clerical and Technical Employees.

[6] See in particular Archibald A. Evans: *Hours of work in industrialised countries* (Geneva, ILO, 1975), especially Ch. II, pp. 53-80; also ILO: *Policies and practices for the improvement of conditions of work and the environment in Europe*, Report III, Third European Regional Conference, 16-25 October 1979.

[7] European Communities: *Report on social developments, year 1979* (Brussels and Luxembourg, Apr. 1980), p. 97.

[8] *Bargaining Report* (London, Labour Research Department), Mar.-Apr. 1980, pp. 2-14.

[9] See in particular International Federation of Commercial, Clerical and Technical Employees (FIET): *Conditions de travail des employés d'assurance et des assurances en Europe, 1978* (Geneva, Feb. 1979), and idem: *Conditions de travail des employés de banque en Europe, 1978* (Geneva, Feb. 1979).

[10] Study by the University of Michigan and the Society of Manufacturing Engineers of Michigan. See "The future of the 4-day week", in *Social and Labour Bulletin* (Geneva, ILO), 4/78, pp. 361-362.

[11] For France see Pierre Boisard: *Bilan de recherches sur la réduction de la durée du travail* (Paris, Ministère du Travail et de la Participation, Centre d'études de l'emploi, Apr. 1979), p. 2; and idem: "Enjeux d'une réduction de la durée du travail", in *Bulletin d'informations* (Paris, Ministère du Travail et de la Participation), Apr. 1979.

[12] John D. Owen: "Hours of work in the long run: Trends, explanations, scenarios and implications", in *Work time and employment*, Special report of the National Commission for Manpower Policy, No. 28 (Washington, DC, Oct. 1978), p. 33.

[13] Janice N. Hedges: "Hours of work in the long run. Comment", ibid., p. 74.

[14] Sar A. Levitan and Richard S. Belous: "Reduced worktime: Tool to fight unemployment", in *Worklife* (Washington, DC, United States Department of Labor, Employment and Training Administration), Apr. 1978, p. 25.

[15] *Employment and earnings* (Washington, DC, United States Department of Labor, Bureau of Labor Statistics), Dec. 1979, table A-26, p. 37. See also Janice Neipert Hedges and Daniel E. Taylor: "Recent trends in worktime: Hours edge downward", in *Monthly Labor Review* (Washington, DC, United States Department of Labor, Bureau of Labor Statistics), Mar. 1980, pp. 3-11.

[16] *Monthly Review of the Employment Situation* (Canberra, Department of Employment and Youth Affairs), Oct. 1979, table 3, p. 2.

[17] Eurostat: *Labour Force Sample Survey, 1977* (Brussels, 1978), table 21, p. 31.

[18] Male workers averaged 6.3 hours overtime a week in April 1979, according to the *New Earnings Survey*. The TUC states that since 35 per cent of manual workers do not work overtime, the real average for those who do would be ten hours per week; in other words, a working week of about 50 hours. *European Trade Union Confederation campaign for reduced working time*, TUC campaign for economic and social advance, *TUC Progress Report No. 1*, Nov. 1979, p. 9.

[19] European Trade Union Institute: *Overtime and the position of trade unions with regard to proposals for the restriction of overtime at European Community level* (Brussels, Aug. 1979).

[20] idem: *La réduction du temps de travail en Europe occidentale*, première partie: *La situation actuelle* (Sep. 1979), p. 16.

[21] Bundesminister für Arbeit und Sozialordnung: *Tarifverträgliche Arbeitsbedingungen im Jahre 1979*, document III a 1-3505 2 (Bonn, Jan. 1980), p. 6.

[22] Pierre Giraudet: *Rapport de mission* (report on an inquiry commissioned by the French Government on the possibilities of adjustment and reduction of working time), 22 Apr. 1980, mimeographed document, pp. 19 ff.

[23] Mario Caomine (Central Secretary of the Swiss Association of Bank Employees): "La réduction de la durée du travail. Une requête des salariés", in *Le mois économique et financier* (Basle, Société de Banque Suisse), 1980/3, pp. 12-13.

[24] See Hedges and Taylor, op. cit.

[25] See in this connection J.J. Dupeyroux: *L'âge de la retraite: principales formules*, mimeographed document prepared for the Commission of the European Communities.

[26] This is the case, for example, in the aerospace industry; see Edward Wasilewski: "Scheduled wage increases and escalator provisions in 1980", in *Monthly Labor Review*, Jan. 1980, pp. 9-13. However, some calculations show that, despite the long-term fall in annual working time — about 1,200 less hours a year than in 1980 — a worker today works more hours over his whole working life than his elders did, because he will live longer; a man born in 1970 will probably work about 6,800 hours more than a man born in 1900. See Juanits M. Kreps and Joseph J. Spengler: "The leisure component of economic growth", in *Technology and the American economy*, Report of the Commission, annex to Vol. II of *The employment impact of technological change*, Studies prepared for the National Commission on Technology, Automation and Economic Progress (Washington, DC, Feb. 1966), p. II-355.

[27] Martin Tracy: *Retirement age practices in ten industrial societies, 1960-1976* (Geneva, International Social Security Association, 1979), Studies and Research, No. 14; and idem: "Flexible

retirement features abroad", in *Social Security Bulletin* (United States Department of Health, Education and Welfare), May 1978, p. 24.

[28] "Les conventions et accords de préretraite", in *Revue française des affaires sociales* (Paris), Apr.-June 1979.

[29] Conseil de l'Europe, Comité directeur pour la sécurité sociale, Comité d'experts en matière de sécurité sociale dans sa composition d'actuaires: *Projet de rapport sur les effets combinés de l'abaissement de l'âge de la retraite et du vieillissement de la population sur le financement des régimes de sécurité sociale relatif aux prestations long terme* (Strasbourg, 22 Feb. 1977; doc. CD/99(77)1).

[30] *Reports of the Quadriennial Advisory Council on Social Security*, 10 Mar. 1975, 94th Congress, 1st Session, House Document No. 9475, p. 63.

AIMS AND EXPECTATIONS

3

The present chapter will try to paint a general picture of the kind of arguments that have been put forward or developed in support of proposals or recommendations for reduction in working time. In accordance with the approach adopted in this study, it seems sufficient to summarise the substance of the arguments, without necessarily identifying the source of any particular one. Hence no attempt will be made at a systematic description of the views expressed by individual writers or organisations;[1] instead, a general background for subsequent examination will be presented. Before entering upon such an examination, it appears necessary to ascertain what kind of effects are expected and what criteria should be used to evaluate them. The intentions of persons in favour of reducing working time and the results they expect would seem to provide useful indications in this respect, at least as far as favourable effects are concerned.

As has already been mentioned, a number of reasons underlie the proposals or recommendations made for reducing working time, each of them being given a different priority according to its origin. Certain objectives are social in character: the aim is to improve conditions of work and thus increase the workers' well-being and job satisfaction, improve the quality of their life outside employment by giving them time to enjoy it, and ensure a fair distribution of the fruits of technical and economic progress, thus reducing the burdens of existence while raising living standards. Other aims are more of an economic nature and relate to absorbing unemployment by reducing working time; that purpose is not usually expected to be achieved by this means alone, and the reduction of working time is often presented as one element in an overall strategy in the field of economic and employment policies. The aims and expectations of the advocates of reduced working time are summarised briefly under four headings in the following pages: quality of life, sharing in the benefits of technical and economic progress, prevention and reduction of unemployment, and parallel measures recommended.

QUALITY OF LIFE

An increase in leisure is being called for in the trade union movement and in wide sectors of public opinion, on human and social grounds. It is considered necessary to enable workers to achieve better physical and mental rest and relaxation and a reduction of nervous tension. It is also considered to be essential in order to enable them to develop their personalities by giving them the time to participate more fully in family life, in recreational, educational and cultural activities, in clubs and societies and civic, trade union and political affairs. This call for improvement in the quality of life takes precedence over all other factors in certain trade union organisations, particularly those in sectors in which unemployment is relatively low.

While it is true that working hours today — whether calculated by the day, the week or the year — no longer reach the very high figures attained in the early years of this century, a reduction is still proposed for the reasons stated above. In support of the claim, mention is made of the fact that the causes of work fatigue — not only physical but also, and increasingly, mental and nervous — still persist and are even multiplying and increasing. These harmful factors may be of a particularly insidious nature in occupations affected by recent technical progress. It has been pointed out in favour of a reduction in working time that the more workers are subjected to output rates imposed by machines, or have to watch lights and dials on a control panel, or keep up with an assembly line or with computers or work in shifts, the more it is necessary to provide them with longer leisure time. Moreover, in some sectors not enough people are employed, particularly in some public services, and this means a greater workload for existing employees, thus damaging their health and accentuating the need for longer rest periods. A reduction in working time is also called for on psychological grounds, as a compensation for the impoverishment in the content of certain jobs. To be sure, efforts must be made to combat or remedy this impoverishment, but it is claimed that there are limits to what can be done in the way of job enrichment: in many fields the possibilities of developing personal creativity are disappearing. Thus, leisure time should be lengthened so that workers can have a life worth living. Furthermore, leisure is of educational value. It offers workers the means of bettering their education and knowledge and thus improves their chance of keeping up with rapid economic and social change.

It is also pointed out that the fact that the average total of hours really worked has dropped over the long term does not necessarily mean that enough progress has been made and that workers today have enough free time for rest and interesting activities outside work. The real decrease in working time without loss of earnings is not always as great as people think, in any event as far as certain categories of workers are concerned. In particular, for a variety of reasons — overtime, "equivalence", exceptions — some categories still work very long hours. Such inequalities must disappear, it is said. Moreover, the long-term fall in working hours ought to have been even more marked, in view of the rise in productivity in recent decades. Finally, the amount of time not actually taken up by work may be taken up by other constraining factors which cut down free time, such as excessive time that has to be spent on travel, administrative and other formalities that are a common feature of modern life, and the effects of breakdowns due to rapid, unplanned urbanisation and the failure of public utilities and services to meet demands placed on them. Such constraining factors become worse as daily life becomes more and more complicated.

In many union claims priority is given to reducing weekly and — especially — daily working hours, in preference to longer annual leave. A reduction in working time is generally considered to be more favourable to bringing about a profound improvement in life styles. The extension of leave is thought of as promoting "getting away from it all" and thus accentuating the divorce between work and life outside work, to the detriment of both. Nevertheless, extension of annual leave is also proposed for its own sake, as a means of improving living and working conditions.

With respect to lowering the normal retirement age, the intention is clear. Workers ought to be able to cease work, free from money worries, at a specific age, the age being lower if they have worked under difficult conditions. This cessation, with maintenance of pension at the same level providing a guarantee of as high a standard of living as possible, is a social objective that is regarded as being valuable in and of itself. Thus retired persons would not be driven to seek employment under financial pressure if they wished to give up paid employment altogether. Similarly, the principle of voluntary retirement and retirement at the age of one's choice is widely recognised as important: on psychological grounds and for reasons of social policy relating to older persons, it is considered essential that workers should be able to postpone or bring forward normal retirement if they so desire.

In practice, there seems to be a certain amount of confusion about systems of early retirement, the main purpose of which is to keep ageing workers from entering the ranks of the unemployed or to transfer them from the unemployment register to retirement. According to a study published in France, the principal trade unions and other occupational associations in that country have as the main plank in their platform the demand that all wage and salary earners should have the opportunity of retiring at the age of 60 with an adequate level of income. The laws concerning premature retirement with full pension for personal reasons (incapacity) or for certain categories of workers (particularly manual workers) are accepted as positive achievements, but a number of organisations in France consider that they introduce inequalities and discrimination among employed persons. With respect to progressive retirement, some people regard it as a "gimmick" while others are more favourably disposed towards it, seeing it as a means of avoiding a too abrupt cessation of a person's working life. According to the same study, progressive retirement is mainly of interest to salaried employees. Wage earners give preference to retiring early, while technical, supervisory and executive staff take the view that the exercise of responsibility is incompatible with part-time status.[2]

In other countries, such as Norway and the United Kingdom, lowering the retirement age is considered to be too costly if it is to be generally applied and is being proposed at present selectively, for social reasons, on behalf of workers in difficult or dangerous jobs.

SHARING IN THE BENEFITS OF TECHNICAL AND ECONOMIC PROGRESS

The idea that technical and economic progress should lead to a gradual reduction in working time, and indeed in the place occupied by work in life as a whole, is mainly based on a theory which has long been widely accepted: the idea that the benefits of increased productivity should be shared.[3] Under this theory, if the same amount can be produced in less working hours, or more in the same number of working hours, as a result of productivity gains, there should be a choice between increased leisure, higher incomes or a combination of the two. Until recently, average living standards have gone on rising while working hours have gone on falling: there has been an increase in real wages, a gradual improvement in payment for annual leave (a trend towards basing such payment on average real earnings rather than on the wage alone), and an improvement in old-age and retirement benefits. However, more recently there have been signs of a fall in the purchasing power of wage earners or households in certain countries, and in these cases a slow-down or stoppage in the trend towards reduced working hours has been observed.

The theory about sharing the benefits of productivity is still very much alive in many trade union movements. In this connection it may be recalled that immediately after the end of the Second World War the International Affairs Committee of the American Federation of Labor submitted a memorandum entitled *International reduction of hours of work as a result of increased productivity* to the Second Session of the Economic and Social Council of the United Nations. The memorandum called for the 40-hour week as an immediate objective, demanded that a further reduction in working hours should be proclaimed as an objective of the ILO, and asked that research should be undertaken with a view to reducing the working week to 30 hours, particularly in the economically most developed countries.[4]

At present many workers' organisations calling for a reduction in working time say that they are ready to give preference to increased leisure as against increases in real earnings. They appear to accept moderation as regards future rises in real wages or even to abandon this claim for the time being, if support for a reduction in working time will contribute to dealing with unemployment. A variety of views are expressed in this regard. The possibility of lower future increases in real wages in return for a reduction in working time is accepted by trade union organisations in Belgium, Canada, the Federal Republic of Germany and Norway, while in the Netherlands the mere maintenance of real wages is not opposed. On the other hand in Sweden, where a reduction in working time is not considered to be a priority for the next three or four years, it is agreed that if such a reduction comes about, it should preferably be accompanied by an increase in real earnings, so that increased leisure can be thoroughly enjoyed.[5]

Mention may be made here in passing of the fact that the question of reduced working time is no longer complicated by the need to maintain normal remuneration — which is the traditional social objective — since there now exists a continuous process of sharing the benefits of improved productivity or of the fruits of economic growth. However, to avoid any misunderstanding, a distinction must be made between two different factors which are involved at one and the same time. Proposals for reducing working time which, if accepted, would lead to decisions to lower statutory or contractual norms in this regard are in principle based on the assumption that the normal wage will not be reduced. Claims for wage increases (and offers to give up such claims in whole or in part for a given period in order to finance the above-mentioned decisions) form part of the process of sharing the fruits of accumulated increases in productivity which is more or less permanently going on in the background.[6] A third distinction should also be made, in addition to the other two, with regard to the efforts made to adjust wages to inflation. These also form part of a continuous process, but the aim is different: to prevent real wages from falling. Any abandonment of wage increases would not imply abandonment of the aim of maintaining the existing purchasing power of wages. These three factors are inextricably bound up with one another.

The claim for full compensation in wages in return for a reduction in the normal working week may also be pressed less strongly, in certain cases, as a result of a policy favouring redistribution of incomes. Thus, it may be proposed to increase the lowest wages when a reduction in the normal working week is introduced or when overtime is compensated for in time off rather than at bonus rates. In the case of higher wages, degressive increases may be accepted.

PREVENTION OR REDUCTION OF UNEMPLOYMENT

The hope that unemployment can be diminished by reducing working time is based on the expected result of certain operations: a raising of the leaving age for compulsory schooling and a lowering of the normal retirement age ought to contribute towards bringing down the supply of labour. An extension of educational leave ought to promote a qualitative adjustment of the balance between labour supply and demand. Dividing up the amount of available work into a larger number of jobs with less working hours ought to contribute towards increasing demand for labour. Millions of unemployed are looking for jobs while millions of workers have longer hours than they want. It therefore seems to be a good idea to share the work that is available among a larger number of workers and, by allowing older workers to obtain full pension sooner, to encourage them to free their jobs for younger people. Despite the practical difficulties involved in such operations, it would be possible, according to this theory, to contribute to absorbing some of the existing full or partial unemployment and to prevent some of the unemployment to be expected because of the continuous arrival of young people on the labour market and of the threat of employment cuts owing to technological change which hangs over many workers. It is also believed that an extension of leisure time would provide a fresh stimulus to sectors of the economy serving needs deriving from use of free time, such as sport, education, tourism, cultural activites and entertainment. New demand deriving from increased leisure time would create jobs.

A reduction in the normal working week is generally considered to be the best way of producing a large volume of work to be shared on a long-term basis; another method is the introduction of a fifth shift in continuous working. It is asserted that if the shift durations laid down by law, agreement or otherwise were to be lowered, this would have the snowball effect required to overcome the slow-down in the long-term trend towards reduction of working hours in spite of continued gains in productivity. Some people believe that productivity gains already made ought to have enabled the working week to be further reduced some time ago. In the United States the proposer of the Bill on the 35-

hour week, already mentioned, pointed out in his remarks in the House of Representatives that labour employed in manufacturing industry had risen by only 3 per cent between 1955 and 1976, while production had doubled; the system of the 40-hour week established in 1938 had built a wall around jobs, and nearly 9 million people had been left outside.[7] In other words, the quantity of work required to produce the same output had been halved; but, because it had remained divided up into a specific number of jobs, on the theoretical basis of one full-time job per 40-hour week, and not less, the number of jobs required to double production had grown only very slightly. On this argument millions of people have been deprived of jobs in manufacturing industry which they would have had if the working week had been cut. According to another hypothesis concerning the whole national economy of the United States, if the long-term trend towards sharing out productivity gains had continued after the Second World War, the normal working week in that country would today be close to 35 hours.[8]

Compensation for overtime in the form of time off, particularly if it is given soon afterwards, is also seen as being a method of ensuring effective reductions in working time and maximising their impact on employment. Shift work is a matter of deep concern in that it causes desynchronisation between personal life and family and social life. Trade unions are seeking to do away with it as far as possible and to substitute systems of work organisation that are more acceptable from the human and social points of view. Where this is not feasible, they put forward a variety of proposals for compensation (longer work breaks, less hours per shift, compensatory rest periods, fifth shift on continuous working, lowering the retirement age). All these measures could lead to providing new job opportunities. Measures to facilitate early retirement and lower the normal retirement age are linked by many trade unions with the possibility of taking on a new worker to take the place of every one who leaves.

Work sharing as it exists at present is increasingly put forward as only one method, and not necessarily the most important, of redistributing the increased employment expected from a reduction in working time. In the United Kingdom the Trades Union Congress has emphasised that it sees the reduction in working time not "in the negative context of sharing out less work, but in the positive context of growth and development".[9] According to a trade union leader who represents workers in the service sector at the international level, the idea of work sharing is out of date in view of the enormous risks which the new technology represents for everybody. He considers that it is time to remodel the whole concept of production and economic processes. Employment, defined according to new principles, ought to be the purpose of all economic activity. He points out that robots will not have bank accounts or take out insurance policies or go on journeys. Consumers will be needed to provide work for these technical miracles: to his mind we have to break away from the logic of capitalism, both liberal and state capitalism.[10]

In discussions about the effects of reductions in working time, frequent use is made of the argument that financial resources would be released because of the expected fall in unemployment: more contributions and lower expenditure for social security schemes, higher tax receipts, and savings on public subsidies to provide jobs for the unemployed. It is argued that these funds could be used to finance the promotion of useful employment. In this connection attention is drawn to the unsatisfied demand for better public services and particularly social services; examples cited include over-burdened telephone exchanges and postal services, long delays in cases before the courts, overcrowding of schools and universities, and lack of services for the care of children, the sick and older people. Reduction in working time is thus seen as part of a wider strategy for stimulating quantitive and qualitative economic growth; it is not regarded as a substitute for appropriate economic, training and employment policies.

Finally, beneficial effects on employment are awaited from the expansion in the total wage bill which would result from the expected fall in unemployment. The stress placed on maintenance of full earnings in the event of a reduction in working time may be explained by the aim of keeping up demand. This is considered to be essential in order to stimulate consumption, production and increased employment. Conversely, reductions in working time accompanied by loss of earnings would aggravate poverty, contract demand for goods and services and therefore increase marketing difficulties, increase unemployment or at best create only very few jobs. There is some scepticism at times about the results of any efforts by workers to be moderate in their wage claims in order to improve the employment situation. Some people believe that maintenance of profits will only lead to stimulating investment in rationalisation, which eliminates jobs, or to the flight of capital, which exports employment. These arguments claim to be based on past experience and assert that official recommendations in favour of austerity, even if they were followed, are no guarantee of return to economic growth, and if they are not followed, can only lead to stagnation. Structural changes would be the pretext for imposing unequal sacrifices.

Arguments in favour of reductions in working time are based in some cases on economic analyses of which some examples are given below. They aim specifically at demonstrating that most undertakings could absorb the cost of the proposed reductions and that the latter would promote a return to economic growth. However, the organisations affiliated to the European Trade Union Confederation, recognising a possible danger of distortion in international competitivity, have stated their preference for a reduction in working time that is co-ordinated at the European level.

PARALLEL MEASURES PROPOSED

Recommendations that working time should be reduced are frequently accompanied by opinions about the context in which such measures should be adopted to ensure that there is a good chance that favourable effects will in fact follow. Some of these conditions have been touched on in passing in earlier pages. Mention will be made here of three specific aspects which often arise in discussion: strategies within the undertaking, general economic and social policy and workers' participation in decisions.

Deliberate strategies comprising programmed control over growth of productivity are considered to be essential, at the level of the undertaking, in order to optimise the effects on employment of reductions in working time. In Belgium, for example, the Confederation of Christian Trade Unions (CSC) has presented an inventory of the parallel measures it regards as essential in this field:[11] it wants the workers to be able to check up on working time, employment and investments, and that action be taken to neutralise counter-attacks by employers. The Confederation considers that employers might purely and simply refuse to reduce working time or offer to improve wages instead, or propose gradual reductions but without taking on any new employees. Employers are also thought to be capable of claiming that new employees are being engaged as a result of reduced working time when in fact the recruitment is due to plans for expansion; or of promising new jobs but without guaranteeing that the level of employment will remain the same in future; or of increasing the number of workers but by increasing the proportion of workers employed on inferior terms (temporary workers, trainees on fixed-term contracts, part-time workers); or of speeding up the work pace or increasing the workload while agreeing to reduce working time, and sometimes even without agreeing to do so.

There are numerous demands for a controlled development of productivity, stressing that it should be achieved by means of technical innovation and not at the cost of an acceleration of the work pace or an aggravation of occupational stress. This growth in productivity ought to be counterbalanced by the development of products that will create new jobs, it is argued. Reduction in working time should be accompanied by qualitative growth concentrating on sectors with a future, on reconversion plans and on areas of activity corresponding to social priorities. There is a great deal of discussion about the economic context required for these reforms. An ETUC working group has set out the principal trade union views in the field of economic theory in a discussion paper. Reduction in working time is mentioned a number of times as one of the measures to be adopted as part of a deliberate economic strategy. Keeping to Keynesian theory as foundation, the paper states that measures for regulating global demand are no longer sufficient and that from now on there must be a combination of general and selective measures with respect to both supply and demand. Growth should come from increased satisfaction of people's needs, a quantitative and qualitative objective which can only be attained if there is a wide social consensus. This means that trade unions must participate in decisions and that their offer to take on their responsibilities in this regard must be accepted.[12] In the United States a trade union expert has pointed out that this paper seeks to propose a new kind of planning incorporating both new and old ideas. According to this author, it should arouse wide interest because it stresses the idea of a new and wider consensus.[13]

The importance of workers' participation in information and decisions within the undertaking has been stressed in many discussions about reducing working time. The Italian metalworkers' federation, for example, claims the right to be informed about the quantity and distribution of overtime worked at the department level, so as to be able to propose measures to eliminate the causes of overtime.[14] In the United Kingdom the Trades Union Congress considers that important gains are to be achieved by linking efficiency bargaining with the reduction of hours. Reductions in working time without loss of pay for the "normal" week can bring substantial public or social benefits in addition to the generation of benefits to the business concerned. In this connection the bargaining process, if taken with the seriousness it deserves, raises many questions as to the disclosure of information and as to joint examination of current patterns of work, pay and working time and the options concerning the efficient development path of the enterprise.[15]

Notes

[1] For the arguments put forward in trade union circles, see the sources given in note 1 to Chapter 1, and International Metalworkers' Federation (IMF), World Conference for the Reduction of Working Time, Geneva, 21-23 August 1979: *Strategy and arguments for the reduction of working time. The effects of the reduction of working time on employment as well as social and economic development*, Document No. 3; also Institut syndical européen: *La réduction du temps de travail en Europe occidentale*, première partie: *La situation actuelle* (Sep. 1979); deuxième partie: *Analyse des conséquences économiques et sociales* (May 1980).

[2] "Les conventions et les accords de préretraite", in *Revue française des affaires sociales* (Paris), Apr.-June 1979, p. 158.

[3] "Sharing the benefits of productivity", in *International Labour Review* (Geneva, ILO), July 1960, pp. 1-25.

[4] *International Labour Code*, 1951, Vol. I (Geneva, ILO, 1954), p. 253, note 367.

[5] International Metalworkers' Federation (IMF), World Conference for the Reduction of Working Time, Geneva, 21-23 August 1979: *Action programme of IMF and its affiliates for shorter work time*, Document No. 2, pp. 8, 11, 23-24, 43, 45, 46 and 54.

[6] For the development of productivity, see in particular Economic Commission for Europe: *Economic survey of Europe in 1978*, Part I: *The European economy in 1978* (New York, United Nations, 1979; Sales No. E.79.II.E.1), pp. 12-13 and table 1.9; and idem: "A. Labour force and employment in western Europe: The prospects in 1985 by major sectors", in *Economic Bulletin for Europe* (New York, United Nations), Vol. 30, No. 2 (Sales No. E.79.II.e.10), pp. 40-42.

[7] Remarks of Hon. John Conyers, Jr., in the House of Representatives, in *Congressional Record* (Washington, DC), Extension of remarks, 18 Oct. 1979, E-5135.

[8] Sar A. Levitan and Richard S. Belous: "Reduced worktime: Tool to fight unemployment", in *Worklife* (Washington, DC, United States Department of Labor, Employment and Training Administration), Apr. 1978, pp. 22-26.

[9] "European Trade Union Confederation campaign for reduced working time", TUC campaign for economic and social advance, in *TUC Progress Report No. 2*, Dec. 1979, p. 2.

[10] Interview with Mr. Heribert Maier, General Secretary of the International Federation of Commercial, Clerical and Technical Employees (FIET), in *Intersocial*, Jan. 1980, pp. 17-19.

[11] "Les 36 heures: imposer un contrôle du temps de travail dans l'entreprise pour répartir l'emploi", in *Syndicaliste* (Brussels, CSC), 25 June 1978, pp. 10-13.

[12] European Trade Union Institute: *Keynes plus. A participatory economy* (Brussels, Euro-Inst. 1979). The chairman of the working group was Clas-Erik Odhner, head of the research department of the Swedish confederation.

[13] Everett M. Kassalow: "Beyond Keynes: European unions formulate new economic program", in *Monthly Labor Review* (Washington, DC), Feb. 1980, pp. 36-40.

[14] *Action programme of IMF and its affiliates for shorter working time*, op. cit., p. 32.

[15] Trade Union Research Unit: *"Efficiency bargaining" over shorter hours*, A preliminary analysis, Technical Note No. 47 (Oxford, Ruskin College, Oct. 1978).

OBJECTIONS AND ARGUMENTS

4

The present chapter is mainly designed to supplement the previous one. It examines the arguments put forward by the opponents of the reduction of working time, or of certain methods of doing so, or in support of the reservations or doubts expressed on this matter. Here again, the intention is essentially methodological in character. It is proposed to set out a general background for subsequent study, by describing the arguments used by the various parties in support of their theories in the debates and controversies concerning the consequences that may have to be foreseen in the event of further reductions in working time. Thus, no systematic attempt has been made to set out in precise terms the positions adopted by the various writers, bodies or governments with regard to this or that kind of harmful or doubtful effect. The following chapters contain numerous references to sources and thus provide this information. The present chapter ought to provide further material in reply to the two questions asked at the outset of this study: What kind of effects should we be looking for? In terms of what criteria, or against what background, should they be assessed?

In pursuing this exploration, an outline of the debates and controversies on the effects of reducing working time seems to be the best way of presenting the fullest possible view of the matter. As will be seen, the arguments put forward are influenced by preconceptions about the causes of depression or recession, or about the causes of unemployment, and about the policies to be followed in dealing with these problems. In the last resort, the question that is being raised here is: What kind of economic system or society do the countries concerned really want? It may be of some interest, despite important differences in the historical context, to delve briefly into the past of the ILO, as an introduction to these issues. In fact, in many respects, they are not new. Moreover, for many years before the Second World War the ILO closely followed the question of the effects of reducing working time and drew its own conclusions from practical experience in this field.

CONTROVERSIES BEFORE THE SECOND WORLD WAR

From 1932 onward the ILO was engaged in a study of the reduction of working time as one of various means of combating unemployment. At first the idea was greeted with fairly general scepticism, but then it was given more and more attention, not only as a method of spreading work among a larger number of workers in times of depression but also as the logical and necessary consequence of the enhanced productive power at the service of industry.[1] It may be recalled in passing that at the same time there was also discussion of other means of combating unemployment, such as lowering the retirement age and lengthening the period of compulsory schooling. Just before the Second World War, when the economic situation and employment were beginning to improve, reduced working time still found many supporters and was considered to be a valid social reform for its own sake, in particular because, as a result of paid annual leave, workers had gained experience of what leisure time really meant.[2]

Debates at the International Labour Conference

Samples of the arguments put forward in 1935 at the International Labour Conference on the possible effects of reducing the normal working week to 40 hours — it was generally 48 hours at that time — and of granting holidays with pay,[3] are given below. It was in 1935 that the Forty-Hour Week Convention (No. 47) was adopted, while the first Convention concerning holidays with pay (No. 52) dates from the following year. The arguments put forward from the workers' side are often very close to those still heard today.

The employers maintained[4] that it was impossible to frame an international Convention on the reduction of the normal working week without at the same time dealing with wages; and that was also impossible. At the national level, a reduction in working hours would mean increased costs and therefore increased selling prices, and the greater the proportion of wages in industry's costs, the greater the increase in the selling prices. These increases would affect all industries using such products. If the reduction were confined only to certain industries, this might result in the use of substitute products produced by other industries. One of the most serious dangers of a progressive reduction in working hours, in the employers' view, was that it would cause discontent and unrest in those industries where working time was not reduced. Moreover, prices of manufactured products would become dearer for agricultural countries, which were already suffering from the low prices received for their products. As for the increased purchasing power expected in the industrialised countries as a result of the increased wages paid, this was illusory, because higher prices would reduce purchasing power. Furthermore, increased labour costs would be an incentive to mechanisation and this would reduce the amount of labour required. Reduced working time would make the unemployment situation worse instead of better.

In the same discussion, another argument put forward on behalf of the employers[5] was that the eight-hour day was now an established fact and that nobody was complaining that it was too long. This question was no longer social but economic. The effects on employment had to be seen in the context of three different classes of industry. For those with continuous processes, it would be possible to organise four shifts instead of three in a 42-hour week. But that would raise the question of the supply of specialised workers, and with workers working a 42-hour week instead of a 56-hour week, there would be a 25 per cent reduction in wages. Would the workers accept this? If not, there would be a total increase in the cost of production of 35 to 40 per cent which neither industry nor the country could bear. The second class of industry comprised sectors in which, for technical reasons, the number of workers could not be increased, as on worksites in the building industry. A reduction in working time would mean a reduction of output and increased costs. The problem of workers' housing would be aggravated. The third class of industry comprised undertakings where an increase in equipment was feasible. If they did not have the required technical and financial means of increasing their mechanisation, their output would fall and prices would increase. Otherwise, there would be increased redundancy.

On the government side, many delegates — including some who said they were themselves heads of undertakings — expressed themselves in favour of reducing the normal working week without lowering living standards.[6] They stressed how important it was to look at what would actually happen in specific industries and cases, taking into account the experience that was being acquired. In their view, workers were entitled to a reduction in their labour, which was now made possible by technical progress, and the problem could not simply be considered from the financial point of view of an undertaking's production costs. Work had become more arduous and the workers needed greater leisure. Life did not consist merely of what went on inside undertakings; what happened in people's homes should also be taken into consideration and households could not survive under the burden of unemployment. Technical progress had completely altered the relationship between wage costs and final production costs, with the result that wages were no longer the determining factor, particularly in manufacturing industry. Other factors of production could have much greater effect on costs, and in their case employers had no alternative but to bear those costs. Why should there be a different attitude towards a worker who "sold" his labour than towards a producer of raw materials who raised his prices? Furthermore, public authorities could have an effect on the financial burdens of undertakings, could combat rises in prices, which were often due to currency speculations, and could also exert an influence on wage levels.

One government delegate[7] questioned the presumptions underlying the arguments to the effect that either wages would have to fall or prices would have to rise if wages rose. On the basis of the reductions in working time that had taken place in his country, he had noted that once such a reduction occurred, the arguments became invalid, because they failed to take into account the imagination, ingenuity and organising ability of the employers. It was necessary to take a double risk: shorter hours and possible higher prices. This was not a simple problem and account must be taken of differences between industries, but it still remained necessary to fix on a maximum which must not be exceeded. This measure, which he regarded as temporary in character, was the best that could be done in the existing situation. There was a latent demand for better living conditions and there were abundant resources available to improve these conditions.

With regard to holidays with pay, the employers stressed the cost burden on undertakings — wage costs and their repercussions on production costs, cost of replacing workers on holiday or, in the absence of replacement, lower production — and also the need for research on the effects of leisure on the workers' health and productivity. On the government side, emphasis was placed on the advantages of this measure, such as increased demand for consumer goods and services, a decrease in social costs due to a reduction in accidents, and a fall in absenteeism due to illness.

Theoretical disputes

To simplify a controversy that is in fact extremely complicated and is still current today, it may be said that these debates were the reflection of two conflicting economic doctrines about ways and means of dealing with the slump. The first, or "classical", theory placed emphasis on regulatory mechanisms inherent in the economic system; all that was needed was laissez-faire. In particular, a fall in production costs due to lower wages would encourage private investment and stimulate production. Any obstacle to this process was therefore to be avoided. As unemployment reduced the workers' ability to defend their living standards, it was in itself a useful regulatory factor and was due, according to this theory, to excessively high wages. If working time was reduced, wages must also be reduced at the same time. The other doctrine has remained associated with the name of Keynes. One of its essential features, from the point of view of the present study, is the importance attached to maintenance of global demand for goods and services — to be achieved mainly by means of public expenditure and investment — as a factor in overcoming an economic depression. Similarly, maintenance of, or increase in, people's purchasing power is considered necessary to assure a satisfactory balance between production and consumption. Through the publications prepared by their officials, the ILO and the League of Nations made a considerable contribution to spreading this conception of how to cope with depressions.[8]

The ILO devoted special attention to the arguments concerning the adoption of progressive social policies in individual countries, since in any event the ILO's mission was to ensure that non-adoption of such measures by any one country should not hinder other countries in their efforts to improve the conditions of their workers. Concerning the arguments against social progress based on the idea that it was harmful to international competitivity, an ILO publication of 1931 had this to say:

... Can one say that countries which make efforts to regulate the labour supply, to introduce vocational and technical education or to protect the workers against sickness and injury arising out of their employment are *ipso facto* at a disadvantage in international competition? And even the reduction of hours of work, the improvement of wages, the protection of children or social insurance surely repay their immediate cost by advantages and incentives of which national industry finally reaps the benefit? Experience appears to show that the countries with the most advanced labour legislations are by no means the least successful in the competition for world markets. The whole question has often been discussed and doubtless will be discussed for long years to come, for social experiments are not carried out in a laboratory where factors of secondary importance can be eliminated, and consequently it is difficult to establish a definite connection of cause and effect in this subject, and the conclusions advanced on both sides are necessarily in the nature of conjectures.[9]

The ILO also tried to establish whether unemployment was caused by wages that were too high. In 1937 the Report of the Director to the Conference stated:

... If a really international test is applied over a number of countries, the only possible conclusion is that the amount paid per hour to the worker is no more than one among a great many factors which go to determine the general level of a nation's economic activity, and by no means the decisive factor. ... To single out one particular factor ... and to proclaim its sovereignty over all others is entirely unscientific and bound to lead to erroneous conclusions.[10]

In fact, improvement in economic conditions and in employment did occur and was associated not with lower wage rates or compression of production costs or deteriorating conditions of work, but with the abandonment of deflation and the adoption of measures of monetary expansion.

Nothing is perhaps more surprising than the effects of the slump on hours of work. In the past, the general tendency in bad times had been to lengthen hours rather than to reduce them, in order that more might be produced for the same or even for a smaller wage. ... Generally speaking, however, so far from the normal working week having been lengthened, a powerful movement has sprung up in the direction of shortening it.[11]

The Report stated that the need for international agreement had become more imperative as the number of countries applying the 40-hour week increased, so as to discourage such countries from imposing protectionist barriers to international trade against competing countries which were still working longer hours.[12]

ILO research on effects

As the Second World War approached it became difficult to discern the effects of the reductions in working time that had taken place in a number of countries because the threat of war and the increase in expenditure on armaments had created special distortions in national economies. Working time had increased in Germany, Japan and Spain. The conclusions of the Director of the ILO about the effects of shortening the working week in France, New Zealand and the United States are summarised below.[13]

In his view, experience in New Zealand and the United States had demonstrated that, under favourable conditions, the 40-hour week could be established without causing serious disturbance. While experience in France had been different, the logical explanation for this was that it was not the 40-hour week *per se*, but the economic conditions in which it had been introduced, that were the cause. According to the report of a tripartite committee on production, the slow-down in production was to be attributed, at least in part, to the way in which the 40-hour week had been introduced. In New Zealand and the United States there had been much more flexibility. In some cases, undertakings had been allowed to spread over a number of weeks the calculation of the average weekly working week. In other cases, additional shifts had been formed so that work could continue without interruption. Employers had sometimes had recourse to overtime, subject to extra payment. Finally, complete, partial or temporary exceptions had been permitted in specific cases. Any radical change in working hours often required major technical adjustments which themselves required time and experimentation. In the French law and its implementing decrees a good deal of latitude had been provided, but advantage had not always been taken of it, particularly because there was no tradition of collective bargaining in the country. This was one of the main reasons for the difficulties that had been encountered.

CURRENT DISCUSSION

Reduction in working time continues to be actively discussed.[14] Some of the methods for bringing about such reductions are the direct concern of public authorities: this is the case with lowering the normal retirement age and with legislative or regulatory action in other fields. Reduction in normal, maximum or actual working time, whether per day, per week or per year, is of more direct concern to the undertaking in its day-to-day operations. However, the arguments set out below concerning possible effects are drawn from a wide variety of sources.

Working time

The opponents of a reduction of working time in any way at all, and in particular of a reduction in the normal maximum working week, place emphasis on the problems that such a change would raise for management, particularly in small and medium-sized undertakings. It is alleged that such a measure would increase unit labour costs and production costs. As a result, either undertakings would have to increase their selling prices, which would reduce the purchasing power of wages while their own competitivity would be endangered, or they would have to reduce their profits, which would affect their capacity for investment and production. In the more or less short term, a fall in production would follow, with dismissals. An increase in employment sought by work-sharing would meet with many difficulties, starting with the shortage of skills in certain occupations, which would become worse. Moreover, instead of taking on new workers, undertakings might prefer to cut back production, work overtime or invest in new equipment, which would increase redundancy. There would be possibilities of absorbing the increased supply of labour by introducing more shift work or extending opening hours of shops, but such measures meet with resistance on the part of the workers concerned or from public opinion. In general, according to these arguments, increases in productivity are necessary to compensate for increases in hourly labour costs; to the extent that such increases are feasible, they will not increase employment. Some economists predict that the negative effects of reduction in working time would extend to the economy as a whole: rapid inflation, reduced ability to compete internationally, harmful effects on the balance of payments and aggravation of unemployment.

These views are favourably received among employers, who repeat them with variations depending on the country or the organisation concerned.[15] Employers insist that conditions of work can be improved only if the costs can be absorbed without affecting the undertaking's output and profitability. Furthermore, a general reduction in working time would not necessarily reduce unemployment, but might mean lower tax receipts. According to the Swedish Employers' Confederation (SAF), a 30-hour week would lead to stagnation in net incomes, make it impossible to improve social services, conditions of work and the environment, make products more expensive, and cause problems with regard to exports and greater difficulties with regard to employment.

Generally speaking, employers' organisations would be ready to consider the possibility of organising a reduction in real working time on an annual basis; such an arrangement would help to combat absenteeism, to take account of individual preferences of workers as regards the organisation of their working time, and to provide more flexibility for undertakings to achieve their production goals. It would be possible to envisage a continuation of the long-term downward trend in working time if growth were maintained and if workers chose to have more leisure time rather than higher wages. However, in periods of economic recession, the choice would have to be made between the status quo and a reduction in working time accompanied by lower wages. Diverse solutions adapted to individual needs and to the situation of each undertaking would be preferable to the disadvantages and rigidity of a general approach.

Many of these views were put forward at the Third European Regional Conference of the ILO. The Employers' Vice-President pointed out that the standard of 40 hours had not yet been met in developing countries or for numbers of workers in European countries and that the level of working time considerably affected ability to compete in world markets. Limitations of working time could be achieved by methods other than that of reducing the normal working week: reduction on an annual basis, extension of paid annual leave, early retirement, restrictions on excessive overtime. In view of the prevailing serious unemployment, and of the desirability of encouraging the private sector to expand its activities so as to create more productive jobs, it was not the moment for a reduction in working time which the employers believed was probable over the long term, as a continuation of a historical trend and as the counterpart of future increases in the productivity of capital. Work-sharing was not a means of combating unemployment. Reduction in working time could only have negative effects on employment in present circumstances, and workers ought to accept the idea that it could be achieved only if it was accompanied by a fall in their income. However, the employers remained receptive to the workers' aspirations for a new kind of arrangement of their working time: flexible hours, job-sharing, part-time working — all these should be encouraged as much as possible.

Other opinions express reservations of varying degrees, caused by the fear of unfavourable effects, while leaving the door open to a wide range of arrangements for reducing working time. They are put forward from various quarters. From an official source, anxieties concerning the danger of unfavourable effects appear in the resolution of the Council of the European Communities on adaptation of working time.[16] These conclusions reflect two main concerns: economic constraints on the one hand, and improved protection of workers and greater participation in social and economic progress, on the other hand. The question of adaptation of working time is set against a background of factors including demographic trends, the prospect of moderate economic growth, the problems of adjustment resulting in particular from the rise in the price of petroleum, the structural problems of the labour market and the progressive introduction of new technologies. The need for an overall strategy aimed at increasing growth potential, competitiveness and innovation, improving the employment situation and responding to the emergence of new social needs is reaffirmed, as well as the need to keep in check any costs of such measures, to take into account the possibility of distributing the gains from the overall increase in productivity between adaptation of working time and wage increases, to promote labour mobility and training and to facilitate the investment or changes required in undertakings in order to encourage new recruitment or avoid redundancies.

In its resolution, the Council stresses that any measures to adapt working time should be assessed in the light of their effects on the production capacity of undertakings, productivity changes and wages, as well as of possibilities of decentralisation, differentiation according to sector or field of activity and phased implementation. It seeks to promote various forms of adaptation of working time including: the application of limits to the systematic use of overtime, due account being taken of the need to keep production processes flexible, of the state of the labour market and the problems which could arise for lower-paid workers; flexible retirement arrangements, with a gradual retirement from working life at the end of the worker's career; development of voluntary part-time work, with appropriate rights and obligations; in the case of shift work, consideration of aspects such as workers' health and working conditions as well as economic aspects such as competitiveness of undertakings. The Council also invited the Commission to consider, with representatives of employers and workers, how a Community approach on the subject of a reduction in annual working time could be formulated, bearing in mind both the improvement of working conditons and the need to avoid redundancies and encourage new recruitment, as well as the need to preserve competitive conditions and curb the effect of such reductions on labour costs.[17]

Despite the multiplicity of theories being advanced, there seems to be general agreement on one point: in the immediate future there is no hope of attaining rates of growth high enough to eliminate unemployment. However, reactions to this state of affairs have their influence on opinions expressed with regard to the need for reductions in working time.[18] When the recession is believed to be temporary and recovery, whether or not it is stimulated, combined with a slow-down in population growth, is thought to be sufficient to absorb unemployment, there is a tendency to prefer to wait upon events, with the idea that effective working time and wage levels should be left to vary in accordance with economic fluctuations, without adopting any irreversible measures. When it is believed that, in spite of a possible recovery in growth and a contraction of the potential active population, technological change would still leave a hard core of unemployment, then this attitude changes.[19] More active, though flexible, measures may then be deemed necessary with regard to reducing working time, together with appropriate employment and manpower policies.[20] Where a reduction in working time is given consideration, a concerted approach is regarded as essential at the regional and international level to diminish any possible negative consequences on inflation and the balance of payments, together with a diversified approach varying with the economic sectors concerned, with maximum support from workers and employers.[21]

Those in favour of restrictive financial and monetary policies on the one hand, and of expansionary policies on the other, are still fighting the same battles. Attitudes in this field continue to have their influence in the form of differing opinions about maintenance of wage levels in the event of reductions in working time. Such maintenance is recommended by persons who are mainly concerned with keeping up the demand for goods and services and with the redistribution of incomes as factors stimulating economic growth; or it is condemned by those mainly concerned with business costs or who think there is a cause-and-effect relationship between profits and investment and between wage increases and inflation, the latter being attributed particularly to excess demand. Experts of the United Nations Economic Commission for Europe questioned not long ago[22] "the validity of discussing and treating inflation in terms of variations in a 'resource gap'". In recent years, however, a growing number of national economies have moved towards restricting demand in the hope of combating inflation.

If inflation is considered as being due to excess demand and to the weight of labour costs in prices, this leads to preference for reduced working time accompanied by lower wages. Partial unemployment is then supposed to play its traditional regulatory role; wage decreases are expected to bring lower costs and prices, and thus promote competitiveness, and protection of profits should stimulate investment and growth. If the intention is to stabilise prices by putting a brake on demand, it is therefore considered necessary from a macro-economic point of view to treat with great caution any attempt to alleviate the employment effects of slow growth by accelerating the progress towards a shorter working week. It is claimed that the inflationary dangers of such moves might be considerable, and would in no way be obviated by an internationally co-ordinated approach to work-sharing. A more promising approach would be to introduce more flexibility into labour markets by reducing the rigidity of wage structures and removing any unnecessary barriers to part-time employment.[23]

From the opposite side it is pointed out that heavy unemployment with its accompanying lower living standard does nothing to reduce inflation. One of the reasons for unemployment is shortage of demand, inflation being mainly due to structural causes or speculation. They therefore favour encouraging demand, among other means by selective programmes financed from public funds and by restructuring economic activities. From this a recovery in consumption, investments and growth is expected, and in that event the maintenance of, or improvements in, wage levels are considered desirable. Some strategies that have been proposed combine massive increases in public investment, reduced working time and wage increases.[24] Such strategies have not yet been tried out in practice. In one country where the idea of such an active policy was favourably received — Austria — there was no question of reducing the normal working week to combat unemployment at a time when it was at a comparatively low level. If the 35-hour week was to be considered, it would mainly be for the purpose of improving the quality of life, unless the employment situation worsened as a result of technological changes.[25]

Finally, some objections raised against reduction in working time derive from the sceptical attitudes towards the supposed improvements to be expected with regard to employment and unemployment. These not only repeat the unfavourable economic forecasts made elsewhere but also put forward arguments based on individual behaviour. It is feared that the number of workers seeking jobs would increase if workers had more free time: they would go over to work in the "black economy" or would go in for "moonlighting", thus depriving unemployed persons of job opportunities. In addition, persons who are not at present seeking jobs would do so because of the attraction of shorter working hours. In any event, the demand for jobs would rise, despite its being already too high for the number of jobs available, and the expected increase in leisure time, which it is claimed would constitute an improvement in the quality of life, would in fact not take place.

Lowering the age of retirement

It is argued by some writers that lowering the normal age of retirement would not necessarily contribute to improving the employment situation. It is claimed that there is no proof that workers who could benefit would in fact choose to do so, or that there would be as many to do so as is expected, or that if they did leave the labour market, they would actually be replaced. Moreover, there is no evidence that once in receipt of a pension many of them would not seek another job (unless such action is prohibited by law), and thus deprive unemployed persons of jobs.

These reservations are based on forecasts of behaviour by individuals and undertakings, and are accompanied by objections of an economic or financial character. They do not appear to be very strong, at least at the level of the undertaking, where lowering the retirement age does not raise a great deal of opposition as long as there is no question of imposing constraints on recruitment or of increasing employers' social charges. But they attract more support at the level of the community as a whole. At this level, calls for a cautious approach are heard: these are based on the demographic situation and on the problems of financial equilibrium in social security schemes. The demographic situation is atypical at the present time in most of the countries under consideration. It is characterised by a rise in the number of young people and a fall in that of people of retirement age: thus there are an exceptionally large number of people entering the labour market, and an exceptionally small number of people leaving it. This trend will cease as a result of the slow-down in population growth, which will begin to show its effects from about 1985 onwards, with variations from one country to another, provided that there is no change in birth rates. It is feared that if working time were to be reduced, there would be a shortage of workers at a future date; furthermore, if people were encouraged to retire, the financial burden on the active population, which is already heavy, would become heavier still.[26] Once measures had been taken to reduce normal working time, it would be very difficult to undo them. However, fears of negative effects are losing strength as the idea of "flexible retirement" gains ground. Under certain conditions, this could provide a means of reconciling financial restraints, difficulties in the labour market and the need for a transition from paid employment to free activity which is apparently felt by many older workers.

In 1976 already, the Council of Europe recommended the grant of an early pension, without reduction, in the five years preceding normal retirement age for workers in certain circumstances (long-term unemployment, incapacity for work, or failure to complete a prescribed qualifying period).[27] The Commission of the European Communities has also put forward three principles to be followed in connection with retirement. The first is that a worker from a certain age (say 60) and before a maximum age, should be entitled freely to choose his retirement age under conditions which ensure that his decision is not unduly influenced by major differences in the amount of pension he would receive according to the choice he makes. The second principle is that of phased retirement. Any loss in income due to a reduction in activity would be compensated, but social security entitlement would be fully maintained. Workers choosing not to benefit from such arrangements would be entitled to engage in part-time employment of various kinds on retirement. The third principle is that, since flexible retirement will have a more direct effect on employment than phased retirement, at least in the short term, "mass" flexible retirement might be encouraged temporarily by financial incentives in periods of chronic unemployment, the jobs thus liberated being refilled; on the other hand, continuation in gainful activity would be encouraged in times of full employment. Model rules would have to be worked out for reconciling social considerations and financial constraints in these various cases.[28]

It may be mentioned in passing that the different forms of retirement that are being introduced do not all correspond to the lowering of the normal retirement age which has been called for, as indicated above, and this has given rise to some confusion. What has been proposed relates in fact to lowering the age at which entitlement to pension at the full rate exists, either because this rate will be paid at an earlier age, or because the fact of having paid contributions for a certain number of years gives entitlement to the full rate, irrespective of age. The other kinds of retirement mentioned above are early retirement, implying an actuarial reduction of the full rate of pension, and pre-retirement under which there is a guarantee of resources, the amount of which may vary, and which is intended to encourage workers who are unemployed or in danger of losing their jobs to leave the labour market and to tide them over until they receive their proper retirement pensions. The effects of these measures are, of course, not the same.

The social demand for leisure

There is at present a growing demand for leisure in the industrialised market economy countries.[29] There are various reasons for this, some of which, such as rising living and educational standards and the increasing problems of daily life, have deep roots. This demand is confirmed by surveys the results of which are normally not comparable between one country and another. One of them, which was carried out in the countries of the European Community in accordance with a uniform methodology, showed that 37 per cent of the employed persons covered were in favour of a reduction in daily or weekly working hours, 25 per cent in favour of longer annual leave and 33 per cent in favour of lowering the retirement age. The second option was of particular interest to younger age groups. There were considerable differences from one country to another. Among employed persons shorter daily or weekly working hours was supported by a higher percentage than longer holidays in six countries — Belgium, Denmark, France, Ireland, Italy and the United Kingdom. A lowering of the retirement age received the highest proportion of votes in Belgium (41 per cent), the Federal Republic of Germany (38 per cent), France (43 per cent), Italy (37 per cent), Luxembourg (49 per cent) and the Netherlands (35 per cent).

For every 100 employed persons covered by the survey, 42 preferred higher wages (for the same working time) and 51 preferred shorter working time (for the same wage); seven expressed no opinion. The percentage of those preferring shorter working time was over 50 in six countries — United Kingdom (51), Belgium (53), France (54), the Federal Republic of Germany (55), the Netherlands (64) and Denmark (66) — and was under 50 in the three others — Luxembourg (20), Ireland (32) and Italy (40). In each country the relative incomes of the respondents had only a slight influence on their preferences.[30]

The way in which questions are framed in such surveys may give rise to misunderstandings. To ask people to choose between "more leisure" and "higher wages" is to ask them to exclude one or the other. In practice, a statutory or contractual reduction in standard working time implies non-reduction of wages corresponding to the previous standard working time; but if time actually worked remains unchanged there will automatically be an increase in earnings for hours that were previously paid at the standard rate and will now be paid as overtime. A choice in favour of shorter standard working hours therefore implies an increase in total remuneration if the employer requires the same number of hours to be actually worked. It is failure to specify "standard working time" that makes all the difference. Moreover, the way the questions were put seemed to indicate that the workers concerned could obtain wage increases by just asking for them: all they had to do was not ask for shorter working time. In practice, both wage increases and reduction in working time are usually obtained only after difficult negotiations and sometimes after bitter conflicts. Furthermore, the questions do not specify whether the wages referred to are real or nominal wages, which is not without importance in the current inflationary situation. Nevertheless, such surveys do play a useful role in revealing certain profound social changes.

The rise in the demand for leisure has encouraged new theoretical approaches in employment and labour policy. Some writers think that attempts should be made to "modulate" the labour supply so that there would be no surplus of applicants for jobs. This might be achieved by changing people's attitude towards work. It would mean finding acceptable remunerated substitutes for work (more education, frequent recycling of skills, or reduction of the length of working life in particular through the introduction of progressive retirement). In the opinion of these writers such a transformation would have a decisive effect both on the labour force participation rate of the population and on the very concept of full employment.[31] Such theories form part of trends in current thinking which seek to revise the definition of the "level of unemployment compatible with full employment", because it is not clear how full employment can be maintained. Labour market specialists seek to establish new policies on working time which both modify the working time of all workers or categories of workers and widen the options available to individuals. These two kinds of measures are not in competition, they believe: "To call for further reductions in working time does not *ipso facto* mean taking a position against greater individualisation and vice versa". The conjunction of all such measures would have beneficial effects on the labour market.[32]

One of the possible individual arrangements of working time attracting particular attention is part-time employment, which has the advantage for the undertaking of being accompanied by lower wages. This kind of short-time working showed a spectacular increase in the past when excess demand for labour was mobilising all available manpower resources. It seems that there is still a steady demand for it in spite of the serious unemployment now prevailing, although in current circumstances it is rather difficult to ascertain whether short-time working is really voluntary or not. In France a report from the General Inspectorate of Social Affairs states that—

The people who dream of working part time are not those who actually experience it. This kind of employment being what it is, everything combines to ensure that the only people who seem to take up such employment are those who are obliged to do so, free choice being far from the most frequent case, contrary to the intentions of the framers of the law of 1973.[33]

Interest in this kind of employment is very lively in official quarters in several countries, and the need to ensure adequate social protection for people in part-time work is generally recognised. A recent draft law in France deals with all employment for periods less than standard working time; it seeks to avoid a too restrictive interpretation of the limits imposed by the Labour Code and hence speaks of "all periods of part-time work lower than the normal hours of work in the undertaking".[34] This draft has met with almost unanimous opposition from trade union organisations. Another draft law would introduce part-time work on an experimental basis in the public service.[35]

According to the ILO, part-time employment is defined as any single, regular and voluntary form of employment with hours of work much shorter than normal.[36] It is recalled that this kind of employment is not dealt with in the present study, because it is merely a form of employment with shorter working time and lower pay, and is thus not to be confused with the traditional social aim of reduction in normal working hours, which is the subject of current controversies. It may suffice here to indicate how useful it would be to undertake research on possible effects of a further spread of this kind of employment.

Discussions about the social demand for leisure rapidly lead into debates about the kind of society or of economic growth that would best meet this new demand. Many people think that giving priority to free time means choosing to "live" instead of to "possess". This choice is said to require a different kind of growth — "qualitative growth" — which would perhaps imply slower accumulation of wealth, but also new and deeper enjoyment of human values.

Standards of living would improve qualitatively because workers would have "more time for living".

Some writers have tried to imagine what kind of development might be based on the idea of a "different use of time",[37] but this has been at a very general and highly theoretical level. It is believed that reductions in working time could take different forms depending on whether the consumer society is accepted as it is (longer weekend and annual leave) or whether a new form of social organisation is proposed (reduction in daily working hours, introduction of a fifth shift, opposition to overtime). What would the implications be? These writers speculate about the demand for new products and services that would result from increased leisure, or about potential individual or collective activities "outside the market economy" that would be either organised or spontaneous and might develop if people had more spare time, and about the measures to be taken to ensure that all this would become reality. Work-sharing in its widest connotation is regarded in this connection essentially as a means of promoting desired social changes. These writers consider that this subject ought not to be reserved for economists, since it is at the crossroads where many of the social sciences meet.

For their part, economists are generally more interested in problems relating to the content of growth. The experts of the Economic Commission for Europe affirm that public discussion has degenerated into a false controversy between "growth" and "no-growth" with the result that not enough attention is being paid to finding other solutions or exploring new opportunities for growth.[38] Some people consider that there is no necessary contradiction between growth and greater leisure. One of them,[39] for example, rejects the idea of "halting" growth, in view of the fact that the basic needs of a large portion of humanity are still far from satisfied, and that the industrialised world will, as pointed out by Fourastié, show an increasing appetite for services. Growth should therefore rather be guided into appropriate channels. It depends on the economic context whether a reduction in working time is a reasonable option or serves as an obstacle to necessary structural change and as a means of distributing poverty. He goes on to say that the transition from quantitative to qualitative growth calls for more than merely a change of adjective: it means changing the type of society we live in, including its economic structures and employment policies. Full employment and higher living standards require changes in aims and priorities involving a number of deliberate choices, among them being the expansion of sensible leisure-time activities.

A reduction in working time could thus be an important factor in redirecting the growth of advanced industrialised economies. More than 20 years ago, a professor of economics put the question whether we should not "reduce working time rather than develop useless products", or keep production as a "first priority, but redirecting it towards what is desirable from the human point of view". He added that "taking a stand on these problems and trying to solve the technical issues involved will no doubt be one of the main tasks of economic science in the future".[40] It may be that the study of this kind of problem has been hampered by a failure to recognise that, in relation to reduced working time, "non-working" time is just as important as working time itself and that both are a source of demand and consumption of specific products and services, irrespective of the nature of the economic and political system. The "leisure society" is not merely of sociological interest: it also gives a different direction to economic growth.

Notes

[1] ILO: *Report of the Director*, International Labour Conference, 19th Session, Geneva, 1935, p. 45.

[2] ibid., 24th Session, Geneva, 1938, p. 43.

[3] ILO: *Record of Proceedings*, International Labour Conference, 19th Session, Geneva, 1935.

[4] ibid., Sixth Sitting, statements by Mr. Oersted, Employers' delegate, Denmark, pp. 65-67.

[5] ibid., Seventh Sitting, statement by Mr. Gérard, Employers' delegate, Belgium, pp. 80-81.

[6] ibid., arguments taken from various statements: Mr. Mahaim (Belgium), pp. 68-69; Mr. J. Godart (France), pp. 70-71; Sir Frederick Stewart (Australia), pp. 75-76; Mrs. Karlsen (Norway), pp. 109-110; Mr. Wauters (Belgium), pp. 534-535.

[7] ibid., statement by Mr. Hamilton (United States), pp. 81-83.

[8] ILO: *The world of industry and labour, 1939*, Report of the Director, International Labour Conference, 25th Session, Geneva, 1939, pp. 14-16.

[9] *The International Labour Organisation: The first decade*, Preface by Albert Thomas (London, Allen and Unwin, 1931), p. 30.

[10] ILO: *Report of the Director*, International Labour Conference, 23rd Session, Geneva, 1937, p. 32.

[11] ibid., p. 34.

[12] ibid., p. 39.

[13] ibid., 24th Session, Geneva, 1938, pp. 48-53. The 40-hour week was introduced in France and New Zealand in 1936; in the United States, the process of reduction to a maximum of 40 hours had begun earlier, though the Fair Labor Standards Act was adopted in 1938.

[14] On this point, see in particular ILO: *Growth, structural change and manpower policy: The challenge of the 1980s*, Report of the Director-General, Third European Regional Conference, Geneva, 1979, with special reference to Ch. 2, pp. 40-65; and idem: *Policies and practices for the improvement of working conditions and working environment in Europe*, Third European Regional Conference, Geneva, 1979, doc. CRE/III-PR 14, pp. 7-9.

[15] See Ch. 1, note 2.

[16] *Official Journal of the European Communities*, "Information and notices", Vol. 23, Part C, 4 Jan. 1980, p. 1.

[17] The question of reducing working time and its possible effects was discussed in the European Parliament in the course of a debate on employment and methods of combating unemployment in the Community; see "Debates of the European Parliament, 1980-1981 Session, Report of Proceedings from 14 to 18 January 1980", in *Official Journal of the European Communities* (Luxembourg, Office for Official Publications of the European Communities), No. 250, Jan. 1980, pp. 45-110.

[18] Since the present study is concerned only with market economy countries, mention may be made in passing of the theories which claim that capitalism is no longer able to ensure full employment. Those who support this view do not appear to consider that a reduction in working time constitutes a problem *per se*, but see it rather as a palliative, the good effects of which will disappear in the long run as a result of technological progress. See, for example, Joan Robinson: *Contributions to modern economics* (Oxford, Blackwell, 1979), 20: "Has capitalism changed?", pp. 227-228, and 21: "Latter-day capitalism", pp. 233-234.

[19] It may be pointed out, however, that the traditional explanation of unemployment as being due to technological progress seems to be no longer so widely accepted. The Economic Commission for Europe has stated, in this connection: "... the view that technical progress 'causes' unemployment has not even the merit of novelty and is no more valid today than it was in the past". See "Labour force and employment in Western Europe: The prospects to 1985 by major sectors", in *Economic Bulletin for Europe* (Geneva, Economic Commission for Europe), Vol. 30, No. 2, p. 48. One economist considers that if this theory about the replacement of men by machines were true,

"France today, after two centuries of technical progress, would have, instead of 20 million employed and 1.5 million unemployed, just the opposite, even allowing for reduction in working time". See Alfred Sauvy: *La machine et le chômage: Le progrès technique et l'emploi*, Preface by Wassily Leontieff (Paris, Dunod, 1980), p. 70.

[20] *Growth, structural change and manpower policy: The challenge of the 1980s*, op. cit., Ch. 2.

[21] Francis Blanchard: "More leisure, more work?", in *ILO Information* (Geneva, ILO), Oct. 1979, pp. 1-2.

[22] Economic Commission for Europe: *Economic Survey of Europe in 1978*, Part I: *The European economy in 1978* (New York, United Nations, 1979; Sales No. E.79.II.E.1), p. 35.

[23] "Economic policy in the early 1980s", in *OECD Economic Outlook* (Paris), Dec. 1979, p. 11.

[24] See, for example, the reference to this kind of proposal in Bernard Keizer: "Les choix de la République fédérale d'Allemagne", in *Economie et politique* (Paris, Institut national de statistique et des études économiques), July-Aug. 1978, p. 48, which also refers to the counter-report by experts supporting this strategy: *Memorandum 78: Alternativen der Wirtschaftspolitik*, prepared by a group of professors at the University of Bremen and ten members of the DIW Institute in Berlin.

[25] "Die 35-Stunden-Woche kommt bestimmt", in *Solidarität*, interview with the Minister, Dr. Weissenberg (Vienna, Austrian Trade Union Confederation), Oct. 1979, pp. 13-14.

[26] Conseil de l'Europe, Comité directeur pour la sécurité sociale, Comité d'experts en matière de sécurité sociale dans sa composition d'actuaires: *Projet de rapport sur les effets combinés de l'abaissement de l'âge de la retraite et du vieillissement de la population sur le financement des régimes de sécurité sociale relatifs aux prestations long terme* (Strasbourg, 22 Feb. 1977; doc. CD/SS(77)1).

[27] Franco Marziale: "Resolution of the Council of Europe on social security measures to be taken in favour of pensioners and persons remaining in activity after pensionable age", in *International Social Security Review* (Geneva, International Social Security Association), 1976, No. 3, pp. 284-289.

[28] Commission of the European Communities: *Community guidelines on flexible retirement*, doc. COM (80) 393 final (Brussels, 14 July 1980).

[29] See, for example, for the United States: "Money versus leisure: A public sector survey", in *Social and Labour Bulletin* (Geneva, ILO), 4/78, pp. 360-361; for Finland: "Reactions to a shorter working day", ibid., 4/79, pp. 381-382. For France, see Jean-Emile Vié (Conseiller-maître la Cour des comptes): *L'aménagement du temps de travail et du temps de loisirs*, Report submitted to Mr. Robert Boulin, Minister of Labour and Participation, January 1979 (Paris, May 1979), pp. 10-11, and Alain Doyelle with the assistance of Françoise Bonnal and Jean-Paul Blanchet: "La perception du temps chez les salariés: Quelques enseignements d'une enquête", in *Travail et emploi* (Paris, Ministère du Travail), Jan. 1980, p. 7. For the Federal Republic of Germany, see Dieter Mertens: "L'aménagement du temps de travail", in *Emploi et nouveaux modes de vie*, international conference, 29-30 November 1979, The Hague (Paris, Institut d'éducation, Fondation européenne de la culture), pp. 22-31.

[30] Commission of the European Communities: *The attitude of the working population to retirement*, Report by Hélène Riffault (Brussels, May 1978; doc. V/457/78-EN), pp. 36-43. The sample survey was carried out at the request of the Commission of the European Communities in October-November 1977 among 8,936 persons representing the active population aged 15 and over. It was made clear that the reduction in working time would be without loss of wages.

[31] Jean Mouly and Robin Broadfield: "Objectives and policies: A reassessment in the wake of the recession", in David H. Freedman (ed.): *Employment: Outlook and insights* (Geneva, ILO, 1979), p. 41.

[32] Mertens, op. cit., p. 20.

[33] Michel Lucas: *Le travail temps partiel*, Report submitted to Mr. Robert Boulin, Minister of Labour and Participation and Mrs. Nicole Pasquier, Secretary of State for Women's Employment, in the series "Pour une politique du travail", No. 10 (Paris, May 1979), p. 33.

[34] The Labour Code defines part-time work as being between one-half and three-quarters of the normal working week (Art. 212-4-2).

[35] Reactions to this draft law include "Fonctionnaires: le temps partiel", in *FO Hebdo* (Paris, Confédération générale du travail — Force ouvrière), 21 May 1980, p. 10.

[36] See in particular ILO: *Date, place and agenda of the 67th (1981) Session of the Conference*, Governing Body, 211th Session (Geneva, 13-16 November 1979), doc. GB.211/2/1, pp. 11-16. Part-time work was recently dealt with by the International Labour Conference as part of the wider question of *Equal opportunities and equal treatment for men and women workers: Workers with family responsibilities*, Reports VI (1) and (2), International Labour Conference, 66th Session, Geneva, 1980.

[37] "Le partage du travail", in *Droit social* (Paris), No. 1, Jan. 1980 (II), report on a symposium organised by the "Travail et Société" research centre at the University of Paris-Dauphine, 3-4 April 1979; in particular "Présentation des travaux du colloque", p. 66; Xavier Greffe and Jocelyne Gaudin: "Partage du travail et mode de développement", pp. 86-89; and Jacques Delors: "Conclusions", pp. 145-147.

[38] "Labour force and employment in Western Europe, the prospects to 1985 by major sectors", op. cit., pp. 45 and 49.

[39] R. Rifflet: "Policy prospects in the European Communities" in Freedman (ed.), op. cit., pp. 29-30.

[40] Jacques Lecaillon: *Les mécanismes de l'économie. Initiation* (Paris, Cujas, 2nd ed., 1967), p. 209.

POTENTIAL IMPLICATIONS
FOR THE INDIVIDUAL

5

There are a number of reasons why it is important to consider the possible effects of any measures for reduction in working time on the individual. In the first place it is for the benefit of individual human beings that such measures are supposed to be taken. Thus we need to know whether the benefits expected in relation to the quality of life are likely to materialise. It is generally accepted nowadays that a reduction in working time is bound to improve living conditions, but how can this best be achieved and in what circumstances? In the second place it is argued that a reduction in working time would bring about changes in people's attitudes to work in their spare time, and one may wonder what those changes would be. The present chapter will seek to identify in particular the changes in attitude which may influence, in one way or another, the more general trends described in Chapter 7.

Proper replies to these questions would need to be supported by research on behaviour and motivation, but very little research has been carried out that would be of direct use for the present purpose: more often than not, scattered references in research carried out for other purposes has to be relied on to throw light on the possible effects of reducing working time. In general, systematic research on the social effects of reducing working time has scarcely begun; it is as though the only effect of such reduction would be to reduce the time available for production. This shortage of information is serious. It is individual human beings who have reactions which — when added together at various levels — constitute "general trends". Because such trends are what trigger off important policy decisions, it is essential that they should be correctly interpreted. In the absence of full and accurate information about individual reactions, assumptions about general trends may in fact be nothing more than hasty generalisations. Besides, in the absence of a sufficiently clear picture of individual reactions, a large part of the social and economic movements set off by measures for reducing working time might remain unknown, and so distort understanding of future trends.

In the following pages attention will be paid in turn to the possible effects of measures for the reduction of working time on life at work, ways of living, and personal attitudes to work in one's spare time. Beforehand, however, a note of caution should be sounded. Such information as is available relates mostly to reductions that have already been carried out to bring down the amount of working time from levels much higher than those existing today. To what extent may we legitimately extrapolate from these higher levels? If current levels were lowered, would the effects be different or less clear? Or should we take into account the "saturation effect" which seems to operate in the long run, according to some observers, once there has been a change in working conditions, and which weakens or neutralises the effects of such changes? If so, should we expect to see the same kind of effects as were noted on the occasion of previous reductions in working time? Or are there new elements in the situation today which would shift the balance in a different way from that of the past?

On all these essential points we shall generally have to be content with guesswork. However, one point seems very likely: the greater the reductions in working time, the more favourable the effects will be in those areas of personal life to be considered here, provided that certain conditions relating to conditions of life are met. But the possibility of some unfavourable effects cannot be ruled out. For example it will be seen that there are some disturbing risks in the field of conditions of work which, in the absence of appropriate measures, would be aggravated by a reduction in working time.

LIFE AT WORK

Possible effects of reduced working time on life at work will be examined below under different headings: attitudes towards work as such; safety, health and welfare; individual production; conditions of work and employment. These distinctions are made to facilitate analysis. It is obvious that they are not so clear-cut in real life.

Attitudes towards the job

Shortening working hours does not of itself change job content. Such a measure cannot therefore be regarded as a substitute for job enrichment or career development. But it may be desirable because of the very nature of the work. Some people believe that hours of work today can be regarded as satisfactory, except for certain categories of workers. Others believe that account must be taken of general factors relating in particular to changes in the nature of certain jobs, the growing difficulty in conditions of life and modifications in the composition of the active population; such factors are said to support the case for a general reduction in working time, without prejudice to more generous selective measures in specific cases. In France the National Agency for Improvement of Conditions of Work (ANACT) emphasises the following factors: the probability of greater nervous fatigue owing in some cases to "speed-up" of production processes, lowering of levels of skill required for certain jobs, increases in time spent on commuting to and from work; and the increased proportion of women in paid employment who, in fact, perform two jobs every working day. There are also some categories of workers who have long weekly working hours, and shiftworkers have special problems.[1]

Thus, while a reduction in working time brings no change in job content, it may — particularly if the reduction is on a large scale — cause jobs that are disagreeable or boring in themselves to be less unattractive. It might help to neutralise the growing alienation from certain jobs that has been noted and is often attributed to the fact that workers are generally better educated, particularly the younger ones, and are therefore more demanding than in the past about the job to which they are obliged to devote a large part of their daily life or their whole existence. Would a reduction in their weekly or annual working time cause them to pay more attention to their job or accept it more readily? Would they stay away from work less often, or for shorter periods? Replies to these questions require research into individual motivation, which is very little understood.

For example the propensity to stay away from work is usually thought of as absenteeism affecting a whole undertaking, and is taken into account in studies of productivity (see Chapter 6). As regards individuals, however, it is the motivation of the person who stays away from work that has to be considered, since we need to try to ascertain how such and such a worker would react if his working time were shortened without loss of earnings; we are dealing with feelings underlying different kinds of behaviour. If it is accepted that some of the motives involved in absence from work while current working hours are in force would find an appropriate response in a reduction of those hours, then we should be correct in thinking that shorter working hours would reduce absenteeism. But we should need to carry out more detailed research on motivation, and motives would have to be expressed in a way that we could understand. Absences from work may be either "with excuse" or "without excuse". Even if there is an excuse because absence was due to illness or accident, there is nothing to say that the accident or illness was not indirectly connected with over-long working time; yet, as we shall see, it is generally difficult, or even impossible, to establish the existence of such a connection. If there is no excuse for absence, it may be due to lack of time to deal with personal affairs, for example; in such cases the reason is not always expressly stated. Or the absence may be due to "not feeling very well", a state that may be assimilated to illness and poor health and may also be connected with over-long working time. A frustrated need for more leisure may create discontent that causes absenteeism. If people do not have enough leisure time to engage in activities that keep them physically and mentally fit, they may fall ill or incur accidents and thus have legitimate cause for their absence from work. In the Netherlands the need for more leisure is listed among the factors responsible for the rising incidence of absences due to illness. In this connection, it would seem that a new scale of values is evolving as the principle of authority in the employment relationship is being questioned, while at the same time leisure activities, in which sport and social contacts play a large part, are growing in importance.[2]

For a number of reasons — some of which have already been mentioned — it is difficult to be definite about the ways in which a reduction in working time would affect the propensity of workers to stay away from work. This is in spite of the large amount of material published on the subject of absenteeism.[3] There are often no significant correlations. Comparisons of the level of absenteeism over a period of time are also unreliable, because the factors that affect it are also constantly changing. In some cases absenteeism seems to have increased over the medium and long term, while working hours have tended to fall; on the other hand many studies on increases in productivity due to shorter working hours have also shown parallel reductions in absenteeism for the same reason. Perhaps these discrepancies are due to the fact that the examples quoted relate to different periods of time — the productivity studies mentioned above covered only short periods. Thus the divergences may be more apparent than real if it is assumed that there is an irreversible urge for more leisure, which will, however, probably become subject to the "saturation effect" in the long run.

Apart from such obvious causes as illness or accident, absence from work is due to various factors. Thus a recent Swedish study of employees who are rarely or never absent provides the following "identikit" portrait: a middle-aged man employed in a small undertaking, living near his work, having some degree of decision about how he does his work and when he takes his "coffee-break", with some variety in the tasks he has to perform and a relatively large degree of independence.[4] Working time is only one factor among many. However, we can try to examine this factor more closely by looking at one feature that is indirectly connected with working time — commuting time, or the distance between home and workplace. It would appear from some research that, at least above a certain level, absenteeism is higher where it takes longer to travel to and from work, or where there are longer distances between home and work. Thus, while it is not possible to displace people's homes, it might be that shorter working hours would help to reduce absenteeism by compensating for time spent on commuting. Furthermore, any positive result thus obtained would no doubt be reinforced if flexible work schedules were introduced. It is generally accepted that absences from work can be reduced by making work schedules more flexible.

A number of studies have established that there is a relationship between absenteeism and poor conditions or an unpleasant atmosphere at work, even if the workers are not paid when they do not come to work, but it is not possible to determine what role the working time factor plays in this. Yet some indications may be found in such studies, even if only indirectly. One Norwegian study shows that of all the factors involved in absences from work, those that are the most directly involved are the effects of workload, stress, nervous strain, fatigue and practical problems having nothing to do with employment.[5] It may well be that a reduction in working time would have a beneficial effect on all these points, even though the factor of working time was not, as such, a subject of the research. At a recent meeting of experts on absence from work and social security, already mentioned above, it was regretted that so little research existed on the effects of shorter working hours — part-time work — on absenteeism; it appeared to be accepted that the effect would be of some importance.[6]

Safety, health and welfare

There seems to be general agreement that the effects of further reductions in working time on workers' safety, health and welfare would be favourable.[7] Unfortunately, in this field as in others relating to the social effects of such reductions, very little relevant research has been done. Similarly, there is scarcely any information about what is considered to be a desirable state of physical, mental and social well-being, other than the absence of illness or injury. It is not only that the borderline between good health and illness is not always clear cut; what is meant by a state of well-being is difficult if not impossible to establish.

Relevant statistics relate essentially to accidents and illnesses, but usually do not provide any clear correlation with working time, and still more rarely with variations in the latter. For occupational accidents and diseases, a number of the factors involved are more decisive in their effects than working time, namely the work environment, personality characteristics, and the relationship between the two. Of course it may be argued that shorter working hours would reduce occupational risks in a number of ways: for example, by limiting the length of time in which workers are exposed to such risks and by reducing fatigue and stress due to work. But accidents can be linked only indirectly with those factors (such as momentary carelessness, mistakes, slow reactions and the effects of stress), and the relationship between working time and fatigue and stress is not at all easy to determine.[8] These states are subjective in nature and hence somewhat indefinable. They may have a variety of causes. For example they may be due not only to working hours that are too long, but also to poor working conditions, too long journeys between home and work, or other causes that have nothing to do with work at all.

It is difficult to establish a quantitative relationship between working hours and accidents at work. When there are statistics on the number of accidents occurring each day in each hour from the start of the shift — and this is very seldom the case — the only conclusion to be drawn is that so many accidents would not have been included in these statistics if so many hours had not been worked. However, it cannot be assumed that the accident curve on the graph would not be modified if working hours were reduced, and the probable benefits of a reduction in fatigue over the whole working day cannot be left out of account. In statistics from Finland covering 1973, for example, it may be seen that for production workers (machine operators and labourers) a fall of 39,969 in the number of accidents resulted from limiting working hours to seven per day, and of 19,165 and 12,100 accidents if both the seventh and the sixth hour were eliminated. Shortening actual working hours to six per day reduced the total number of accidents from 144,386 to 85,252; the 19,165 accidents due to the addition of the seventh hour represent more than double the number occurring in the first hour of the shift (9,886).[9]

A French report arrives at the general conclusion that the two main risk factors in accidents during the working day are the start-up period and accumulated fatigue. At the beginning of the working day (preceded by a tiring journey to work), the start of the production process and an increasing rate of production are responsible for a high level of risk. After about three hours there is a transition from a situation in which acts and movements are controlled by the will to a state where they are automatic. This is a dangerous period. There is then a less difficult period up to the fifth hour followed by fatigue which is responsible for further risks, despite a slow-down in the rate of production towards the end of the shift. In fact weekly working hours seem to have very little effect on risks but, in some occupations (metal trades and wood working) the degree of risk may be clearly and positively influenced: an increase of one hour per week would bring about a 30 per cent rise in the indicators for the metal trades.[10]

It is not possible to provide reliable figures on the possible effects of shorter working hours on the number of occupational accidents, if only because it is difficult to determine what the situation was before and after the reduction, "all other things being equal". Moreover, we cannot say what would happen if the reduction in working time caused the undertaking to take on new workers in compensation; would the newcomers incur more or fewer accidents? How serious would these be? The frequency and gravity of accidents in part-time, as compared with full-time employment, would provide a useful indication for evaluating the possible effects of a big reduction in working time. This kind of information is not readily available, however. It is often stated that there are relatively fewer accidents in part-time work, but a general statement of this kind is not enough to enable us to draw definite conclusions.

Nevertheless, even if accidents are not necessarily more numerous towards the end of the working day or on the last day of the working week, they do happen at that time and on that day and they are often more serious towards the end of a shift. Shorter working hours would probably reduce their number, though perhaps not proportionately. Similarly, if the normal working week were "compressed" (four days instead of five, for example), the number of journeys to and from work would be automatically reduced and so would the number of accidents occurring on such journeys. In connection with accidents, it should be recalled that fatigue and tension due to work may be the cause of accidents away from work, just as fatigue and tension caused by factors unrelated to work may be reflected in the number of occupational accidents. The same is true with regard to illnesses.

In connection with occupational diseases, the length of time a person is exposed to risk, in the widest sense of the term, obviously plays an important role, but in many cases the relationship with a possible reduction in working time is even more difficult to establish than in the case of occupational accidents. In some work processes (for example in the chemical industry) the relationship between the duration cf exposure to risks and adverse effects on health can perhaps be determined in a relatively conclusive manner. The fact that limits for exposure are laid down by law reflects this situation. For certain carcinogens and other highly toxic substances the limit should be zero. On the other hand there are many cases where the limits of exposure have been established on the basis of an eight- to 10-hour day or a 40-hour week. They reflect the present state of scientific knowledge and do not take into account the personal vulnerability of each worker. As knowledge, experience and information progress there is always a tendency for authorised limits of exposure to be reduced. To be sure, if there were a reduction in working time that reduced exposure to risks below the statutory limit, this would increase the safety margin in practice. In view of the relative uncertainty of knowledge in these fields, it may be assumed that the benefits would be significant. It should be noted that the less obvious hazards stemming from mental and nervous tension are increasingly frequent in certain occupations nowadays. The consequences of this trend would have to be measured in relation to the whole working life, and not only in relation to working hours: workers may sometimes accumulate occupational stress over a period of years, only to die at the very moment when they have the opportunity to relax provided by retirement.

Many of the effects described above constitute only strong probabilities. It is often impossible, in the current state of knowledge, to establish one cause in a quantifiable way, in isolation from other factors. This is why these matters are usually left out of account in evaluations of the economic effects of possible reductions in working time. Yet no one denies that they exist, or that they involve heavy losses in hours and days of work, or that their cost is reflected in the sale prices of products. They also oblige the community to spend considerable sums on medical or surgical treatment, rehabilitation and various cash benefits (sickness and invalidity allowances, and benefits payable on decease, such as survivors' benefits). When standards of safety, health and welfare are breached, most of the persons affected suffer varying degrees of incapacity, which in turn make it more difficult for them to reintegrate themselves normally in employment and cause a fall in their living standards.[11]

Individual output

It is also likely that reductions in working time would have favourable effects on individual output per hour, both quantitatively and qualitatively. Unfortunately, we have almost no information about this. In the past, conclusions contradicting this hypothesis were put forward in systematic research on the relationship between working time and individual productivity; but this research took place in the special circumstances of wartime, and the positive correlation that was found between increased individual output and longer working hours related in the main to workers paid by results.[12] In any event, even if there is a probable positive relation between lower working hours and individual output, it could only be established for a small proportion of employees — those whose output can be measured, namely workers contributing directly to the making of material goods. The concept of "individual output" is almost impossible to define, in so far as a large and growing number of jobs in advanced industrial societies are concerned. It should be used sparingly and with caution. It has been pointed out in connection with repetitive jobs involving mental effort (visual inspection, supervision of machines) that efficiency falls as time goes by, though there may be irregularities in the slope of the downward curve.[13]

However, it is now generally accepted that productivity would rise if working time were reduced. But various factors that differ according to the individual, such as a fall in absenteeism and in the number of mistakes, rejects and breakdowns, would play a role in addition to increases in individual output. Moreover, a rise in productivity might also be the result of rationalisation or modernisation of equipment; such measures are almost always adopted at the same time as working time is reduced.

Terms of employment and conditions of work

A reduction in working time involves a risk of causing a deterioration in terms of employment and conditions of work. This may arise in various ways as a result of the adoption of measures intended to compensate for the cost of the reduction or to reduce it to a minimum: the workload may be increased (directly by increasing the amount of work to be performed, indirectly by not replacing workers during their additional leave or by economising on supporting staff); production processes may be speeded up; shift work may be introduced or extended; and night work may also be introduced. The risk of increases in workload is particularly difficult to resist for managerial, supervisory, professional and technical staff.[14] In the case of manual workers and salaried employees longer breaks and selective heavier cuts in working hours may help to obviate this risk. Such measures are among those recently put forward in the various proposals made, and the agreements reached, in connection with shortening working time. There may also be a deterioration in terms of employment with an increase in vulnerability and insecurity if employers make use of more employees with uncertain status or without the protection afforded by collective agreements in order to make up the working hours lost as a result of reduced working time. When an individual worker's hours are reduced in connection with progressive retirement it may sometimes be necessary, for technical reasons, to change his functions. A change of this kind may have unfavourable consequences if it means a fall in the worker's status and is not made in full agreement with the worker concerned. Again, if it is decided that working time shall in future be calculated on an annual basis, the weekend breaks that are essential to workers' health may be adversely affected and their leisure time may be subordinated to the production needs of the undertaking, unless appropriate safeguards are established.

In evaluating the effects of possible reductions in working time on the quality of life at work, we must see what safeguards are introduced in each case to ensure that such measures do not operate to the disadvantage of the workers concerned. Any deterioration in conditions of work and employment is contrary to the social objectives of shorter working hours. The Third European Regional Conference of the ILO pointed out that a reduction in normal working hours should not result in increased workloads.[15] Intensification of effort may be counter-productive because it gives rise to hidden production costs within each undertaking as well as to remedial or compensatory social costs which fall in the last analysis on the community as a whole, because they have to be paid for.

Shift work and night work have received a special share of attention up to now because of the particularly serious problems they raise from a social and human point of view.[16] In addition, however, there is a risk that if working hours were shortened, shift work and night work would be increased in order to keep machines and equipment running economically. Workers' organisations, supported by certain writers in this field, call for selective compensatory measures such as heavy reductions in working time, the introduction of a fifth shift (giving a working week of just over 33 hours), and a lowering of the normal retirement age for workers in proportion to the periods of time spent on these kinds of work. In connection with shift work one writer has put forward the idea of different combinations of shifts (fixed or alternating) of six hours each, with weeks comprising 36, 35 or even 30 hours. By such arrangements, and by adjusting timetables, it becomes possible for the workers to take their main meals with their families or to follow a more natural alternation of sleep and wakefulness and thus diminish or remove the harmful effects of this kind of work. With shifts of six or six-and-a-half hours, two shifts could work in daytime.[17] Other writers stress the harmful effects of night work and make daring suggestions for a reduction in working time for shift work to a weekly average of 28 hours.[18] However, even in such cases, the strict weekly framework may need to be broken, and this raises objections on the part of workers and their families, who look on the weekend break as a significant social gain. Some arrangements of working time that would compensate for the cost of reductions — for example extension of opening hours for shops, including on Sundays, also meet with strong resistance.

WAYS OF LIFE

Nowadays no one would think of questioning the need for leisure.[19] A certain number of social evils are associated with too much work, thus adding to the stress of modern life.

Of the effect of long hours on general well-being and the quality of life there can be no argument: leisure is needed for the full development of the personality, of the arts of living and of deeper social relationships.[20]

Nevertheless it is difficult to see what effects further reductions in working time would have on the use of leisure time, or even on their extent. The concept of "spare time" needs to be defined. Leisure in the true sense of the term is often defined as corresponding only to relaxation, recreation and personal development and fulfilment.[21] Part of the time which is not occupied by work or commuting between home and workplace is taken up by activities which are not really freely chosen, such as those corresponding to physiological needs or domestic constraints, and the errands that form an unavoidable part of daily life.

The possible effects of further reductions in working time on ways of life have to be guessed at with the help of indications most of which are indirect in character. Some research on intentions and actual behaviour with regard to utilisation of leisure and on preferences concerning possible arrangements for reducing working time may be used for this purpose. However, we are obliged to rely on our imagination to try to determine the possible effects of an increase in the time not occupied by work on the economic behaviour of individuals (in terms of such economic concepts as the standard of living, consumption and savings) and hence on the economy as a whole.

How would increased leisure be used? Asked about a possible reduction of the working week to below 30 hours, 53 per cent of French people (50 for women and 57 for men) replied that they would devote more time to their family; 39 per cent (35 for men and 42 for women) said they would make more things themselves and buy less in shops. Then came training for another occupation such as carpentry and dress-making (32 per cent); reading and theatre-going (32 per cent); participation in local administration (25 per cent); social life (22 per cent); and television (9 per cent).[22] It would be helpful if there were more surveys of this kind. There is more information available about the use of leisure existing today than there is about people's intentions in the event of increased leisure. It reflects a wide variety of behaviour, differing according to sex, income, education, type of job and age. Comparisons made at different times might enable us to detect trends. It must not be assumed, however, that trends can be simply extrapolated from the present into the future, if only because technological change also has its effect on the ways in which leisure is utilised, sometimes in quite unforeseeable fashion. Other factors may play their part, such as the energy crisis: the rise in the price of petrol may encourage people to stay at home more, make workers more demanding about the quality of their housing and their day-to-day environment, and stimulate "do-it-yourself" activities.

Other surveys relate to individual preferences with regard to possible ways of reducing working time. Using the results, we can try to imagine what kinds of economic and social activities would develop in each case, but unfortunately there have been very few such surveys and it is possible to draw only very general conclusions. The above-mentioned survey carried out in the countries of the European Communities gives an idea, as we have seen, of the proportion of employed persons interested in longer paid annual leave; this proportion is higher in the lower age groups. But the survey makes no distinction between two possible ways of reducing working hours: on a daily or on a weekly basis. A survey carried out in 1978 in the Federal Republic of Germany[23] made this distinction and also allows comparisons to be made with a similar survey in 1971. This shows that 18.9 per cent of the persons covered (as against 16.7 per cent in 1971) were in favour of less hours per day, and 24.5 per cent (31.2 per cent in 1971) wanted a longer free weekend; 53.2 per cent favoured longer holidays as against 43.7 per cent in 1971. Another survey, also dating from 1978, but including lower retirement age as one of the possible ways of reducing working time, gave the following results: out of 100 persons questioned, 35 were in favour of this last method (34 per cent for women), 23 preferred longer holidays (24 for women), 22 preferred the four-day week (20 for women) and 11 preferred a shorter working day (12 for women).[24] Preferences vary from one country to another.

Such surveys do not go into sufficient detail about personal preferences and the underlying reasons to provide guidance for decisions concerning shorter working time or to allow forecasts of their economic and social consequences. At best we can put forward theories, using as a starting-point the idea that the way in which leisure time is increased will influence the way in which it is used.

It is often said, for instance, that women seem to be more interested in a shorter working day, no doubt because household chores have to be done throughout the year; men might be readier to share these tasks if they had more time to do so. This arrangement might be a factor in a strategy for equalising the status of the sexes.[25] Reduction in daily or weekly working hours would certainly bring profound changes in ways of living, since they would make daily life easier, contribute to a better balance between life at work and life away from work, benefit family life and perhaps stimulate the birth rate, favour social relationships and promote trade union, civic, group and cultural activities and sport. Combined with flexible work schedules, it would space out traffic rush-hours, thus reducing both commuting time and the risk of road accidents. A day or two lopped off the working week might give rise to new problems if total weekly working hours were not reduced at the same time, but it would also reduce the time spent on commuting. If people had more leisure at the weekend they would be more inclined to seek a change of scene, which might take such forms as regional tourism, increased contact with nature for city dwellers, and purchase of a second home. Extension of annual leave would encourage more extensive travel, bringing regions and peoples into closer contact and widening cultural horizons. If people were free to make their own arrangements for their annual total working time there would be a wider variety of ways in which leisure would be used.

Leisure has become a major element in everyone's life. More and more, people organise their lives around their leisure activities, which to a large extent determine their life style. A fundamental change seems to be taking place in this field and the fact that, in very many cases, people make financial sacrifices to maintain the proportion of expenditure on leisure activities in the family budget, even when their income or purchasing power falls,[26] shows how deep-rooted this change is. However, it should be mentioned that the more "time for living" there is, the more dissatisfaction seems to increase; and some sociologists[27] see this as a manifestation of the evils of industrial society, irrespective of political or economic systems. Views are expressed that leisure liberates previously repressed internal urges in the individual who then becomes a battlefield where consumption and creation, social conformism and personal liberation, activities involving social participation and activities inspired by infantile escapism are in conflict with one another. As a result, work is experienced as something even less tolerable. There is often a vicious circle uniting tiring and stultifying work with poor quality of leisure activities.[28] A worker who has little opportunity of exercising his capacity for independence or decision in his work may also find his capacity for enjoying his leisure is affected. Leisure may then lose its attraction. In Sweden, according to preliminary results of a survey, progressive retirement seems to have particularly attracted workers who have already had a rich and well-filled life.[29] But the source of this information does not specify the jobs or earnings of the workers concerned.

The vicious circle involving quality of work and quality of leisure is the reason for the variety of reactions concerning the priority to be given to reducing working time in comparison with other methods of improving working and living conditions. Some management specialists[30] have tried to find out whether job satisfaction increased with shorter working time. From a survey they discovered that this was the case with "white-collar" workers even though working hours for many of them were already lower than for manual workers. In the case of the latter, dissatisfaction did not diminish with shorter working hours; it was closely linked with discontent about the work itself and with the feeling that they were badly paid. Utilisation of leisure appeared to differ as between the two categories — more manual and "do-it-yourself" activities among salaried employees, more time spent in front of the television set or in general social relationships among manual workers. These specialists conclude that increased job satisfaction and the introduction of equitable wage systems would be better received among manual workers than a reduction in working time. Many specialists in the sociology of labour, however, stress that to bring about an improvement in workers' conditions, work and leisure must be treated together as a whole.

In principle, if one is in receipt of a retirement pension one can enjoy unlimited spare time. If the normal age of entitlement to pension is lowered, the pension would become available at a period in life at which a person's capacities for all kinds of personal and collective activities are better preserved. This could have an effect on pensioners' ways of living, with specific consequences for the economy and social transfers. If this measure were combined with a reduction in working time, the health of future pensioners would probably be improved in comparison with that of workers reaching retirement age nowadays. But there might be contrary effects. On the one hand there is certainly a correlation between good health and the pursuit of an activity after retirement. On the other hand workers now nearing retirement belong to a generation who have had experience of holidays during their working life and value their leisure. Ways of using leisure would therefore be modified in favour of activities to which these new pensioners had become accustomed before retirement.[31] However, opportunities for using leisure are more limited after retirement because income is lower. This is why people with low income often feel a mixture of anxiety and satisfaction at the idea of retiring, while those who are better off look forward to the prospect more eagerly.[32] However, an improvement in the financial conditions of retirement is in progress almost everywhere.

Notwithstanding this, it would be particularly dangerous to forecast the possible effects of lowering the normal retirement age on people's ways of life. Ideas change rapidly in this regard. As has already been mentioned, we are moving away from the concepts of an age of retirement and cessation of activity on retirement. We may even be moving towards abandonment of the traditional life sequence of education first, then work, then rest.[33]

Spare time should also be looked at from the economic point of view, because a worker is also a consumer, a saver and a handyman about the house. Leisure gives rise to consumption of a variety of goods and services, thus stimulating production: this is consumption in the true sense because time is needed to buy goods and use what one has bought, just as time is needed to produce what is bought,[34] while there is also consumption of the many goods and services directly connected with various ways of utilising leisure. "Do-it-yourself" is also an important aspect of the use of leisure. Such activities as household maintenance, repairs and improvement, the preparation of food and the making and maintenance of clothing represent contributions to total production, even though they are not included in existing systems of national accounts. They also contribute to raising living standards, both of themselves and because they free income for other expenditure. If people have time to shop around and buy more cheaply, this also makes a contribution to improved living standards and is one essential condition, among others, for ensuring that competition, which is regarded as important in market economies, shall not be distorted. An increase in spare time ought to result in savings in cash or in kind. How would it influence real incomes, or the propensity to save or invest? How would "do-it-yourself" influence the kind of goods that would be bought? Such questions elicit no reply, or are not even asked.

PERSONAL ATTITUDES TO WORK

In the following pages we shall examine the possible effects of a reduction in working time on personal attitudes from three points of view: whether employed workers will seek additional work; whether people will be more inclined to drop out of the labour market if the normal retirement age is lowered; and whether persons who have retired will be attracted back to work if new full-time jobs with shorter normal hours are created.

We need to know what economically active (and inactive) persons would do if they had more spare time, because this knowledge will help to detect trends that may either promote or impede reduction of unemployment. For example, if workers had more spare time, would they use it to work overtime, or openly take a second or even a third job, or work while concealing the fact from the authorities? If normal working hours were lower, would people without jobs seek employment with the new, more attractive working hours, or would workers in part-time employment seek full-time jobs? If the normal retirement age were to be lowered, would many of the workers entitled to do so decline to retire if they were free to choose? Would those who did retire still wish to carry on in gainful employment? As we have seen, these are the questions which are usually raised in this connection. If the replies are in the affirmative, it is to be feared that imbalances in the labour market will be aggravated. These questions are important not only from the point of view of the labour market. From another point of view — that of improvement of quality of life — any progress that is expected from a reduction in working time would not take place if the additional spare time were not used for leisure.

Three general remarks need to be made before giving closer consideration to these various possibilities. First, contrary to what was contemplated in the previous section, it is likely that the bigger the reduction in working time, the greater the risk that people's behaviour will take a form that will be unfavourable to an improvement in the employment situation. In the second place, however, in the hypothetical situations under consideration, which concern only a reduction in working time without loss of earnings and a lowering of the normal retirement age without reduction in pension, there would be no loss of "normal" income (wages or pension) to be compensated for. Thus, any financial incentive to follow one of the courses of behaviour listed above would be reduced to a minimum. Finally, in practice, it is not enough merely to hope to obtain a job: the job must be found, and that is not easy in a saturated labour market, so that there may be a wide gap between what people intend and what they can actually do. Furthermore, from the point of view of reducing unemployment, it is important to know whether the jobs sought would actually be of interest to unemployed workers.

Search for additional employment

We shall try to ascertain the extent to which persons in employment would seek additional employment if they had more spare time every day or every weekend, or during their annual leave. The additional employment to be considered here comprises overtime, holding more than one job, and working without declaring the fact. We shall then try to see whether such employment, if it can be shown to exist, would deprive the unemployed of job opportunities.

There is very little directly relevant information available on the first point. In the Federal Republic of Germany the author of the above-mentioned study tried to obtain such information in his research on individual choices between leisure and income.[35] He did not rule out the possibility that a growing proportion of employed persons would carry on two jobs, one of them without declaring it, if working time were reduced below a certain level; however, he noted that a third of employed persons stated that they would prefer to have more spare time, even if this meant earning less, and that only 5 per cent preferred to work more and have higher earnings. He concludes that the risk of an expansion in multiple jobholding would probably not be very great. He also notes that only workers belonging to certain specific occupations (building trades, for example) are in a position to carry on a second job, whether officially or otherwise, and that there is no unsatisfied demand for most workers' qualifications. The same author points out, furthermore, that the amount of overtime worked has remained remarkably stable over the long term and that no correlation can be found between it and trends in working time. These considerations are typical of the kind of indirect deductions that have to be made on little evidence and of the wide range of criteria that have to be used if we are to try to respond objectively to the questions set out here.

It is more than likely that if financial need is the dominant consideration, in the event of an increase in their spare time workers will try to obtain additional income wherever possible. Financial need is chronic among the poorer classes of the population, and it may also exist from time to time among members of other classes when faced with non-recurrent expenses. Overtime comprises a special financial incentive since it is paid at premium or bonus rates. If it were decided to reduce the working week, this would mean that bonus rates would be paid for hours that were previously paid at normal rates. The financial incentive to work overtime would be further strengthened if premium rates were increased so as to discourage employers from having recourse to overtime. However, since premium rates would apply from a lower level of working time, previous earnings would be attained without the need to work as many hours as before.

For people working on the sly or who hold more than one job, inadequate pay for the main job would seem to be an important factor; indeed, because of this, the main job may take second place. A vicious circle may thus be created linking work on the sly and absenteeism. According to some surveys, it is possible to programme absences, and also work overtime, so as to raise average earnings while reducing the actual hours worked for the principal employer.[36] However, these are isolated examples and we cannot draw general conclusions from them. Other factors play their part and in some cases we can conclude that a mere reduction in working time would not be enough in itself to encourage workers to take on additional employment. According to a recent survey carried out in Spain, 45 per cent of the persons questioned work longer hours than they wish because their occupation or their employer obliges them to do so. More than a third of the persons having a second job stated that they would prefer not to have it if circumstances allowed.[37]

The improvement in material standards of living over the past decades may have reduced the proportion of workers for whom financial reasons would play a major role in causing them to seek additional employment if they had more spare time. But we do not know what the specific effect of actual experience of leisure would be. It may be that exposure to this experience would strengthen people's propensity to enjoy their spare time, and this would explain the results of certain surveys mentioned above, concerning choice between leisure and income. Are we justified in thinking that an extension of compensatory leave for overtime would have such an effect in the future, for example? It has been pointed out that in the United Kingdom, where overtime is particularly prevalent, it has fallen significantly in cases where agreements provide for compensation in the form of time off: having experienced more leisure, the workers covered by these agreements have become more attached to it.[38] This observation should be compared with the finding that there seems to be a scale of levels in this regard, though it is difficult to generalise. In France it is said that workers on short time, working only 32 hours per week with lower wages, do not want to have a second, undeclared job, or to work overtime, or to work at the weekends or on holidays; with a 32-hour week, workers had started to enjoy life again.[39] However, reactions of this kind would probably only occur if working time were greatly reduced, and this is unlikely in the present state of affairs.

We also need to know the reasons, other than financial ones, which cause workers to work overtime, to take on a second or a third job, or to enter undeclared employment, if we are to try to understand why such persons may use any additional spare time for this purpose. Sometimes the explanation is to be found in interest in the work, or in career ambitions; extra spare time may be used to satisfy these needs. However, reasons of this kind would no doubt be more valid in the case of undeclared employment or multiple job holding than of overtime, because in the latter case it would seem that financial reasons predominate. Workers who devote long hours to their main job because they find it interesting are normally those with relatively high earnings who do not work "overtime" as this is understood in legislation and collective agreements.[40] They are often the possessors of exceptional qualifications, which explains why they are in such demand, even after they have retired. It is possible that the tendency of such persons to devote their spare time to the pursuit of their profession acts as a brake on the creation of new jobs in the professions concerned, but this situation does not seem to have aroused much attention. At the present time, extra work by those with rare qualifications cannot be harmful to the job prospects of unemployed persons since, by definition, there is already a shortage of the required qualifications and there is every reason to believe that the unemployed do not have these qualifications.

Work on the sly makes it possible to avoid income tax and social security contributions. However, it often occurs for reasons of friendship or neighbourliness, and may also be wanted because it is inherently interesting and because it is not subject to the constraints of wage-earning employment, or because it affords an opportunity to use skills which are not used, or are badly used, in the main job. In the case of persons holding more than one job, we have more complete information about non-financial reasons. For example in the United States, according to a survey carried out in 1977, about 20 per cent of the persons questioned (many more Whites than Blacks and more married women than married men) said that they had more than one job because they found pleasure in the second job; a very small proportion of these people were using this second job as a means of acquiring experience to enable them to change their main occupation, to set up their own business or to help friends and relatives in need of part-time help.[41] When causes of this kind are involved, they are more likely to operate if people have more spare time. However, since such activities provide a source of personal satisfaction for the workers concerned, we cannot but view them favourably, even though they may reduce the number of normal job vacancies.

In any event, each type of additional employment raises its own specific problems. In the case of overtime we need to know whether it is the workers who volunteer or the employer who imposes overtime. Yet we have very little information about the workers' freedom to refuse to work overtime. According to a study concerning 422,500 workers covered by major collective agreements in the United States, fewer than one out of six could refuse to work overtime without creating difficulties for themselves; in the majority of cases the worker had to present a reasonable excuse and a substitute had to be available for the excuse to be accepted.[42] Another study[43] noted some progress in this regard: between 1969 and 1977 the proportion of workers who were free to choose whether to work overtime, or who could refuse to do so without being penalised, rose from 36 to 52 per cent of the workers covered by the study. It would seem that custom and practice, with the collusion of management and unions, also have an influence in the field of overtime.[44]

From the point of view of the present study it is of particular importance to know whether the amount of overtime would increase or would remain unchanged in the event of a reduction in the normal working week. It would be enough for it to remain unchanged for there to be a reduction in time actually worked. According to research relating to the countries of the European Communities, the actual number of hours worked per week has evolved over the long term parallel with nominal working hours, leaving aside temporary fluctuations.[45] This would tend to refute the theory that overtime would permanently increase in the event of a reduction in normal working time, though there might be a temporary short-term increase. This point has given rise to controversy. In the United Kingdom the Department of Employment had assumed that overtime would increase if there were a reduction in working time. In support of this hypothesis it pointed out that when the normal working week for most workers fell from 44 to 40 hours between 1964 and 1966, overtime absorbed nearly half the potential new jobs thus created.[46] On the other hand the research department of the Trades Union Congress maintained that the evolution of hours actually worked and of normal working time in all sectors of the economy had been parallel between the two dates. For workers in manufacturing industry the number of hours actually worked had fallen by three-and-a-half between the mid-1950s and the beginning of the slump, while the normal working week had fallen by four hours.[47]

It is difficult to decide whether persons taking on additional employment are depriving the unemployed of job opportunities if one does not know what additional employment is involved and whether it would be offered to unemployed persons and be acceptable to them. On the first and third points, we need to know the preferences and motives both of persons whose working time is reduced and of the unemployed.

If the additional employment is not declared, it is by definition largely unknown. It seems to be quite widespread,[48] no doubt as a result of unemployment, but it may well be that the market for such jobs is more or less saturated in a number of countries. We do not know whether people working on the sly are already employed, or retired, or partially or fully unemployed. In any event some writers take the view that to a very large extent, concealed employment meets a demand that would otherwise not be met at current market prices, and thus contributes to supporting the economy.[49] If the number of hours spent on additional employment is low, this will not correspond to the normal full-time job most unemployed persons are seeking; nor will casual jobs performed in response to casual demand.

It has been estimated that in Italy the majority of workers having a second or third job devote at least 20 hours per week to them.[50] In the United States a growing number of women have more than one job; in a quarter of the cases workers combine paid employment with an independent activity. In May 1977 half the women holding more than one job had two part-time jobs, while most men had at least one full-time job.[51] In May 1976 the average number of hours devoted to outside employment was 16 per week for craftsmen (22 hours or more for a quarter of them), ten for professionals and seven and nine respectively for persons employed in private households and in education services.[52]

The question whether reducing weekly working time would help to create unemployment by encouraging people to hold more than one job was raised in the United States in 1966. At that time it was considered that a reduction of weekly hours could not be the cause of the relatively high unemployment that had existed for some years. Similarly, there seemed to be little practical use in trying to eliminate the practice so as to create a possible source of new job opportunities. It appeared unlikely that a reasonable reduction in the working week would lead to an increase in multiple jobholding, particularly because the workers concerned were wage earners working over 40 hours in their main job rather than salaried employees with a work-week of between 35 and 40 hours. Part-time employees were more likely to hold a second job, as were certain workers employed under specific conditions (in particular shift work) which left a good deal of spare time during the day.[53]

At present, studies carried out in the same country show marked preferences for longer holidays rather than other forms of reduced working time.[54] Being concentrated in a limited space of time, holidays are less conducive in practice to regular additional employment than are the shorter working day or week. Nevertheless, a need to earn more money may also cause people to take on lucrative extra jobs during their holidays. It would therefore be useful to know whether people feel an overriding need for more money. According to one survey 62.7 per cent (as against 56 per cent ten years earlier) of a sample of manual and non-manual workers in the public sector surveyed in 1976 would have preferred to work longer and earn more in consequence, rather than to work less for the same earnings (16.2 per cent) or to work less and earn less (21.1 per cent).[55] Thus the empirical approach indicated above would seem to produce contradictory evidence with regard to whether employed persons were likely to take advantage of any increase in their spare time to look for additional work.

Propensity to withdraw from employment

In principle, lowering the normal retirement age is intended to enable workers to take well-earned rest and to spend most of their later years as agreeably as possible. By stopping work at an earlier age, these new retirees would, it is hoped, provide more job opportunities for younger people. What do we know about possible individual reactions to a lower normal retirement age? In proposals made in this connection, mention is usually made of voluntary retirement. This is why we shall examine first whether, if the retirement age were lowered, there would be as many cessations of employment as hoped, and whether those who retire would leave all forms of employment altogether. We shall then look into the question of the effects of individual behaviour in this connection on job opportunities for the unemployed.

The sample survey carried out in the nine EEC countries, which has already been mentioned a number of times,[56] gives important information about attitudes of employed persons towards retirement. But it considers retirement at the age now fixed, or early retirement with corresponding reduction in the pension, or early retirement with pension maintained at the level of accrued contributions. Thus, information relevant to the present study can be drawn only indirectly from the survey. The proportion of persons questioned who stated that they were looking forward to retirement with satisfaction did not exceed 50 per cent. Women were slightly fewer than men in this case, while in categories having moderate or high income the balance shifted definitely towards satisfaction. From 40 years of age onwards, 55 per cent of wage earners, 49 per cent of salaried employees and 37 per cent of the self-employed were looking forward to retirement. In the Benelux countries the proportion of people having this attitude was two or three times higher than that of people facing retirement with anxiety, while in Denmark and Italy people facing retirement with anxiety were in the clear majority.

According to the same survey the proportion of people wishing to cease all employment on becoming entitled to retirement pension was 57 per cent; 24 per cent intended to look for some form of paid employment, and 19 per cent did not know what they would do. The reasons given by the 24 per cent intending to seek paid employment were: for 17, just because they wanted to keep active; for 6, because they wanted to increase their income; and for the remaining 1 per cent, other reasons. With regard to the choice of early retirement with actuarial reduction of pension, 33 per cent intended to take it, 48 per cent were against and 19 per cent had no opinion. Of the 33 per cent intending to take early retirement, the reasons given were: health (7), poor working conditions or uninteresting work (3), the wish to pursue leisure activities (17), the fact that the spouse would already have retired (2), and other reasons (4). People closer to retirement age were clearly less desirous of giving up work than others. Among employed persons, 45 per cent were interested in the idea of an individual contribution that would make it possible to take retirement one year earlier; this proportion dropped to 36 per cent in Denmark and 28 per cent in Ireland, but rose to 53 per cent in Italy and 54 per cent in Belgium. Finally, the idea of arranging a transition between active employment and retirement was received very favourably among employed persons in general (72 per cent) and among the public (71 per cent); the most enthusiastic were people who were attracted by early retirement and who also intended to look for other paid employment (5 per cent of all employed persons). Interest in progressive retirement has been confirmed by Swedish experience. It should be recalled that it was introduced in Sweden in order to improve the quality of life and not for employment reasons.[57]

The desire for retirement appears to be strong in the industrialised countries. One study about these countries shows a trend in the past towards lowering the age at which retirement was granted, even though this had not been specially encouraged; attempts made in some cases to promote postponement of retirement by increasing benefits had met with only very limited success.[58] This information relates to decisions concerning the grant of retirement pensions and tells us nothing about possible continuation of activity afterwards. In Austria, where since 1961 retirement on full pension has gradually become possible at 60, subject only to a period of 35 years' contribution, while early retirement of older unemployed persons has also been made possible, the proportion of pensions awarded to male workers before the age of 65 jumped from 5 per cent of the total number of new pensions granted in 1960 to 51 per cent in 1976. In the Federal Republic of Germany what happened went far beyond forecasts. Since 1973 workers may choose retirement on full pension after 35 years' contributions three years before the normal age of 65 (five years since 1978) and long-term unemployed workers may also take retirement on full pension at 60, subject to 15 years' contributions. The proportion of retirement pensions granted to men under 65 rose from 5 to 61 per cent between 1960 and 1976; however, this rise is said to be attributable to the effects of economic recession in the years 1967-72. The nature of the pension scheme plays an important role. In France rates of pension are highly progressive between the ages of 60 and 65 in the general scheme and therefore discourage early retirement. It was calculated that if entitlement were at 60 instead of 65 (general scheme and supplementary scheme together), there would be 350,000 additional persons willing to retire.[59]

The desire for retirement may have various causes, such as a need for rest and leisure, state of health, invalidity, or difficulty in adapting to jobs that are changing rapidly. It cannot be fulfilled without taking account of other factors which may work in its favour or against it and which explain the possible discrepancy between the interest expressed in early retirement and what people actually do in this regard. Those factors include expected income, family situation and state of the labour market, in particular. There are also differences according to sex: in many countries the proportion of women in the employed population has risen in the higher age groups and has partly compensated for a decline in male employment due in part to provisions favourable to early retirement.[60]

The reasons for decisions about retirement have been closely studied in the United States,[61] as well as the reasons why a person in receipt of pension continues to work or not, so as to determine what measures should be adopted to meet the serious problem of the rapid decline in the proportion of older men in employment. For the future, however, it is not sure that the attraction of early retirement will persist.[62] Various factors might bring about a change in trends almost everywhere: inflation and delays in adjusting levels of taxation, which always bite into the purchasing power of pensions; the degree of unemployment, which may mean that potential beneficiaries of measures for lowering the retirement age may fear that they will be unable to find paid employment if they need to do so. Unemployment has already obliged many people to retire "voluntarily".

As for the propensity of retired persons to seek paid employment, we have seen that interesting studies have been made on the subject. Here again, the factors involved are complex, not least because of the diversity of regulations concerning the cumulation of a retirement pension and earnings from employment, including the application of a ceiling on income.[63] In Italy many public servants retiring at 55 with full pension have taken another job.[64] In France it is estimated that between 25 and 30 per cent of retired persons were still working for pay.[65] On the occasion of a survey carried out in 1978, one pensioner out of ten said that he was doing so, and the same proportion of persons who had not yet retired also declared their intention of doing so. In most cases part-time jobs were involved: half of the retired persons did not work more than 20 hours per week, and only one out of three worked more than 31 hours. Such employment consisted either of "odd jobs" (looking after children, selling newspapers, household chores, maintenance, etc.) taken to earn extra money, or of the pursuit on a part-time basis of a previous occupation requiring high qualifications — a retired barrister acting as a legal adviser, a former chief accountant doing the books for small tradesmen, a former manager of a small undertaking acting as a management consultant. People who had retired at the age of 55 were proportionately no more numerous in this kind of activity than those who had retired at 65 (11 per cent in both cases).[66]

Lowering the normal retirement age while maintaining full pension would no doubt encourage people to retire, as experience has shown. This assumption is confirmed by the decisions taken to retire with a pension lower than the full rate, but considerations concerning income are obviously of major importance. In the United Kingdom a "job release scheme" started in 1976 and enabling workers to retire one year in advance if their jobs were filled by unemployed persons seems to have had very little effect.[67] According to one study the allowance paid was inadequate and workers feared an unfavourable reaction from their employer if they asked to be allowed to benefit under the scheme.[68] The paid employment of retired people has the same possible effects on job opportunities for the unemployed as undeclared employment or the holding of more than one job. It may perhaps be added that if retirement is granted to people who have been unemployed for a long time, it is likely that there would not be much demand for their services, since they have already been difficult to place in employment and have undergone a loss of skills due to lengthy enforced idleness. In any event, a number of early retirement schemes prohibit people from taking another job until after they have reached the normal retirement age, and this must make it even more difficult for them to find a new job.

If it were considered desirable in the future to reverse the trend towards a lower retirement age so as to reduce the cost of retirement pensions and halt the narrowing of the financial base of pension schemes predicted on the basis of demographic trends, would this reversal be favourably received by individuals? A number of authorities do not think so. In the Federal Republic of Germany planners estimated that about two-thirds of those entitled to retire at 63 (about 335,000 in 1973 and 1.7 million by 1985) would continue to ask to do so; and once they had been without employment for two years it was not expected that those people would return to the labour market at 65, the age at which they would be entitled to cumulate full pension and earnings.[69] However, the situation in the labour market also plays its part: if there is a strong demand for workers people may be encouraged to apply, while a saturated labour market will discourage applicants. It is also possible that other trends in individual behaviour may help to strengthen the financial bases of pension schemes just at the time when this is most needed. As already mentioned, there is a certain tendency for women to stay in employment longer. It is a fact that it is only after a certain age that gainful employment begins to be really attractive for many women who have brought up their children. This trend would no doubt be reinforced by a reduction in working time. It would bring in more social security contributions, and the same effect would be obtained if unemployed persons re-entered the labour market. We shall see below how likely this would be if normal full-time employment were reduced.

Possible attraction of full-time employment with shorter normal hours

The fear has been expressed that a reduction in working time (either of the working day or of the working week) would encourage persons without employment to look for jobs because the shorter new full-time work schedules would be more attractive. It may also be that part-time employees would be interested in full-time jobs with shorter hours, because such jobs would involve working hours closer to what they already work, but with full-time pay. This kind of question raises the difficult problem, which has been very little explored, of the connection between short-time working, normal working hours that are reduced, and part-time employment. This connection is not always very clear.[70] A reduction in time actually worked would in practice blur the difference between the new, shorter full-time work schedule and part-time work, and statistics on part-time employment do not always make a distinction between partially employed workers (i.e. those on short time) and part-time employees. In the statistics of some countries the limit between full-time and part-time employment is fixed at 35 hours a week.[71]

We can only guess what individual reactions might be to the possibility of full-time jobs with shorter normal hours. It may well be that they would attract people into the labour market only if the new schedules became very close to current hours for part-time employment. This would mean that weekly working hours would have to be very considerably reduced, which is most unlikely. But we also need to know whether present working hours in part-time jobs correspond to what holders of such jobs actually want or whether they would have preferred longer hours. This is the most important point, and it is not always easy to determine, since statistics usually give actual or average working hours, without indicating what the workers concerned were really looking for.

Statistics on part-time employment show very different schedules, but the weekly average is noticeably below 35 hours. In 1977 the average number of hours actually worked by employees having a main part-time job was 20.3 in the European Communities (22.4 for men and 20.1 for women); for people working casually on a part-time basis it was 17.7 (20.6 for men and 16.8 for women).[72] A relatively high proportion of persons having a main part-time job worked rather few hours. In industry 48.4 per cent worked between 15 and 24 hours, 32.8 per cent between 25 and 34 hours, and 11.1 per cent between one and 14 hours; the corresponding percentages in service trades were 47.9, 21.4 and 25.9 respectively. In comparison with 1973 the proportion of persons working from one to 14 hours and from 15 to 24 hours had increased in industry and services, while the proportion of those working 25 to 34 hours had fallen.[72]

These statistics tell us nothing about what the workers concerned really wanted. However, they relate to hours actually worked by employees having a main part-time job and include work schedules of up to "48 hours and above", which no doubt means that they include persons having more than one part-time job. If we assume that the percentage of part-time employees working more than 34 hours per week is symptomatic of the demand, or of preferences for working hours close to full time, it may be interesting to note that 2.6 per cent of those concerned worked between 35 and 29 hours in services (3.5 per cent in 1973), and 4.3 per cent in industry (5.9 per cent in 1973); those working 40 to 41 hours comprised 1.3 per cent in services and 2.3 per cent in industry. The proportions for hours above 41 were well below 1 per cent.[72] According to statistics from Canada, out of 1,423,000 part-time employees who worked an average of 14 weekly hours in January 1980, 438,000 did not want full-time jobs, 691,000 had no choice either because they were in educational institutions (513,000) or because of personal or family obligations (178,000), while 214,000 had not been able to find other employment.[73] In Australia, out of 996,900 part-time employees in November 1979, 847,000 did not want to work longer hours; the weekly average was 15.4 hours.[74] In the United States, also in November 1979, out of 15,918,000 persons normally working less than 35 hours per week, 14,013,000 either could not or did not wish to have a full-time job, and average number of hours per week for those normally working part time for reasons other than financial ones was 18.5.[75]

The demand for part-time jobs is thus not the same as a demand for a shorter full-time job — even reduced to 35 hours — and there is no reason to think that a shorter normal working week, even a considerably shorter one, would bring more than a negligible increase in the number of people seeking employment. Housewives who do their own housework can devote only a limited amount of time to outside employment. From a survey carried out in the Federal Republic of Germany it appears that this consideration determines part-time employment as it is usually found in practice, with a strong emphasis on work for half-days.[76] Limitations of time are also strict for people trying to work while pursuing their studies.

The demand for part-time jobs by persons already in employment is a different matter. It is more diverse in character and seems to be due to more complicated causes. According to the above-mentioned survey in the Federal Republic, 40 per cent of the employed persons covered would have liked to work 20 hours a week, provided that they would continue to be covered by social security, while the vast majority wished to work between 30 and 40 hours. A reduction in the normal working week to below 40 hours would therefore keep a number of people in normal full-time employment who were apparently ready to accept part-time jobs. It would therefore absorb a potential demand for part-time employment, that is employment with lower earnings. It is hard to gauge the size of this fringe demand for part-time jobs that would be eliminated if the normal working week were shortened; but it would be restricted to employed persons who wanted only a small reduction in their working hours, and we need to make a distinction between what people say they intend to do and what they actually do. It would appear that many people who say they want a part-time job hesitate when it comes to putting their declared intention into practice.[77] When questions are asked about people's intentions, it is not always made clear that part-time employment would be accompanied by lower earnings. In any event, these people are already in employment. Furthermore, in the case of persons with more than one job the demand for part-time employment cannot really be very different from that for full-time jobs. As has been seen, it is not infrequent for people (particularly women) to have two or more part-time jobs, perhaps because in some cases they need to work but could not find full-time jobs. Holding more than one part-time job is one way of having the equivalent of a full-time job.

Unlike what would probably happen with reductions in the normal working week, the development of new part-time jobs might, however, cause a flood of new entrants into the labour market and thus aggravate its present saturation. On the other hand, the entry into employment of married women would reduce the number of persons able to work who receive benefits and services provided by the community without paying taxes or social security contributions. They would thus widen the financial basis of social security schemes. Moreover, systematic development of part-time jobs would help the expansion of progressive retirement schemes, and therefore partial withdrawals from employment, because the shortage of such jobs is recognised as an obstacle to the implementation of these schemes, which have aroused great interest as we have seen.

Notes

[1] "La réduction de la durée du travail", in *Lettre d'information* (Montrouge, Hauts-de-Seine, Agence nationale pour l'amélioration des conditions de travail), Oct. 1979, p. 4.

[2] L. Lamers: *Social insurance and accident prevention in the Netherlands*, Paper submitted to an ILO meeting of experts on occupational accident prevention and compensation, Geneva, 29 January-2 February 1979 (doc. OAPC/1979/D.14).

[3] The International Social Security Association organised a meeting of experts on absenteeism and social security from 28 to 30 April 1980.

[4] *Jenkins work report* (Paris, Social and Economic Studies), No. 21, Nov. 1979, p. 63.

[5] Svein Johansen: "Quality of working life, absence and action: Some aspects of an action research project on absence from work", in *Absenteeism and social security* (Geneva, ISSA, 1981), Ch. VIII, pp. 86-100. This chapter reports the preliminary results of the first stage of a survey of wages in five food industry enterprises in different parts of Norway.

[6] F. Heilbronner: "Work absence: An introductory analysis", ibid., Ch. I, pp. 1-11.

[7] ILO: *Encylopaedia of occupational health and safety*, Vol. 1 (Geneva, 3rd ed., 1983), under "Hours of work".

[8] International Occupational Safety and Health Information Centre (CIS): *Human factors and safety*, Information sheet 15 (Geneva, ILO, May 1967), in particular pp. 20-22, 54-57 and 79.

[9] National Board of Labour Protection: *Työtapaturmat olycksfall i arbete* (Industrial accidents), Official Statistics of Finland 1973-1974-1975 (Helsinki, 1976), pp. 24-25, Table 4. In Finland normal working time has been 40 hours per week and eight hours per day for manual workers since 1970; the daily maximum is nine hours per day, with the possibility of exceptional schedules of up to 12 hours. Some categories of salaried employees work seven hours per day and 37½ hours per week. See Henrik Lagus: "Introduction of the forty-hour week in Finland", in *International Labour Review* (Geneva, ILO), July 1968, pp. 27-38.

[10] Bernard Solins: "Une exploration des statistiques nationales d'accidents du travail", in *Revue économique* (Paris, Armand Colin), Vol. XXVII, No. 3 (*Economie de la santé*), May 1976, pp. 467-470. The occupational accidents analysed were those affecting persons insured under the general social security scheme, in particular those covered by the 15 national technical committees. The latter are responsible for most secondary activities (industry) and tertiary activities (commerce and services).

[11] Research is in progress in the ILO on the cost of industrial accidents and occupational diseases to workers, undertakings and the community.

[12] United States Department of Labor, Bureau of Labor Statistics: *Hours of work and output* (Washington, DC, 1947), Bulletin No. 917.

[13] Peter Colquhoun: "Working efficiency, personality and body rhythms", in *Department of Employment Gazette* (London), June 1978, pp. 682-685. This research appears to confirm the hypothesis that there are "ultradian" rhythms (completed in less than a day) which affect performance. For example, there is a rhythm of about 90 minutes in the ability to detect critical events. When we know more about these rhythms we may be able to use them to determine the optimum intervals for rest breaks, or changes in job, for individual workers. But it is early days for this, says the author.

[14] Rolande Cuvillier: "Intellectual workers and their work in social theory and practice", in *International Labour Review*, Apr. 1974, pp. 313-314. See also "Du temps pour vivre ... et le temps qui compte", in *Cadres et maîtrise* (Paris, Confédération générale des cadres), 22 Apr. 1978, pp. 13-15.

[15] ILO: *Record of the Third European Regional Conference (Geneva, 16-25 October 1979)*, doc. GB.212/2/1, Resolution concerning the improvement of working conditions and the working environment in Europe, para. 12.

[16] See in particular ILO: *Night work*, Working paper prepared for the Tripartite Advisory Meeting on Night Work, Geneva, 26 September-3 October 1978 (doc. TAMNW/1978/I), and idem: *Management of working time in industrialised countries*, Main documents of an ILO symposium on arrangement of working time and social problems connected with shift work in industrialised countries, Geneva, 3-11 May 1977.

[17] Marc Maurice: *Shift work : Economic advantages and social costs* (Geneva, ILO, 1975), p. 101.

[18] J. Carpentier and P. Cazamian: *Night work : Its effects on the health and welfare of the worker* (Geneva, ILO, 1977), especially pp. 57-64.

[19] See, for example, for the past, Edward P. Thompson: "Time, labour and industrial capitalism", in *Past and Present* (Oxford, Corpus Christi College, The Past and Present Society), Dec. 1967. Already in 1924, the ILO Recommendation (No. 21) concerning the development of facilities for the utilisation of workers' spare time made special reference to the need for "action against the misuse of alcohol ... venereal disease and gambling" (Part II (*b*)).

[20] ILO: *Encyclopaedia of occupational health and safety*, op. cit., Vol. 1, p. 1057.

[21] According to J. Dumazedier: "Current problems of the sociology of leisure", in *International Social Science Journal* (Paris, UNESCO), 1960, No. 4, p. 522.

[22] Michel Bosquet: "Quand les chômeurs seront heureux", in *Le Nouvel Observateur* (Paris), 4 Dec. 1978, pp. 79-96. The total exceeds 100 because the persons questioned in the survey may have given more than one answer.

[23] Dieter Mertens: "L'aménagement du temps de travail", in *Emploi et nouveaux modes de vie*, conférence internationale, 29-30 novembre 1979, La Haye (Paris, Institut d'éducation, Fondation européenne de la culture), p. 24.

[24] Survey by the Allensbach Public Opinion Institute for the magazine *Stern*. Results quoted in the source given in the previous note. For other surveys, see Alain Doyelle, in collaboration with Françoise Bonnal and Jean-Paul Blanchet: "La perception du temps chez les salariés: quelques enseignements d'une enquête", in *Travail et emploi* (Paris, Ministère du Travail), Jan. 1980; for Finland, Karl Gröhn: *Views on shortening daily working hours* (Helsinki, Ministry of Social Affairs and Health, Research Department, Oct. 1979), Julkaisuja Publications, No. 15; for the United States, Fred Best: "Preferences on worklife scheduling and work-leisure tradeoffs", in *Monthly Labor Review* (Washington, DC, United States Department of Labor), June 1978, pp. 31-37.

[25] "Equal opportunities for women", in *OECD Observer* (Paris), Mar. 1979, pp. 27-32.

[26] See report by M. Maldague (Canada) in Fondation Van Clé: *Temps libre et accomplissement*, Congrès pour une charte des loisirs, congrès mondial, 5-7 avril 1976 (Antwerp), pp. 74-88. See also "Evolution des loisirs et leur coût, Etats-Unis", in *UIMM Documentation étrangère* (Paris, Union des industries métallurgiques et minières), Oct. 1973, p. 19 (taken from *Business in Brief* (New York, Chase Manhattan Bank), Apr. 1973).

[27] Jean-Marie Dupont: "Joffre Dumazedier et le temps de vivre", in *Le Monde* (Paris), 16 Mar. 1980, p. XIII.

[28] See for example Gunnela Westlander: *La relation entre les heures de loisir et le travail: quelques perspectives et résultats de recherche en Suède* (Stockholm, Rädet för personal- och arbetskivsfragor, 1978, Arbetsrapport fran forskningsavdelningen), No. 10, conférence présentée au dixième Congrès international de la promotion du travail et des travailleurs, Institut international pour les problèmes humains du travail, 11-13 octobre 1977. See also Stanley Parker: *The future of work and leisure* (London, Paladin, 1972), especially Ch. 5.

[29] Lars-Ake Aström: *Gradual transition from full-time work to retirement, with income deriving in part from work and in part from a reduced pension*, Report IX, XIXth General Assembly of the International Social Security Association, Madrid, 4-14 October 1977, pp. 1-12; Göran Crona: *Partial retirement in Sweden. Developments and experiences*, Paper submitted to the Ninth World Congress of Sociology, Upsala, Sweden, 14-19 August 1978.

[30] K. Roberts et al.: "How many hours in a week", in *Personnel Management* (London, Institute of Personnel Management), June 1974, pp. 33-41. Study conducted amongst a sample of 474 economically active men in a suburban area of Liverpool.

[31] This remark was made in connection with tourism by older people. See "Le temps des loisirs du troisième âge", in *Espaces* (Paris, Association pour la culture et les loisirs pour le tourisme), published in 1974.

[32] Commission of the European Communities: *The attitude of the working population to retirement*, Report by Hélène Riffault (Brussels, May 1978; doc. V/457/78-EN), p. 12.

[33] This is the case with systems allowing individuals a sort of "drawing right" on pension funds to "break up" the traditional sequence (time for study — time for work — time for rest) throughout life, as proposed in Gösta Rehn: "Vers une société de libre choix (temps de travail et temps de loisir)", in *Droit social* (Paris), July-Aug. 1978, pp. 314-332. See also Fred Best and Barry Stern: "Education, work and leisure: Must they come in that order?", in *Monthly Labor Review*, July 1977, pp. 3-10.

[34] On this point see for example Staffan Burenstam Linder: *The harried leisure class* (New York and London, Columbia University Press, 1970).

[35] Mertens, op. cit., p. 10.

[36] A. Mikalachki and D.C. Chapple: "Absenteeism and overtime: Double jeopardy", in *Relations industrielles* (Quebec, Laval University), 1977, No. 4, pp. 532-545. Survey of absenteeism based on company records of automobile plant workers. Absenteeism is higher among skilled workers, who have more control over their own overtime, than among production workers.

[37] Survey by the Emopublica group for the Dirección general del medio ambiente, in *El Correo Catalán* (Barcelona), 11 Aug. 1979, p. 23.

[38] *Overtime and shift-working*, A guide for negotiators (London, Trades Union Congress, 1973), p. 7.

[39] Adret: *Travailler deux heures par jour* (Paris, Editions du Seuil, 1977), Ch. 1: "Le temps en '3 x 8'", pp. 26-27.

[40] In the United States more than half the employees working 41 to 48 hours received premium pay in May 1977, as against a quarter of those working 60 hours or more. Among the latter, many held supervisory positions not covered by collective agreements or legal provisions on overtime. See Earl F. Mellor: "Working a long week and getting premium pay", in *Monthly Labor Review*, Apr. 1978, pp. 46-48.

[41] Scott Campbell Brown: "Moonlighting increased sharply in 1977, particularly among women", ibid., Jan. 1978, pp. 27-30.

[42] Sar A. Levitan and Richard S. Belous: "Reduced worktime, tool to fight unemployment", in *Worklife* (Washington, DC, United States Department of Labor, Employment and Training Administration), Apr. 1978, p. 25.

[43] Graham L. Staines and Robert P. Quinn: "American workers evaluate the quality of their jobs", in *Monthly Labor Review*, Jan. 1979, pp. 3-12. Results of a survey by the Survey Research Center of the University of Michigan.

[44] See for example E. G. Whybrew: "Overtime and the reduction of the working week: A comparison of British and Dutch experience", in *British Journal of Industrial Relations* (London School of Economics and Political Science), July 1964, pp. 149-164; and Derek Leslie: "Hours and overtime in British and United States manufacturing industries: A comparison", ibid., July 1976, pp. 194-201.

[45] "Adaptation of working time: Impact of a reduction in the annual duration of work", in *European Economy* (Luxembourg, Commission of the European Communities, Directorate-General for Economic and Financial Affairs), Mar. 1980, p. 83 and table 2.3, p. 91.

[46] "Measures to alleviate unemployment in the medium term: Work-sharing", in *Department of Employment Gazette* (London, HM Stationery Office), Apr. 1978, p. 400.

[47] John Hughes: "A shorter working week: How the Department of Employment got it wrong", in *Workers' Control Bulletin* (Nottingham, Institute for Workers' Control), 1978, No. 6, pp. 14-19.

[48] Raffaele de Grazia: "Clandestine employment: A problem of our times", in *International Labour Review* (Geneva, ILO), Sep.-Oct. 1980, pp. 549-564. Between 30 and 35 per cent of all employment in Italy was unofficial, according to ILO: *Youth employment in industrialised market economy countries*, Proceedings of an informal consultants' meeting, Geneva, 2-4 November 1977; mimeographed World Employment Programme research working paper; restricted, p. 57. In France it is estimated that there are between 800,000 and 1,500,000 people who are steadily engaged in unreported employment (André Fourcans: "Le travail noir encouragé par la loi de finances pour 1980", in *Le Monde*, 11 Dec. 1979, pp. 23 and 26). The figure of 800,000 is given for France in "Le travail clandestin peut très mal finir", in *Le Figaro* (Paris), 4 May 1979, p. 12, and in "Un nouveau rapport sur le travail noir", in *Libération* (Paris), 23 Apr. 1980, p. 3 (concerning the Delerozoy report).

[49] See for example "Le travail clandestin peut très mal finir", loc. cit. This article estimates that only 50,000 jobs in France are lost to craftsmen or the registered unemployed because of unreported employment.

[50] "Povert e segmentazione del mercato del lavoro", in *Economia e lavoro* (Rome, Fondazione Giacomo Brodolini), July-Sep. 1979, pp. 423-424.

[51] Campbell Brown, op. cit.

[52] Kopp Michelotti: "Multiple jobholding rate remained unchanged in 1976", in *Monthly Labor Review*, June 1977, p. 47.

[53] Myron L. Joseph: "Hours of work and leisure", Part 4 of *The employment impact of technological change*, Studies prepared for the National Commission on Technology, Automation and Economic Progress (Washington, DC), Feb. 1966, pp. II/343-344.

[54] Best, op. cit. Interest in long leave, including sabbatical leave, was confirmed in a national survey covering 2,000 persons.

[55] Best, op. cit.

[56] Commission of the European Communities: *The attitude of the working population to retirement*, Report by Hélène Riffault (Brussels, May 1978; doc. V/547/78-EN).

[57] Aström, op. cit., pp. 1-12; and Crona, op. cit.

[58] See Martin B. Tracy: *Retirement age practices in ten industrial societies, 1960-1976* (Geneva, International Social Security Association, 1979); and idem: "Flexible retirement features abroad", in Social Security Bulletin (United States Department of Health, Education, and Welfare), May 1978.

[59] Commissariat général du plan: *Rapport du Comité emploi et travail*, préparation du VIIe Plan (Paris, La Documentation française, 1976), pp. 329-331. The effects of possible measures modifying the choice of age of entitlement to retirement pension have been analysed on the basis of a model assuming a certain choice between income and fatigue (or unpleasantness of work) on the one hand, and income in retirement, on the other. See also in this connection J.P. Launay: "Les effets de l'abaissement de l'âge de la retraite sur la population active: une méthode d'évaluation", in *Economie et statistique* (Paris, Institut National de la Statistique et des Etudes Economiques), Nov. 1975, pp. 53-60.

[60] Trend noted in Great Britain for persons over 65 in 1976 (Audrey Hunt: "The elderly: Age differences in the quality of life", in *Population Trends* (London, Office of Population Censuses and

Surveys), No. 11, Spring 1978, pp. 10-15); and for persons between the ages of 55 and 64 in Belgium, France, the Federal Republic of Germany, Norway, Sweden and the United Kingdom (Tracy: "Flexible retirement features abroad", op. cit., p. 5). See also Carl Rosenfeld and Scott Campbell Brown: "The labour force status of older workers", in *Monthly Labor Review*, Nov. 1979, pp. 12-18, which found that "labor force activity has declined sharply among men 60 to 64 years of age", contrary to what was found for women in the same age group.

[61] Michael J. Boskin: "Social security and retirement decisions", in *Economic Inquiry* (Long Beach, California, Western Economic Association), Jan. 1977, pp. 1-25; Leonore Bixby: "Retirement patterns in the United States", in *Implications for social security of research on aging and retirement* (Geneva, International Social Security Association, 1977), Studies and Research, No. 9, pp. 27-43; and Arden Hall and Terry R. Johnson: *Social security, health and retirement plans* (Menlo Park, California, SRI International, 1978).

[62] See, for example, "Personnel aides see reverse of the trend to early retirement: Survey says directors expect employees to work longer as a result of inflation", in *Wall Street Journal*, 24 Oct. 1979.

[63] Elizabeth Kreitler Kirkpatrick: "The retirement test: An international study", in *Social Security Bulletin* (Washington, DC, United States Department of Health, Education, and Welfare), July 1974, pp. 3-14.

[64] ILO: *Youth unemployment in industrialised market economy countries*, op. cit., p. 60.

[65] Commissariat général du plan: *Rapport du Comité emploi et travail*, op. cit.

[66] Alain Monnier: "Les limites de la vie active et la retraite. II: Les conditions de passage la retraite: realités et projets", in *Population* (Paris, Institut national d'études démographiques), Jan.-Feb. 1980, pp. 109-135. Survey made by the Institute in question among older people, of whom 1,404 were employed and 953 had retired.

[67] "Measures to alleviate unemployment in the medium term: Early retirement", in *Department of Employment Gazette* (London), Mar. 1978.

[68] Richard Layard: "The costs and benefits of selective employment policies: The British case", in *British Journal of Industrial Relations*, July 1979, pp. 187-204.

[69] Kirkpatrick, op. cit., p. 11.

[70] Olive Robinson: "Part-time employment in the European Economic Community", in *International Labour Review*, May-June 1979, pp. 299-314.

[71] Australia, United States, Ireland. These statistics include all reduced-time employment, whatever the reason for it, and not only part-time employment in the strict sense.

[72] Eurostat, Luxembourg: *Durée du travail: Résultats principaux d'enquêtes menées au niveau communautaire*, Employment and Unemployment Rapid Information, Demographic and Social Statistics 3-79, 8 Oct. 1979, tables 6.1, p. 11 and 6.5, pp. 15-17.

[73] Statistics Canada: *The Labor Force, February 1980* (Ottawa), tables 28 and 33, pp. 48 and 53. The average was 14.8 hours, if persons not working in that particular week were excluded.

[74] Australian Bureau of Statistics: *The labour force, Australia, November 1979* (Canberra), tables 18 and 16, pp. 18 and 17. Hours actually worked, not hours paid.

[75] *Employment and earnings, December 1979* (Washington, DC, United States Department of Labor, Bureau of Labor Statistics), Vol. 26, No. 12, table A-27, p. 38. The economic reasons were: lack of employment, shortage of raw materials or repairs to equipment, taking a new job or leaving a job during the week and inability to find anything other than part-time work; average part-time hours for these categories were 20.2 hours per week.

[76] Christian Brinkmann: "The desire for part-time employment on the part of employed and non-employed women", in *Mitteilungen aus der Arbeitsmarkt- und Berufsforschung* (Stuttgart, Berlin, Cologne, Mainz), Vol. 12, No. 3, pp. 403-412 (in German with summary in English p. 459). According to surveys carried out in 1969 and 1978, the desire to work part time had considerably increased: in 1978 most young people in part-time jobs did not want full-time employment.

[77] In France, in a preliminary survey in 1976 in a number of banks, 81 per cent of the 840 replies received to 1,500 questionnaires were in favour of part-time work; in September 1978 only 25 persons had put their intention into practice, and one year later 53; it was presumed that this was because their income would have dropped ("Le travail temps partiel", in *Femme pratique* (Paris), Mar. 1980, pp. 50-63). The gap between potential demand and actual demand may be very wide, as we have seen.

POTENTIAL IMPLICATIONS AT THE LEVEL OF THE ESTABLISHMENT

6

The possible consequences of reductions in working time at the level of the establishment have been outlined in a number of general studies which are for the most part rather theoretical in character. They are summarised in the first part of this chapter. We then consider two specific problems (that of costs and that of effects on employment) with respect to which a good deal of new theoretical writing is being produced, and which are vital to the running of an establishment in practice. Some theoretical assumptions have been supplemented by research at the micro-economic level. However, this research is recent and reveals many gaps which will have to be filled if we are to have an idea of the real reaction at the level of the establishment. The research places great emphasis on the probable or actual effects of reduced working time in the field of employment, which may include the creation of more jobs, a reduction of partial unemployment, or the avoidance of dismissals. The multiplicity of factors that play their part in each separate case usually prevents us from establishing close correlations with reduction in working time in the strict sense of the term. Moreover, measures for reducing working time are considered in isolation, that is to say, without reference to any accompanying or supporting measures that may be considered or proposed to help to reduce unemployment.

The vast majority of the relevant studies concern only industrial and commercial undertakings, which account for only a part of the economic operation of advanced industrial societies: other employing establishments or bodies (administrative agencies, non-profit-making services and more generally all activities whose product cannot be quantified) are generally left to one side, even though they also contribute an essential part of the national product. Moreover, even within this limited framework, emphasis is generally concentrated at certain levels: the workshop or building site, workers visibly and directly connected with a certain item of capital equipment or a physical product, and those who are paid on an hourly basis. Thus most of these studies concern only a small fraction of the employed population and, moreover, one that is diminishing in advanced industrial societies.

GENERAL THEORIES

General theories on the possible effects of reductions in working time at the level of the undertaking will be summarised in this section.[1] In the first part they are based essentially on the economics of the firm. The following two parts are then devoted to two types of effects which, while relating to practical problems, do not often give rise to other than theoretical consideration. These are the risk of shortage of personnel and certain problems of scale.

Economics of the firm

In studies relating to the general economics of the firm, reductions in working time are generally regarded as measures resulting from external constraints such as legislation or trade union pressure. They are not thought of as part of the trend towards reduced working time which prevailed for several decades. The theories put forward seem to relate to a static situation, without reference to the momentum acquired by this trend.

It seems to be generally accepted that reductions in working time in industrial and commercial undertakings ought to result in loss of production, since productive capacity would be used for shorter periods. These losses would be reduced by productivity gains resulting from the reductions in working time itself, since the workers' fatigue would be lessened and absenteeism would diminish[2] and there would be a reduction in idle time. But these effects vary according to the firm and the sector of the economy. In part they depend on the method of remuneration and the technical conditions in which production is carried out, and specifically on the extent to which work rates are controlled by machines. In practice, it is impossible to isolate the effect of measures which firms would probably take to increase global productivity from such factors as modernisation of equipment, various rationalisation measures such as reorganisation of production or work (shift work, for example), or stricter cost management. Opinions vary about the relative importance of productivity gains resulting from further reductions in working time.

It appears to be generally accepted that "other things being equal", either a reduction in normal working time without loss of earnings or an extension of paid annual leave would increase the hourly wage cost but not the total wage bill unless arrangements are made to work the hours that would otherwise be lost. In principle, workers' earnings do not increase but are redistributed over shorter working time; thus the hourly wage is increased. Moreover, unit production costs increase because overall production costs relate to lower production. Additional expenditure may be caused as a result of practical arrangements required because of new work schedules (various types of reorganisation, penalty payments for delays in deliveries, for example). Reorganisation of work schedules and particularly the introduction or extension of shift work apparently brings about considerable gains in productivity and means that equipment and machinery are used for longer periods, but this would also mean increased expenditure on bonuses for overtime, shift work, night work or weekend work. Opinions differ as to what additional costs are to be expected as a result of the reductions in working time and as to the capacity of the firm to meet these further costs.

Possible effects on employment are closely linked with the decisions that the firm takes with regard to its production and its investment (in rationalisation or in capacity). Generally speaking, the greater the productivity gains the less employment should increase, and vice versa. In order to know how employment may evolve, we also need to know what decisions the firm will take with regard to its output, because a reduction in working time may lead to a fall in output. If the firm decides to maintain its previous output or to increase it, there may be scope for absorbing increases in unit costs. A number of measures may be adopted for this purpose with different consequences as regards costs and employment.[3] If the firm has not been working to capacity, with personnel or equipment not employed as fully as possible, it may use this reserve capacity of factors of production already in use without effect on employment. It may also bring back into use previously idle equipment (some of which may have been less efficient), or develop shift work: the more intensive utilisation of such idle equipment, if it is accompanied by the engagement of new workers, will increase the total wage bill. A third method is to invest in supplementary equipment which may play a decisive part in obtaining hourly productivity gains and may accelerate substitution of capital equipment for labour. New workers will be taken on in proportion to the requirements of the new equipment and to the extent that the latter does not make it possible to economise on manpower. Such investment in itself, as well as the taking on of any new workers, would involve supplementary costs. Many of the other methods proposed would also increase overall costs.

Direct effects on employment will therefore be nil if the firm reduces its output. If it compensates for lost working time, various solutions may offer themselves, some of them in combination with one another, with variable consequences as regards costs. If we assume that the firm has recourse to overtime there will be no positive effect on employment, and wage costs will increase. If it takes on new workers the effect on employment will be favourable, but the total wage bill will increase and indirect costs are to be expected as well: administrative costs in recruiting personnel, and induction and possible further training costs. If the firm has workers who are underemployed or partially unemployed, the effects on employment will be invisible; in the latter case the firm would also lose the benefit of public assistance in connection with partial unemployment. If the firm decides not to dismiss workers, the effects on employment will also be invisible; unemployment will merely not increase. Generally speaking, unless there is a very great expansion in business, the higher productivity gains are, the less the probable increase in employment will be. It should be noted in this connection that although reductions in working time are proposed by many trade unions so as to promote an improvement in the employment situation, in practice in a large number of collective agreements that have been made the employees benefiting from such reductions in working time undertake to increase productivity to the extent that such an increase lies within their power so as to avoid or limit cost increases.

The consequences of cost increases on a firm's competitiveness give rise to much argument. It has been said that if the firm passes on cost increases in its selling prices, it puts itself at a disadvantage with its competitors and loses part of its market. If it reduces profits to maintain prices, its margin for investment is reduced and therefore, in the long run, its output and its market position are compromised. In both cases, even if there are immediate positive effects on employment, they may well be nullified later and it may even be necessary to lay off workers. There are differences of opinion about the capacity of firms to shoulder new burdens. In any event all decisions concerning output — whether to lower it, maintain it or increase it — depend on existing or expected outlets in the market. This is also true of decisions concerning technical equipment and human resources.[4] The effects on the firm's ability to compete depend on a great variety of factors, particularly trends in demand and the pricing policy the firm can follow in view of the degree of control that it has over the market and the degree of elasticity or inelasticity of demand for the goods and services it produces. But the determining factor in the last analysis is the extent to which the firm's products find a market, and that determines whether the firm makes a profit and what its earnings will be.

Other practical problems are often discussed in this connection, and firms are said to be more or less well equipped to solve them according to their size, the sector of the economy to which they belong and their financial situation. Two are often mentioned. One is the danger of increasing shortages of personnel having certain skills or in certain regions. This would have implications for costs since to overcome such shortages the firm may be obliged to have more overtime worked, to offer higher wages to attract the few workers available, or to incur expenditure on training. The other problem lies in the possible difficulty of creating jobs that will correspond to the demand for labour that emerges if there is a reduction in working hours.

Risks of shortages of personnel

There does not seem to be any information available about the risks of personnel shortages in the event of reductions in working time. However, various observations have been made on the subject, and are summarised below. In fact, shortages of personnel with particular skills or in particular regions are a permanent problem; they are considered to be an integral feature of economic development and there have always been changes and movements in the labour force to meet them. The flexibility and adaptability resulting from such changes is well known. To take only one example, in the Federal Republic of Germany about 10 million workers change jobs every year.[5] There would seem to be more possibilities of inter-occupational substitution and mobility than one would expect, particularly in service trades, and the margin of initiative left to the employer to meet his needs for particular skills is not negligible.[6]

According to a United Kingdom study, inappropriate conditions of work and employment and wastage of skills may cause shortages over which the employer may have some control.[7] In France it would appear that the sectors with the highest rates of pay are usually those in which working hours were substantially reduced in the past.[8] In addition to the influence of the workers themselves, who exert strong pressure for such reductions when they belong to the relatively better-paid categories, management practice would partially explain this situation: one of the obstacles to taking on new workers to compensate for reductions in working hours lies in manpower shortages, and it is easiest to overcome this difficulty in the sectors with the highest wages.

According to the writer who made this observation, the existence of higher wages is a sign that special attention has been given to personnel management, of which working time is one aspect. Higher labour costs are of course easier to accept when the wage bill represents only a small part of sales prices, or in industries which do not have to face much foreign competition.

To evaluate the risk that reductions of working time may create bottlenecks in occupations requiring certain skills, a number of factors have to be taken into account. For example it is more and more generally recognised that it is increasingly uncommon for the effective capacity to perform specific tasks and functions to be obtained without lengthy practical experience of doing the job under normal conditions; therefore it is inside the undertaking itself that a major part of the skill necessary to perform such functions has to be acquired. Moreover, there are today many programmes of assistance to business which take over some of the cost, including wage costs, involved in the training of workers. Some are linked with particular employment creation objectives; there are so many examples of such programmes that one need do no more than mention their existence.

Furthermore, we should not lose sight of labour mobility within undertakings when jobs requiring skill and experience are to be filled: this has been more clearly seen with the replacement of workers who retire, and who are normally very experienced, but it is also generally true when a job which becomes vacant for any reason is filled, as it often is, by promotion. Outside recruitment will take place only after a series of internal transfers, and may in the end mean the recruitment of workers with little or no skill.

Problems of scale

According to certain analyses, the size of the undertaking, and in particular the number of persons employed, if it falls below a certain level, may restrict the management's practical possibility of creating new full-time jobs on the basis of work made available by reductions in working time. For example, if the working week is lowered from 40 to 35 hours and only five workers are employed, there will be new employment available for only 25 hours, which is enough for a part-time job but no more. If the reduction is less, the limited amount of new employment available will be even more marked. Moreover, the employment available will be in jobs requiring differing skills which would therefore require multi-skilled workers to do all the work becoming available in the various jobs. Small firms would be at a particular disadvantage in such cases.

Very little research has been done on these specific aspects of the effects of a reduction in working time. One survey published in the Federal Republic of Germany warns against too mechanical an approach to this problem. It appears that in small and medium-sized undertakings some workers are often underutilised to some extent; thus even if the work made available by a reduction in working hours is not sufficient to create a full-time job, there would not necessarily be a need to engage someone on a new full-time job. Moreover, if this problem of scale means that no new jobs are created in an undertaking below a certain size, and if the result is that output and supply fall and that prices rise, some firms might decide to produce more and engage new workers.[9] Another observation concerns the "round figure argument". This is that there is a continual process of adjustment of working time to the number of available jobs, and management is used to dealing with the organisational problems resulting from small reductions in working time.[10] It is also possible that full-time jobs can be created by organising combinations of skills; this would be in conformity with programmes of job enrichment, which are fashionable today. In any event the restructuring of jobs requires certain adjustments, and would involve problems of the same kind as the establishment of part-time jobs; the idea of developing part-time employment seems to have made progress, which would imply that the practical problems involved are not necessarily insurmountable.

Problems of scale should not, in any case, arise except within strict limits, with regard to certain jobs. This leads us to consider the relationship between the nature of work and employment.[11] Many activities for which output cannot be directly measured are occupying a dominant place in advanced industrial societies, and in those cases there is no linear relationship between work and employment, no mechanical relationship between a given quantity of labour and a given number of jobs, and also no real, significant relationship between time spent in a given place and a given amount of output. The volume of final output depends on the large number of factors, among which working time is not necessarily decisive. Moreover, in many sectors there is not a fixed quantity of work, established once and for all.

COSTS

Analyses of effects on costs[12] reveal a fundamental uncertainty: they must necessarily take account of the influence of reductions in working time on employment in the undertaking, since any change in total wage costs is the result of certain employment effects and not of reductions in working time as such; yet this influence cannot easily be foreseen. But that is only one reason among many why cost estimates raise problems. In the following pages we shall successively consider the difficulties of evaluating productivity gains, various examples of cost estimates, the special problems raised by overtime, and finally the reasons why a case-by-case approach is necessary in this connection. This does not, of course, exhaust the question of costs, and that is why they will reappear in the following section in which specific cases are in fact examined. As regards shift work, given the complexity of the subject it has seemed preferable to deal with it as a whole in the last part of the chapter, under the heading of work organisation, in relation to its combined implications for employment and costs.

Estimates of productivity gains

It has been estimated that a reduction of 1 per cent in working time corresponds to a gain in productivity of 0.5 per cent, that is to say, a fall of only 0.5 per cent in output. However, this figure has given rise to considerable dispute. It is an estimate that was made in the past, and the author accompanied his conclusions with various reservations. In his study[13] he showed in particular the variety of hypotheses used in this field in different countries. In the United States, on the basis of the usual working time in 1957 (2,069 hours per year of 39.8 hours per week over 52 weeks), the author believed that a small reduction in working time would be compensated to the extent of 40 per cent. But in the Federal Republic of Germany, for example, complete compensation was foreseen, owing mainly to increases in output resulting from the substitution of capital for labour.[14] In France different evaluations were made, varying with the method of reducing working time; the increase in productivity was negligible in the case of extension of annual leave but in the case of a shorter working week the compensation for this reduction due to productivity gains could reach 40 per cent.[15] A study published by the ILO in 1975 includes a comparative summing-up of the various evaluations of productivity gains made on the occasion of previous reductions in working time.[16]

If there were further reductions today, would the productivity gains to be expected be in fact less? Some authors believe so. They hold that because working time is not as long as it used to be, workers are less tired; these writers also argue that the margin for improvement in productivity is becoming exhausted as a result of the efforts made to overcome the depression. In response to such arguments other writers point to the increasing fatigue and stress due to the difficulties of daily life and to the possibilities afforded by technological advances and the spectacular gains in productivity to be expected from scientific and technical progress. Experience of productivity gains obtained when there was a transition from full-time to part-time employment may perhaps furnish useful indications in this regard because the reductions in working hours in that connection were often quite substantial. Considerable gains have been noted in a number of studies.[17] Among the factors most often mentioned are increased efficiency, more flexible use of manpower, lower rates of sickness and absenteeism, fewer accidents at work, improved opportunities for using human resources at the regional level. It is true, however, that part-time employment is sometimes precarious and this may lead the workers concerned to react in such a way that generalisations would be hazardous.

In the United Kingdom the Trade Union Research Unit of the Trades Union Congress considers that a reduction in working time can stimulate increased productivity. Lengthy working hours are often a symptom of inefficiency. By remedying this situation, it would be possible to reduce overtime, lower costs and improve competitiveness. Excessively long working hours sap workers' morale and output and increase absenteeism; they may encourage the undertaking to go on using out-of-date machinery and thus put a brake on investment in new and more efficient processes. A reduction in working time would stimulate management to be imaginative and would promote better utilisation of resources; moreover, fixing positive objectives with regard to leisure and employment would contribute to the creation of a favourable atmosphere for technological change and reduce resistance to it.[18] The Unit has analysed various methods of reducing working time, linking this measure to economies in unit costs and to various gains in industrial and commercial efficiency.[19]

Estimates of productivity gains that might result from further reductions in working time have been made for the purpose of macro-economic research; they have probably only a very distant relationship with what actually happens in individual undertakings. In any event, they do not give a clear picture. Thus an advisory committee appointed by the Swedish Government to study a trade union proposal for a 30-hour week thought that a reduction in working time would, as in the past, have beneficial effects on production (these estimates were based on the possibility of a reduction of 2.5 hours per week up to 1983).[20] In the United Kingdom in 1978 the Department of Employment put forward the hypothesis that productivity gains would compensate for 40 per cent of losses in potential output if the working week was shortened to 35 hours, on varying assumptions about changes in overtime, output and employment.[21] On the other hand, in the Netherlands the Central Planning Bureau expected only a small improvement in hourly labour productivity if there were such a reduction.[22]

Gains in productivity resulting from further reductions in working time would probably differ, depending on the sector of the economy where the reductions were made. According to a study made in Italy some years ago relating to the possible effects of a reduction in the working week to below 40 hours, for every reduction of 5 per cent (two hours) the increase in hourly productivity would vary according to the sector between 0.5 per cent for electricity, gas and water, and 3.5 per cent for construction. A reduction of 10 per cent (four hours) would bring about greater increases, varying between 1 per cent in the first sector mentioned above and 8 per cent in mining and construction, with 6 per cent for textiles, clothing, wood and furniture. For industry as a whole hourly productivity gains were 2.2. per cent in the first case and 5 per cent in the second.[23] One point appears to have been generally ignored: that is the real importance of productivity gains to be foreseen in sectors other than those producing actual goods, which are the only ones that can be measured with current techniques, or where workers are paid otherwise than by the hour. For some sectors or categories use is made of estimates of a purely conventional character. In France, for example, in recent econometric models a compensation of 100 per cent is assumed for commerce and services.[24] It should be recalled that in a number of service occupations, assumed to be "unproductive", which accompany and promote the so-called "productive" sectors, estimates of productivity gains could be only of academic interest at the level of the undertaking since these activities produce effects on productivity that are integrated in the results attributed to other sectors.

Consequences of further reductions in working time would no doubt also differ according to the methods by which they were made. Opinions do not always agree upon these differences. The French Democratic Labour Confederation (CFDT) and IG Metall in the Federal Republic of Germany, for example, consider that a compensation of 50 per cent due to productivity gains, which they assume in the event of a shorter working week, would also be valid if annual leave were extended; the positive effects of the latter measure would be felt after the leave and not throughout the year, but it is recalled that leave is often granted at times when business is relatively slack. The author of the study made in the Federal Republic of Germany concerning the metalworking industry, which is based on practical experience and some statistical data, points out that an increase in productivity is not to be expected in the first year in which holidays are extended. In his view, the productivity gains mentioned by IG Metall on the basis of a survey by the IFO Institute in Munich relate to the past and are no longer valid for a reduction in the working week.[25]

As regards a reduction in overtime, a study by the European Trade Union Institute states that the productivity gains to be expected would exceed those obtained from a shorter normal working week. It points out in support of this claim that the fall in productivity tends to be proportionate to the number of hours worked every day and accelerates above a certain level (generally after six hours), while payments for overtime weigh heavily on labour costs.[26]

The way in which weekly working hours are reduced should also be of importance. If the normal reduced week of 35 or 32 hours were compressed into four or four-and-a-half days, productivity gains might be considerable, according to some research. A survey published in the United States in 1975 reports on the experience of 16 firms that had introduced the compressed week. It included a number of cases where the normal week of 32 to 35 hours was spread over three or four days. The survey gave a number of examples of positive effects on the volume of business (the transition to the "compressed" week was accompanied by an extension of opening hours), employment and utilisation of equipment, and in the form of reduced absenteeism and overtime, but the authors warn against drawing generalisations from only a few cases.[27] According to more recent experience, if the undertaking is closed for longer periods, it may make important savings in overheads, for example on heating and lighting. In some cases, productivity gains of up to 30 per cent have been recorded on Mondays following the suppression of work on Friday afternoon.[28]

The "compressed" week does not appear to arouse much interest in trade union circles, if all it does is to redistribute the same number of hours of work per week. In the United States trade unions appear to be moving towards a compressed week without longer daily hours. Automobile workers now have "personal" paid leave (five days per year since the end of 1976, and seven days since the following year), which they hope they can increase until the working week is reduced to four days.[29] Some supervisors believe that the four-day week would increase production, reduce absenteeism, and improve job satisfaction; in particular, there would be less absenteeism because the loss of wages is higher when the worker misses a day in a four-day week than it would be in a five-day week.[30]

Major gains in productivity are also expected from a reduction in total annual working time, although discussion is somewhat theoretical on this point. In particular, this method would, it is believed, reduce absenteeism and be more profitable to undertakings because it would allow them to adapt goods and services to seasonal and other variations in demand.

A "think tank"[31] has made the following evaluations of the advantages and disadvantages of various ways of reducing working time so as to obtain a 2 per cent reduction in the 40-hour working week; its conclusions are based on actual cases of reductions in working time made in the past. In its view the grant of five extra days of leave at weekends or of days at choice would make it easier to adjust to economic fluctuations. Moreover, since there is already a lot of absenteeism before and after weekends and public holidays, the loss of output would be limited; if need be, it should be possible to have recourse to temporary staff and volunteers. Reductions in the working day are, however, without major effect on output and do not mean much to employees because they are too small. With regard to a reduction on the Friday afternoon, immediately before the weekend, some managers had doubts about the desirability of shortening one afternoon out of five, and feared that this arrangement would ultimately result in a rather unproductive Friday afternoon. It was generally agreed that if a fifth week of leave were introduced, it would be advisable to give it outside the summer, either at Christmas, or on the occasion of half-term school holidays in February. As regards any loss of output, it would no doubt be small with a daily reduction of ten minutes in working time, but would be greater if there were 50 minutes less work on Fridays. The fifth week of leave, it is generally believed, would cause a loss of output roughly proportional to the reduction in working time. This would also be one of the more costly solutions from the point of view of recruitment of extra staff, since its effects would be concentrated over a short period. Different methods of reducing working time also have advantages and disadvantages, with unforeseeable effects on costs in such fields as stocks, welfare services (such as canteens, dispensaries and transport), maintenance of equipment and relations with suppliers and subcontractors.

Estimates of costs

Various estimates of the increases in costs to be expected from reductions in working time have been made. In general they reflect the double uncertainty that exists about possible effects on employment and on gains in productivity. Moreover, the basis on which the figures put forward in controversies on this subject have been established are not always explained, and it is consequently often difficult to say whether the estimates are really comparable. The discussions place great emphasis on effects relating to wage costs and on the extent to which it will be possible to compensate for any increases in them by gains in productivity.

Some of the estimates have been made by employers' organisations. Thus in the Federal Republic of Germany it has been estimated that in one metallurgical undertaking one hour's reduction in working time corresponds to a wage increase of 2.6 per cent. With full wage compensation, the cost to the entire industry would amount to DM7,000 million. The 35-hour week would result in an increase of 18 to 24 per cent in production costs. One additional day of paid annual leave would mean a rise of 1 per cent in wages and would cost the industry DM2,500 million.[32] The employers' federation of Belgium has estimated that reducing weekly working hours from 40 to 36 would raise hourly wage costs by 11.1 per cent over three years, or 3.7 per cent per year. Other charges would have to be added to this, including that resulting from lower utilisation of productive equipment (since machines would work 36 hours instead of 40 and would cost 11.1 per cent more per product) and those due to increased investment to maintain the level of production. In addition, there would be the costs already foreseen in collective agreements.[33] The Confederation of Australian Industry believes that it would cost at least 12 per cent more to do the same work in the event of a reduction in weekly working hours from 40 to 35, and at least 20 per cent more if account were taken of the fact that shortages in certain skilled occupations would make it necessary to have recourse to increased overtime.[34] In the view of the Swedish Employers' Confederation, to reduce the working week from 40 to 30 hours, without reducing real income, increases in productivity of at least 33 per cent would be necessary. This figure might even reach 50 per cent in manufacturing industry, given the fall in the profitability of investments.[35]

In general, employers' organisations fear that reductions in working time with maintenance of wages will endanger the financial situation of the firm, particularly if it is of small or medium size. The Belgian Employers' Federation considers it impossible to absorb the increased costs that would result from shortening weekly working hours to 36, which would oblige them to increase the number of employees by 3 per cent, even if social charges were reduced as the Government proposes, and if wage increases were restricted to following the cost-of-living index, though doubts were expressed as to whether it was possible to respect such a restriction in practice.[36]

Estimates have also been made on the trade union side. Research workers at the European Trade Union Institute[37] consider that a reduction in weekly working hours to 36 would be compensated to the extent of 50 per cent by gains in productivity. Additional jobs would be required to make up the remaining 50 per cent. The wage bill would rise by 5.5 per cent. The increase in overall costs would be 6.5 per cent, if an increase of 1 per cent in capital costs is assumed. The way in which the reduction is to be brought about, in particular how it is to be spread over time in order to take account of the situation of each firm, should be considered as an integral part of the trade union programme, including wage claims. Extension of annual leave from four to six weeks would require an average increase in employment of 3.48 per cent; the total cost (wage costs plus supplementary capital costs) would be 3.9 per cent. Limitation of overtime would promote the creation of new jobs. On the average, the elimination of one hour of overtime per week, or 48 hours per year, will call for a 1 per cent increase in the workforce with a corresponding rise in overall wage costs; the inclusion of capital costs will result in increased total costs of 1.24 per cent. The introduction of a fifth shift in shift work would have the same effect as a simple reduction in weekly working hours, except that the reduction would be greater and would not involve supplementary capital cost.

Various arguments put forward by trade unions attempt to show that undertakings could absorb the foreseeable new costs. Like any other benefit having economic effects, a reduction in working time must cost something, but it is contended that the technological advances which make it possible also help firms to bear the cost. It has also been pointed out (for example in the Belgian trade union movement) that if issues of cost were as decisive as is claimed, some firms would not insist on offering higher wages rather than reducing working time.[38] On the other hand, one reason put forward in Denmark to explain the growing importance that has been assumed by the claim for reduced working time is the refusal of employers to meet wage claims.[39] It is also argued that the cost of shortening weekly working hours would be lessened in any case by resulting gains in productivity, and could be spread out over a certain period of time. It would not be much greater on average than cost increases to be expected from normal wage negotiations. As a rule, wage increases are budgeted for in company accounts. Since many trade unions have offered to moderate their claims for future increases, these budgeted wage rises could be used to absorb the cost of reductions in working time.

An Italian analysis examines the various consequences resulting from the change-over from a system of two eight-hour shifts, five days a week, to one of three shifts of six hours 20 minutes each, with a six-day week. The normal weekly working hours are assumed to fall from 40 to 38, and hours actually worked, previously 42, to fall by 10 per cent. At 38 hours, there would be no more overtime. An assumed initial total of 100 workers would rise to 110; there would be a 10 per cent increase in production (rising from 4,200 to 4,600 units) and an equivalent rise in average hourly productivity. What would remain unchanged would be the total number of hours worked, weekly production per worker, weekly wages, the cost of fixed capital and labour cost per unit produced. The price of the product would not change. There would be a 10 per cent increase in average hourly wages, in the total wage bill, in receipts and in variable costs (raw materials). This analysis concludes that profits would rise by 40 per cent.[40]

Estimates have also been made by other private and official bodies. To take one example from an official source, the Department of Employment in the United Kingdom has calculated that a 6 to 8 per cent rise in labour costs would result from a general reduction in working hours to 35 per week. This estimate is close to that coming from the Confederation of British Industry, which gives 8.5 per cent, while the Trade Union Research Unit puts forward an estimate of 7 per cent.[41] On the trade union side, it is pointed out that if they were spread over three or four years, the increases in unit labour costs would amount to about 1.5 or 2.5 per cent per year; this should be compared with cost increases of over 90 per cent in the previous four years, which the system had managed to absorb, despite the difficulties.[42]

Another survey analyses in detail the costs resulting from an extension of paid holidays in the metalworking industry in the Federal Republic of Germany. It concludes that each extra day of leave adds a little less than 0.7 per cent per hour of labour cost to direct personnel costs, to which must also be added indirect costs of 0.1 to 0.3 per cent. Progressive extension of annual leave by an average of 4.5 days would result in a total increase in labour costs of between 3.3. and 4.2 per cent.[43] Another study sets out a model based on empirical data, to calculate the cost of extending paid holidays for different categories of employees. The average estimated cost is 0.4 per cent on the wage bill for every day of leave. This is a ceiling because, if the increase is related to total costs, including capital, the result would be lower, though probably not by much. On the same bases the author estimates that a 1.3 per cent increase in wage costs would result from a reduction of one hour in weekly working time.[44] In the United Kingdom it is recognised that work is heaviest at holiday time in sectors such as the postal services and the railways. It is then necessary to pay more overtime to workers who are not on holiday or to take on casual workers. In addition, work on holidays entitles workers to wage bonuses and compensatory time off.[45]

Special problems relating to overtime

Overtime is regarded as advantageous to an undertaking because it enables the employer to adapt flexibly and rapidly to fluctuations in production and orders and to overcome shortages of certain skills, notwithstanding the increased wage rates and premiums that have to be paid. In addition, overtime is performed by workers already employed by the firm, and the fact that they are familiar with their jobs and with the routine of the undertaking often results in considerable savings. Premium rates for overtime are normal practice and in principle are supposed to discourage employers, but this effect is often counterbalanced, more or less depending on the particular case, by another factor. This is the result of the provisions applicable to social charges under which recourse to overtime is advantageous either because social security contributions are not payable in respect of overtime pay, as in the United States, or because there is a ceiling on earnings used as a basis for contributions, as is the case in many other countries. In the latter case the hours used by the employer to offset any reduction in working hours are the hours that cost him least in social security contributions. In calculating the financial costs and benefits, attention has to be paid to the occupations and grades concerned (whether they are low paid or well paid), and the nature of social security schemes applicable.

The effects to be expected from increased penalisation of overtime have received particular attention in the United States. This question was raised about 1965, and it proved to be difficult to evaluate the effects of the law in this field, except indirectly.[46] Today, the debate continues and concerns the relationship between penalisation of overtime and employment. It is pointed out that the cost of overtime premiums represents a decreasing part of labour costs, which are increased by the development of "fringe benefits" (which represented 36.1 per cent of wage costs in 1975, as compared with 16.8 per cent in 1953). If this trend persists, the dissuasive effect of overtime premiums will continue to diminish.[47] Reduction of weekly hours to 35 or 32 would lower the limit at which premium rates would become payable. Assuming that earnings corresponding to the 40-hour week were maintained, it would be necessary to increase the hourly wage rate by 14.3 per cent in the first case and 25 per cent in the second; this could no doubt be absorbed by annual increases in productivity, if workers simultaneously abandoned claims for wage increases. The author of this estimate did not recommend an increase in overtime premiums, so as not to increase unit labour costs.[48]

In Japan the Sohyo trade union federation states that large undertakings tend to have more recourse to overtime in order to overcome economic fluctuations, while small and medium-sized firms "hire and fire" as the economy fluctuates. Comparing premium payments for overtime with the cost of recruiting new workers, Sohyo considers that the bigger the undertaking, the lower the cost of these premiums as compared with the cost of recruitment. It is to the advantage of large undertakings to prolong working hours until overtime premiums reach a level of 70 per cent more than normal hourly wages. Reduction of overtime when there is a downturn in economic activity also has its advantages: reduction in costs, and (since there are no dismissals) peaceful relations with the workers. Sohyo believes that a very big increase in premium rates would be necessary to counter this kind of conduct on the part of big undertakings successfully.[49]

Accounting for working time on an annual basis makes the concept of overtime less clear-cut. If overtime disappears as a result, some savings may be made (hours that would be regarded as overtime within the limits used at present to calculate weekly averages would cease to be so regarded and would no longer be paid at higher rates). To judge this kind of situation, it is important to know whether weekly working time would still be calculated at intervals within the year. The annual basis of calculation of working time also raises problems with regard to the regular rest periods at present prescribed in labour legislation, and the increases in wage rates laid down for work at weekends or on holidays.

Need for a case-by-case approach

In the field of costs, perhaps more than in any other, a case-by-case approach is necessary, because the factors involved are extraordinarily complex.

In the first place, available information is far from sufficient. No systematic account appears, as yet, to be kept of production costs.[50] This observation seems to be particularly true of labour costs and some other forms of expenditure which many undertakings seem to resign themselves to bear without trying to quantify them.[51] In one case study[52] it is noted that accounting procedures in use seem unsuitable for evaluating the cost of a decision about shorter working time. For example, in accounting terms, cost per hour worked increases if the total wage bill is unchanged but the number of hours falls; yet in fact, actual expenditure remains stable. Again, if a reduction in working hours leads to an increase in stocks, the cost factor applied to these stocks is likely to be based on units of area. Yet there will be no additional expense if storage capacity is not fully used, and if it is, the expense will be much greater than that shown in production costs. The concept of hourly labour productivity itself needs to be used with care. It is merely a standard of measurement. The exercise of relating productivity to a given factor (per working hour in this case) does not mean that there is a cause-and-effect relationship between one and the other.

The way firms proceed with regard to costs connected with working time gave rise to the following observations, which should be borne in mind, though without making any hasty generalisations.

The National Board for Prices and Incomes in the United Kingdom noted that a very high proportion of firms made no calculation of the effects that changes in working time might have on costs and profits.[53] This was true for overtime and in cases in which shift-work systems were introduced. An informal study in the United States found that relatively few firms made any detailed cost analysis on which to base their decisions regarding overtime and fringe benefits.[54] In France it has been found that the introduction of new systems of shift work that reconcile financial and welfare considerations meet with resistance from industrialists, who often prefer to keep to the traditional systems, while paying bonuses or granting additional days off.[55] Some studies of systems of arrangement of working time conclude that there is no consciously directed policy designed to optimise its utilisation; generally management does not seem to try to evaluate the cost of work-time arrangements. Considerations such as the system of internal operations of the undertaking and the balance of power between the employer and the unions apparently play a more important role in such decisions.

A case-by-case approach to the question of costs is also necessary since the effect on costs of measures for reducing working time must be evaluated on the basis of the whole economic, technical and organisational context of which these costs form a part. Wages are only one part of labour costs. The latter are only one factor among many in production costs, a factor which varies from one undertaking to another and from one sector of the economy to another. The incidence of an increase in total wages has to be weighted in consequence. Besides, the cost of production is only one of the many factors to be taken into account in determining sales prices. To the extent that profit considerations intervene, account must be taken of the fact that, as a result of systems of taxation of company profits, final net profits may in some cases decrease less than proportionately to the increase in costs. The cost of production is only one factor among others affecting the ability to compete: other considerations such as choice, conception and reliability of the product, punctuality of deliveries, quality of the after-sale service, availability of spares and exogenous factors such as exchange rates all play their part.[56] Finally, each undertaking reserves to itself the choice of its own financial margin of manoeuvre, and this will vary from one firm to another.

Thirdly, the productivity gains induced by reductions in working time are additional to the long-term trend in productivity. This long-term trend must therefore also be taken into account in evaluating capacity to absorb the additional costs. Thus, if the productivity trend is generally positive, it would be more accurate to refer to the gains resulting from shorter working time as an "acceleration" of the rise in productivity. Here again a case-by-case approach is necessary since trends differ widely from sector to sector.[57]

EMPLOYMENT

The possible effects of measures for reducing working time in the field of employment will first of all be considered on the basis of an examination of the plans and actual record of particular undertakings. Separate sections will then be devoted to the specific influence of the organisation of work and of methods of reducing working time.

Analysis of actual situations reveals that there is much less rigidity and more flexibility and dynamism than theoretical reasoning might lead us to suppose. Empirical findings seem to indicate that the work-sharing problem lies essentially in the field of short-time working intended as a means of avoiding lay-offs or dismissals. To be sure, the management of an undertaking has no reason to create jobs just for the sake of providing employment. If it is found that shorter working time has had positive employment effects, they are apparently due in most cases to the fact that the situation of the undertaking made it possible. If on the other hand the effects are negative, this may be because irrespective of cost considerations, the substitution of machinery for labour is one way of avoiding having to resolve difficult problems of personnel administration and human resources management, or having to face the possibility of labour disputes (machines do not go on strike) or having to deal with a multiplicity of complicated regulations.

The effects on employment of measures for reducing working time are generally particularly difficult to determine for two reasons. First, if the undertaking decides to make up for the hours lost by using additional personnel, it can do so in a number of ways. The new workers may be put into part-time or temporary (interim, short-term) jobs, or may be employed under subcontracts or even without reporting the fact. In principle, such methods are less costly than recourse to overtime or the creation of long-term full-time jobs. It is not always easy, and may be impossible, to work out how many jobs are involved. The extent of these kinds of employment, which have advantages from the point of view of flexibility in management, has been widely recognised and is mentioned in many case studies in connection with reductions in working time. It is not new. In the United States, when the "penalties" payable over and above 44 hours in order to discourage overtime were extended in 1963 to retail trade establishments, the result was a marked fall in the proportion of employees working more than 44 hours a week, but an increase in the proportion of part-time employees.[58]

Secondly, it is often hard to distinguish in the operations of undertakings between what is due to shorter working time as such and what is due to economic conditions, or the specific characteristics of the undertaking itself and its policy with regard to production, investments, modernisation and sales. Reductions in working time may merely bring forward decisions that would have been taken in any case. This is perhaps particularly the case in respect of technology. The rapid application of the results of scientific and technical progress is one of the most powerful factors for success in the competition among industrialised countries themselves, and in the growing competition between the latter and the developing countries. Some people even believe that the substitution of capital for human beings will go on, whatever labour costs may be and at whatever level of wages.[59]

Intentions

One way of ascertaining what the probable effects of reduced working time would be on employment is to put the question to the managers themselves. One French survey, the results of which are set out below, reveals both the complexity of the decisions to be taken after such measures and also how few undertakings intend to take on new workers.[60]

It was assumed that working time would be reduced by 2.5 per cent (one hour a week or five days a year). Out of 100 heads of undertakings, 46.4 replied that they would maintain their production in the year following the reduction, with the same equipment and number of employees, which implied that reserves of capacity existed, while 50.8 would not do so; the survey does not say whether the latter would raise or lower their production. With regard to investments, 59 industrialists would consider various measures, such as installing more productive equipment (24), having recourse to overtime (nine), introducing or extending shift working (nine), or using certain equipment more intensively (15). In addition, 51 per cent did not expect any particular effects; 17 would recruit new workers, 14 would call for overtime, and 14 would occasionally take on interim workers (a survey in 1969 had given 4 and 6 per cent respectively for the last two measures, and 12 per cent for those intending to recruit). Of the managers questioned, 73 per cent were of the opinion that shorter hours would provide jobs only if there were a proportionate reduction in wages (31.1. per cent) or a partial one (42.2. per cent). Finally, when asked about how large a reduction in weekly hours would have to be in order to oblige them to take on more workers, 38.1 per cent replied that two to four hours would be needed, 29.9 per cent said more than four hours and 24.2. per cent said one to two hours.

A survey carried out in the same year in the metal trades in the Federal Republic of Germany also deserves to be quoted, even though it envisages shorter working time without maintenance of earnings, because it demonstrates that policies will change according to the time perspective, even within the same undertaking.[61] The replies reveal that a reduction of two hours a week would be made up for to the extent of 60 per cent by further rationalisation measures, and 14 per cent by overtime in the production sector; in the administration sector the corresponding percentages were 78 and 7. In the short term, the percentage of undertakings expecting to take on more workers or eliminate redundancies was 46 in the production sector and 33 in the administration sector; in the medium term these percentages rose to 48 and 35 respectively. Almost none of the small undertakings mentioned the possibility of taking on additional workers. The proportion of undertakings expecting to have recourse to overtime was much smaller in the medium term than in the short. Finally, with regard to effects on production (in the production sector only) 9 per cent of the undertakings questioned expected a fall in the short term and 13 per cent in the medium term. These low percentages may be compared with a remark made by the Director of the Institute for Employment and Occupational Research of the Federal Labour Office, who said that even in a period of full employment production had never fallen solely because there had been a reduction in working time.[62]

Another survey, carried out by the engineers' and executives' union of the French Democratic Labour Confederation (CFDT), obtained estimates from 578 executives belonging to about 350 undertakings on the probable effects of a reduction in weekly hours from 40 to 35 (less than 12.5 per cent) on the number of employees under their responsibility. Of these executives, 71 per cent expected some increase in the number of workers, differing according to categories: 10.8 per cent for those on shift work, 8.7 per cent for office employees, 8 per cent for workers not on shift work, 8 per cent for secretarial staff, 7 per cent for foremen, 9.5 per cent for technicians, 7.2 per cent for middle-level executives and 7.4 per cent for high-level executives. The survey revealed that 39.4 per cent of executives worked more than 45 hours a week and 16.7 per cent more than 50 hours. Most of them hoped that a reduction in working time would be achieved by reducing the number of working days per year.[63]

In Denmark a survey made within different government departments with a view to ascertaining the extent to which limitation of overtime might be translated into new permanent jobs revealed that in all cases additional costs would have to be assumed. One of the reasons given was that overtime is distributed unequally in the course of the year.[64]

The record

Surveys of intentions reveal possible developments which it is useful to know about for purposes of forecasting, but it is important to be able to supplement them by information about what undertakings actually do. Examples of reductions in working time negotiated at the level of the undertaking or of the industry seem to be becoming more numerous, and case studies now exist for a number of countries.[65] The studies reviewed in this section relate mainly to France. They therefore represent only a small fraction of the available material. However, they furnish striking examples of the wide gap between the supposed "rationality" of economic agents and their actual behaviour, the logic of which largely escapes our understanding.

A first series of French studies[66] revealed the particular psychological importance attached to the figure of 40 hours. Despite being unsuitable to certain aspects of the operation of undertakings, "make-work" expedients were sometimes found to bring lower work schedules up to 40 hours a week. However, according to these studies, if the existing standard of 40 hours were to be lowered there would not necessarily be a rise in the number of employees in the circumstances then prevailing. Organisations based exclusively on daytime working seemed to make up for shorter weekly hours by increased productivity, though it did not appear to be possible to identify this clearly. Those working shifts showed a non-proportional rise in the number of employees, to the extent that during the early stages the additional shift absorbed workers who were already employed, but not on shift work.

These studies also show that there is no obvious link between shorter working time and other major factors traditionally mentioned in this connection (productivity, absenteeism, investment policy, etc.), at least as far as it is possible to judge from subsequent analyses of examples of reductions in working time. In general, among both workers' and employers' organisations, there is a great deal of uncertainty about the whole complex of problems relating to reductions of working time, and in negotiations between them the outcome is determined less by an informed choice between clearly defined positions than in terms of defence of general principles and acquired rights. The studies also show that personnel questions are often regarded by management "as a kind of pollution that prevents them from 'getting on with their real job', and even chiefs of personnel themselves often seem to consider that these questions do not merit serious research".[67]

The need to situate these problems in a wide context is emphasised in another study, published in the Federal Republic of Germany.[68] Its author recommends that reduction of working time should not be studied in a static situation, but in relation to the changing nature of the undertaking itself, the policies it follows concerning rationalisation and innovation and the resulting changes that occur in its internal organisation. It would be possible to compensate for cost increases by various measures such as intensified utilisation of the factors of production, substitution of factors, modification of equipment, intermediate products and final products, and managerial changes. Some of the undertakings might thus overcome the financial problems arising from reduced working time. The bottlenecks that occur are not due to the reduction itself but to the difficulties that arise in moving from one arrangement of working time to another. To judge from the results of this research, lack of information on both the employers' and the workers' sides is an obstacle that has to be surmounted in order to have a reasonable chance of overcoming these difficulties.

Another French study analyses the situation resulting from 241 agreements or unilateral decisions to reduce working time, most of which came into effect in 1978 or 1979.[69] It shows that many reductions in weekly hours took place as a form of adjustment to changes in market conditions. The average of the reductions considered, with or without maintenance of previous earnings, brought average weekly hours down from 42 to 40.6. Reductions to below 40 hours concerned shiftworkers almost exclusively: in these cases, previous working hours were already 40 or less, and were reduced to an average of 37.7. Agreements and decisions concerning workers not on shift work brought the largest reductions. Only about 50 undertakings provided any information about the effects of the reductions on recruitment. With regard to all the reductions made, with or without maintenance of previous earnings, there was recruitment of more workers in 50 per cent of cases and stoppage of dismissals in 10 per cent. In undertakings which recruited workers, the number recruited amounted to 7 per cent of the number affected by the reduction, or 4 to 5 per cent of the total staff. In undertakings making large-scale reductions in working hours, the average amount of "work-sharing" resulting from them was in the neighbourhood of 60 per cent. When recruitment was on a large scale, previous earnings were not fully maintained.

If we take into account only the subject of the present study, namely shorter working time with maintenance of previous earnings, we can come to the following conclusions, on the basis of a summary analysis given in a table annexed to the above-mentioned study. Out of 247 cases of undertakings surveyed, about 140 maintained previous earnings in full.[70] Only 33 of these provided information about the effects on employment. From this it appears that there was some recruitment of workers in 16 cases and none in 17; among the latter, dismissals linked with automation were avoided in one case, whereas in another, mechanisation resulted in a significant reduction of the workforce. In eight cases where recruitment occurred, working hours were reduced to under 40, in most cases to 38 (or close to 38) and in one case to 35; these reductions related to shift work. The same concentration around 38 hours and the same predominance of shift work are to be found in cases in which no recruitment occurred but working hours were reduced to below 40; there was one reduction to 35 hours (with improvement in work organisation), and another to $35^1/_2$ (with new investments). Whether new workers are taken on or not, the situation varies considerably from one undertaking to another as regards the adoption of measures in such fields as work organisation, the installation of new equipment, and investment specifically intended to improve productivity. Such investment does not preclude recruitment. It is hard to draw general conclusions on all these points.

Work organisation

A great deal of discussion is going on about the possibility of combining reductions in working time with different forms of work organisation, so as to reduce costs to a minimum while achieving optimum effects on employment and the workers' quality of life. This discussion has been very far-ranging in theory, but up to now has concentrated most attention on shift work.

Many writers — both theoreticians and practitioners — stress the need for an intense effort of imagination, innovation and organisation to put reduction of working time into practice in the best conditions. Some personnel management experts regard the constraints created by trade union pressure, the need to avoid disturbances at work, and cost requirements as challenges to stimulate creativity in work organisation. In the United Kingdom one writer[71] believes that, if it is combined with greater flexibility in work schedules, a reduction in working time can provide opportunities for improving productivity and services without necessarily becoming a source of increased labour costs that have to be conceded to employees after a fight. Calculation of working time on a yearly basis may reduce the costs for the employer and give workers longer periods of free time. Emphasis is placed on the wide range of possible methods. For example a reduction of the working week to 35 hours may be carried out with an intermediate stage of $37^1/_2$ hours, although in cases in which large numbers of workers are on shift work and changes in work schedules raise very complex problems a direct move to 35 hours may be preferable. The writer also considers the advantages of combining the 35-hour week with an extension of part-time working or job-sharing. Part-time work, for example, may help to fill in reduced schedules and perhaps lengthen the periods during which services are provided (as in the retail trades) or the duration of utilisation of machinery. Among the other advantages it offers are: it makes it possible to meet demand at peak periods and to replace workers who are ill or on holiday; it facilitates recruitment, since many women are looking for part-time work; it widens the basis of selection and promotion of personnel, since the number of workers is larger; it widens the range of skills and experience available and allows undertakings to benefit from the higher morale and higher productivity of part-time employees. Job-sharing raises special problems relating to social charges, but they do not always work to the disadvantage of this method.

Much has already been written on shift work and its possible combination with reduction in working time.[72] Where it cannot be eliminated altogether, many trade unions call for systems of 6 × 6 and 4 × 9 hours, implying a normal working week of 36 hours, or, with continuous working, for a fifth shift, implying a working week of a little more than 33 hours. The unions claim that these systems would have a favourable effect on employment. Introduction of a fifth shift would oblige employers to take on more workers in continuous working. Employment might also be promoted by introducing shift work or increasing the number of shifts in cases where the degree of utilisation of equipment is in direct proportion to the number of shifts multiplied by a reduced standard weekly working time. The system of two day-shifts seems to reduce the disadvantages of shift work for workers to a minimum. In fact, however, it is hard for unions to define the extent to which one shift work pattern may be considered more acceptable than another.[73]

In Sweden some reservations have been expressed about certain experiments with a fifth shift, and even with a sixth shift: they did not result in shorter daily hours but only in more free time, and their effects on employment are uncertain.[74] In the timber and paper industries, where the normal working week is 36 hours (1,654 hours per year), the introduction of a fifth shift has not necessarily resulted in more employment because many factories had surplus manpower. The employers' representatives for the timber industry consider that the introduction of a sixth shift in a minority of factories was mistaken in current economic conditions, because timber is scarce.

In the Netherlands a collective agreement, the first of its kind, was recently concluded in the European Container Terminus in Rotterdam. This provided for both a shorter working week for 800 shiftworkers and the creation of 200 new jobs in the change from a four-shift to a five-shift system. After a transitional period the employees concerned will work 21 shifts in each five-week period, with an average of $32^1/_2$ hours per week. The workers have abandoned their claim for wage increases and holiday bonuses, and if that is not enough to compensate for additional costs, shift work bonuses may be reduced. The effects on costs have still to be determined.[75]

A French study[76] emphasises that in most cases there is a complementary relationship between workforce and equipment; it warns against taking the purely arithmetical view, which is to assume there is a given volume of production and a given hourly productivity and to go on to deduce a total number of hours worked, which is then divided in terms of working time and the number of employees. It is often necessary to extend the period of utilisation of equipment. Leaving aside cases where capacity is underemployed, it is likely that in the event of a reduction in working time most undertakings will have to look for other solutions. Against an uncertain economic background, the development of shift work (particularly on the most productive machinery) is perhaps the most suitable method. Nevertheless, management seems to be still in favour of investing in more productive equipment. The proportion of workers on successive shifts is said to have fallen between 1974 and 1977, the system of two alternating shifts apparently gaining ground among the various shift work systems in use.[77]

Two solutions are put forward to avoid a reduction in the period of utilisation of equipment: to reinforce the shifts, which would mean taking on new workers and higher costs (but it is the only solution possible with continuous working), or to introduce another system of shift work, on condition that there are markets for the products or that capital intensiveness in the production process is high enough to absorb the increased wage costs per unit produced. If this is not the case and it is desired to shorten working hours as well as to prolong the period of utilisation of equipment, the two solutions must be combined. These various possibilities have been practised or envisaged in 11 cases analysed in the study just mentioned.[78] The reductions in working time were sometimes large, and favourable results were obtained or were expected with respect to recruitment and cost in many cases. Almost all these examples related to reductions in working time with maintenance of earnings (except in three cases where part-time work was introduced). On the basis of these actual cases, the author of the study prepared theoretical models designed to keep costs down and reduce disturbances to a minimum. The result is that in the event of a large increase in the duration of utilisation of equipment (50 per cent or more), the fall in production costs may reach between 10 and 15 per cent in a plant with heavy capital investment and a high amortisation rate; it would thus be possible to offer employees benefits that are even more "motivating" than those envisaged (36 or 33.6 hours per week with maintenance of earnings). In several cases decreases in costs can be achieved with systems of work organisation that are closer to the workers' interests, as in all cases where there is a change-over from single-shift working to an alternating two-shift system. Other methods may be combined with a reduction in working time,[79] but they require management to think in terms of a three-month or yearly average, and not week by week.

Another study[80] shows how important it is not to limit analysis of employment effects to those parts of an undertaking on continuous working. In the case considered weekly working hours were reduced from 40 to 38 and there was no increase in the number of employees although there was continuous working; this is contrary to the conclusions arrived at on the basis of theoretical reasoning. There was a need for extra workers for continuous shift work, but these were found by reducing the number of hours spent on supporting activities such as examining rejects to see whether they should be scrapped or reworked. Moreover, a situation in which there is at first no recruitment of workers for shift work may give way in the long run to one in which there is a shortage of daytime employees. The study also shows how necessary it is to examine each case on its merits, not only from the technical and economic points of view but also from the human angle, taking into account such factors as the interests represented by employers' and workers' organisations and their general objectives, the different ways in which difficulties and disturbances affect them, cultural background and, in particular, the attraction exercised by simple, striking figures such as 40 and 35 hours, and readily quantifiable variations. Neglect of such factors may lead people to reject changes that would have been both economically and socially progressive.

Influence of methods by which working time is reduced

In the examples considered so far, attention has been focused chiefly on shortening hours worked per week. We shall deal below at greater length with other methods of reducing working time.

On the basis of theory and deductive reasoning, the expected results of reducing working time in the form of productivity increases can be transposed into the field of employment. We may recall here the general observation that the higher the expected increases in productivity, the less will be the positive effects on employment, and vice versa. To be sure, experience shows that reality is much more complicated but, if we bear this general observation in mind, we can assume that a reduction in working time calculated on a yearly basis will not create many jobs, since expected productivity gains are high in this case. Can we expect this method to be widely followed? It raises organisational problems and account must be taken of acquired rights.[81] It may also be difficult to administer, because it is complicated. Thus, a firm reply to the question would be premature. Another observation that has been made is that calculation of reductions in working time on a yearly basis would make it possible to eliminate periods of inactivity which would otherwise have been classified as short-time working (partial unemployment) or seasonal work.

In addition to possible effects on employment that may be deduced from expected effect on productivity, we should perhaps also see whether a prolongation of paid annual leave would not lead to the development of certain kinds of employment that enable undertakings to meet temporary production needs. With regard to the chances of increasing employment by this means, a study carried out in Ireland shows that the risks of disturbing production are greater if annual holidays are lengthened, which normally results in closing the undertaking, than if the working week is shortened. In addition, undertakings can try to adjust to longer annual holidays by having more overtime worked before the holiday season, as usually happens before the Christmas break. Thus, the expected fall in the annual total of working hours would not materialise. Unfavourable effects would also be likely in the field of costs and as a result of difficulty in finding workers to make up lost working time, as in the case of reductions in weekly hours; but, in addition, there would be a greater risk that workers with much longer holidays would seek temporary jobs during their absence.[82]

The possibility of expanding employment by limiting overtime would vary, depending on whether overtime is compensated by time off or not; if so, the effects on employment ought in principle to be more favourable. National characteristics and the peculiarities of each occupation are also significant. Thus, if it is hoped to create new job opportunities by restricting overtime, the scope for manoeuvre will differ from one country to another. Recourse to overtime is relatively frequent in Australia, Ireland and the United Kingdom, for example, while it is relatively rare in the Netherlands and Switzerland. It also varies from one occupation to another. It concerns manual workers in particular, and on the whole affects women much less than men. It has been estimated in Ireland that if the maximum weekly hours were fixed at 44, the percentage of employees affected would be, for men, 5.6 in retail trade and 5.9 in wholesale; almost no women would be affected. Generally speaking, overtime is more prevalent in industry. For some industries there are peak periods of seasonal demand and these industries are the most affected.[82] In the United Kingdom the Trade Union Research Unit in its arguments with the Department of Employment relied on differences in working hours and overtime between one sector and another to support its case in favour of reducing the standard working week to 35 hours; this measure would have more direct effect on the working population as a whole.

The effect on employment of restrictions on overtime would depend on the kind of restrictions applied and, in particular, on the extent to which it would be possible to reduce the attraction of overtime for management and labour, without compromising the flexibility of production. According to a study by the

European Trade Union Institute, simultaneous measures with regard to the standard working week and overtime would have a better chance of producing positive results. However it would be difficult, if not impossible, to evaluate the effects of shorter working hours on employment, particularly because of the differences in the levels of working hours laid down in collective agreements, differences between economic sectors, the variety of systems of work organisation, and the inclusion of short-time working and part-time work in employment statistics. One vital condition for obtaining the desired favourable effects on employment would be to make it compulsory for overtime to be compensated by time off in the form of complete days, to be taken within prescribed periods of one or two months after the overtime is worked. The principle of computing overtime on an annual basis should be rejected, because of the risk of "annualising" the volume of work; for the purpose of compensation, totals should in any event be worked out only for short periods such as a week or a month. It would be more simple and effective to fix a single level above which compensation in the form of time off would become compulsory.[83]

With regard to the possible consequences on employment of lowering the retirement age, the main problem is to know whether the undertaking will replace workers who retire. A number of considerations will affect that decision. Replacing retiring workers by new recruits involves various costs: recruitment, initiation, training among others. But young recruits may cost less because they are less well paid than were the retirees. Younger workers are normally better educated and more adaptable when faced with new technologies; recruitment of such workers may make it easier to carry out necessary economic reorganisation. Moreover, the departure of older workers may unblock career opportunities, help to keep better workers and make it possible to overcome certain problems connected with ageing. On the other hand, the loss of experienced workers who are hard to replace may also endanger the survival of small undertakings. In addition, some time is required before new recruits become accustomed to the requirements of their jobs. Progressive retirement raises specific problems: calculation of what previous "full time" meant in the case of some occupations; complexity of calculation of work schedules; holidays; the difficulty of creating enough part-time jobs. Yet it enables undertakings to benefit longer from the experience of older workers. If it is properly co-ordinated with the progressive entry of young people into employment, it may help to improve their training by integrating them better into the day-to-day reality of working life.[84]

There is a mass of statistics about how many workers retire, but very little information about management's attitude concerning their replacement. In the Federal Republic of Germany the survey of intentions already mentioned above showed that, in the event of a lower retirement age, management was more likely to recruit new workers than to adopt rationalisation measures, and that it would move faster to fill vacated jobs; one reason given for this is that, more often than not, the replacements are already employed in the undertaking. But we cannot be sure whether, at the bottom end of the series of internal promotions, a new worker would be recruited from outside.[85] In France the effects of the flexible retirement system over a certain period were studied by analysing the complex pattern within undertakings formed by direct recruitment and internal mobility followed by recruitment. Where the initial aim of the system had been to reduce the workforce, the achievement of that aim was followed after a time by a stage at which normal replacements occurred; if the aim had been to have a younger workforce or to respond to trade union pressure, full replacement of all workers was often carried out rapidly.[86]

In Sweden, out of 28 undertakings questioned in a survey, half had not taken on new employees to work the hours lost as a result of the introduction of part-time working combined with progressive retirement. The reasons given were: rationalisation measures, shutting down production units, and improved efficiency due to part-time working.[87] It is worth recalling that the difficulties involved in creating a sufficient number of part-time jobs is one of the most frequently mentioned obstacles to the implementation of progressive retirement schemes.

Notes

[1] For references, see in particular sources from employers' circles quoted above, and also "Le plan économique et social du gouvernement: une mauvaise thérapie", Speech by Mr. Raymond Pulinckx on Radio-Télévision flamande (BRT), 25 April 1979, in *Bulletin de la Fédération des entreprises de Belgique* (Brussels), 1 May 1979, pp. 1695-1699; for the attitude of the Engineering Employers' Federation in the United Kingdom, see "Shorter working hours", in *British Journal of Industrial Relations* (London), Mar. 1979, p. 113; Oliver Drague: *Vers une autre durée du travail* (Paris, Chotard et Associés, 1979). See also references from trade union organisations quoted above, and L. Hujoel: "La réduction de la durée du travail", in *Socialisme* (Brussels), Feb. 1979, pp. 5-18, and Raphael Nedzynski, in *Free Labour World* (Brussels, International Confederation of Trade Unions), Jan.-Feb. 1980. Use has also been made of studies by specialists and official publications which have been cited already or will be cited subsequently.

[2] See on this particular point *Absentéisme*, report of an international symposium organised by the Union des industries métallurgiques et minières, Paris, 29-30 April 1980.

[3] See on this subject the classic analysis by François Eymard-Duvernay: "Les 40 heures: 1936 ou ... 1980?", in *Economie et statistique* (Paris, Institut National de la Statistique et des Etudes Economiques), June 1977, pp. 3-23.

[4] See in particular on this subject Robert Clark; *Adjusting hours to increase jobs: An analysis of the options*, Special report of the National Commission for Manpower Policy (Washington, DC, Special Report No. 15, Sep. 1977).

[5] Dieter Mertens: "L'aménagement du temps de travail", in *Emploi et nouveaux modes de vie*, International conference, 29-30 November, The Hague (Paris, Institut d'éducation, Fondation européenne de la culture), p. 12.

[6] See Gabriel Ducray: "Vocational training today: The changing relationship between training and employment", in *International Labour Review* (Geneva, ILO), May-June 1979, pp. 265-281. On the importance of manpower planning in the undertaking and its internal adjustment machinery, see John Fyfe: "A future for company manpower planning", in *Department of Employment Gazette* (London), Mar. 1978, pp. 286-288.

[7] "Skill shortages in British industry", ibid., May 1979, pp. 433-436.

[8] Eymard-Duvernay, op. cit. in note 3.

[9] Rolf Kasiske and Fred Manske: "Labour, technology and company size as factors influencing the effects on employment of reductions in working time", in *Mitteilungen aus der Arbeitsmarkt- und Berufsforschung* (Stuttgart, Berlin, Cologne, Mainz), 1979, No. 3, pp. 340-348 (in German with summary in English on p. 456).

[10] Mertens, op. cit. in note 5, pp. 12-13.

[11] See, for example, Alain Cotta: "Quelques interrogations sur le concept de travail, d'emploi et de chômage", in *Travail et emploi* (Paris, Ministère du Travail et de la Participation), Sep. 1979, p. 715.

[12] In addition to the references already given, see Jacques H. Drèze: *Salaires, emploi et durée du travail*, conférence pour le Colloque "Inflation, emploi et change" marquant le cinquantième anniversaire de l'Institut de recherches économiques et sociales de l'Université catholique de Louvain, sur la base d'une étude de l'auteur et de Franco Modigliani (1979, mimeographed). See also Michel Praderie and Daniel Baroin: "L'entreprise et la durée du travail: un enjeu social", in *Droit social* (Paris), Jan. 1980 (II), issue dealing with work sharing, pp. 75-80.

[13] Edward F. Denison: *Why growth rates differ: Postwar experience in nine Western countries* (Washington, DC, Brookings Institution, 1967), Ch. 6, pp. 54-69. See also Irving F. Leveson: "Reductions in hours of work as a source of productivity growth", in *Journal of Political Economy* (Chicago), Apr. 1967, pp. 199-204, and references there.

[14] Studies made by research institutes at the request of the Government; the results are quoted in Denison, op. cit., p. 61. The size of the reductions is not indicated.

[15] Estimates made for the Fifth Plan, quoted in Denison, op. cit., pp. 60-61.

[16] Archibald A. Evans: *Hours of work in industrialised countries* (Geneva, ILO, 1975), Ch. II, section entitled "Hours of work, productivity and economic growth", pp. 67-80.

[17] For example the study by the Norwegian productivity institute quoted in *Intersocial* (Paris), No. 48, Apr. 1979, p. 2; W. Friedrich et al.: "On the employment expectations, available job reserves and the potential of additional part-time jobs in the manufacturing and in the construction industry: Results of a sample survey", in *Mitteilungen aus der Arbeitsmarkt- und Berufsforschung*, 1978, No. 2, p. 235 (in German with summary in English on p. 259).

[18] *The campaign for economic and social advance*, European Trade Union Confederation campaign for reduced working time, TUC Progress Report No. 2, Dec. 1979.

[19] Trade Union Research Unit: *"Efficiency bargaining" over shorter hours: A preliminary analysis*, Technical note No. 47 (Oxford, Ruskin College, Oct. 1979).

[20] "Working hours cut could boost productivity", in *Industrial Relations — Europe*, July 1979, p. 6. The Committee is mentioned under the initials DELFA.

[21] "Measures to alleviate unemployment in the medium term: Work-sharing", in *Department of Employment Gazette*, Apr. 1978, pp. 400-402.

[22] Centraal Plan Bureau: *Centraal Economisch Plan, 1979* (The Hague, Mar. 1979), p. 114.

[23] Estimates by the Istituto di Studi nelle Relazioni Industriali e di Lavoro (ISRIL) quoted in Evans, op. cit., p. 72.

[24] Gilles Oudiz, Emmanuel Raoul and Henri Sterdyniak: "Réduire la durée du travail, quelles conséquences?", in *Economie et statistique*, May 1979, pp. 3-16.

[25] Wolfgang Bartel: "The costs involved in extending holidays in the metal industry", in *Mitteilungen aus der Arbeitsmarkt- und Berufsforschung*, 1979, No. 3, p. 355 (in German with summary in English on p. 457).

[26] European Trade Union Institute: *La réduction du temps de travail en Europe*, Partie II. *Analyse des conséquences économiques et sociales* (Brussels, Euro-Inst., May 1980), pp. 39-40.

[27] United States Department of Labor, Bureau of Labor Statistics: *The revised workweek: Results of a pilot study of 16 firms*, Bulletin 1846 (Washington, DC, 1975). The survey covered five manufacturing firms, three banks, two insurance companies, two automobile dealers and one wholesale trade firm, one hospital, and two government agencies.

[28] Statement by a property development group. "Travailler moins pour travailler tous et vivre mieux: un leurre ou une possibilité?", in *Radio TV — Je vois tout* (Lausanne), Broadcast by the Télévision Suisse Romande, 25 October 1979.

[29] Paulette Bourgeois: "Vers une réduction de la semaine de travail", in *Gazette du travail* (Ottawa), Nov.-Dec. 1979, pp. 498-499.

[30] Results of a study by Richard Hartmann and Mark Weaver: "Four factors influencing conversion to a four-day work week", in *Human Resource Management* (Ann Arbor, Michigan), Spring 1977, pp. 24-27. The study related to 400 of the 700 United States companies which had adopted a compressed working week with longer daily working hours.

[31] M. Pépin et D. Tonneau: "Le comportement des entreprises face la réduction des horaires de travail: le cas d'un groupe automobile (IIᵉ partie)", in *Travail et emploi*, Sep. 1979, p. 53. This was a working party comprising representatives of various services (finance, research, personnel) and production units, and of the Centre de gestion scientifique of the Ecole des mines de Paris.

[32] *Was tun?*, pamphlet by the General Economic Institute for employees, quoted in *UIMM — Documentation étrangère* (Paris, Union des industries métallurgiques et minières), Jan. 1979, p. 3; and "La réduction de la durée de travail en Europe", in *Intersocial*, p. 13.

[33] *Bulletin de la Fédération des entreprises de Belgique*, 1 May 1979, op. cit. in note 1.

[34] Confederation of Australian Industry, National Employers' Industrial Council: *Will a reduction in hours of work bring back full employment? We say No!* (information leaflet).

[35] *Social and Labour Bulletin* (Geneva, ILO), 1/79, pp. 33-34.

[36] In Belgium undertakings creating additional jobs after a reduction in working hours receive payments from the State for five years. It is hoped to create 100,000 jobs by this means. *Bulletin de la Fédération des entreprises de Belgique*, loc. cit. in note 1.

[37] Nedzynski, op. cit., and Hujoel, op. cit., both in note 1.

[38] "Les 36 heures: imposer un contrôle du temps de travail dans l'entreprise pour répartir l'emploi", in *Syndicaliste* (Brussels, CSC), 25 June 1978, pp. 10-13.

[39] International Metalworkers' Federation: *Action programme of IMF and its affiliates for shorter work time*, Document No. 2, World conference for the reduction of working time.

[40] Giuseppe Bianchi and Domenico Laise: "Proposta ISRIL relativa al problema della riduzione degli orari di lavoro", in *Contrattazione* (Rome, CISL), July-Oct. 1978 (*Riduzione dell'orario di lavoro e occupazione, prima parte: studi e proporte*), pp. 106-111.

[41] Simplified summary of complex studies in *Technical Notes*, Nos. 43, 46 and 47 of the Trade Union Research Unit, and "Measures to alleviate unemployment in the medium term: Work-sharing", loc. cit. in note 21. See also John Hughes: "Shiftwork and the shorter working week: Two ways to make jobs", in *Personnel Management* (London), May 1977, pp. 18-20; idem: "A shorter working week: The CBI shows its true colours (and its intellectual bankruptcy)", and "A shorter working week: How the Department of Employment got it wrong", in *Workers' Control Bulletin* (Nottingham, Institute for Workers' Control), 1978, No. 6, pp. 10-18.

[42] Hughes: "A shorter working week", op. cit., p. 12.

[43] Bartel, op. cit. in note 25, pp. 355-361.

[44] Karl H. Pitz: "The costs of shortening working hours (with reference to holidays)", in *Mitteilungen aus der Arbeitsmarkt- und Berufsforschung*, 1979, No. 3, pp. 349-354 (in German with summary in English on p. 456).

[45] Incomes Data Series: IDS Study 206 — Holidays 1979, summarised by Patricia Tisdall: "Doing a deal on longer holidays", in *The Times* (London), 16 Apr. 1980, p. 19.

[46] Myron L. Joseph: "Hours of work issues", Annex to *The employment impact of technological change*, Studies prepared for the National Commission on Technology, Automation and Economic Progress (Washington, DC), Feb. 1966, pp. II/336-343.

[47] Joyce M. Nussbaum and Donald E. Wise: "The overtime pay premium and employment", in *Work time and employment*, Special report of the National Commission for Manpower Policy (Washington, DC, Special Report No. 28, Oct. 1978), pp. 317-337. The fringe benefits include employers' contributions, pensions and insurance paid by the employer, annual leave and paid holidays.

[48] Clark, op. cit. in note 4, pp. 26-28 and 54-65.

[49] "White paper on the 1980 spring struggle", in *Sohyo News* (Tokyo), 15 Mar. 1980, pp. 40-42.

[50] Even today, "many undertakings do not calculate what their production costs are, or get them wrong". Jean Fourastié: *La productivité* (Paris, Presses Universitaires de France, collection "Que sais-je?", 1980), p. 88.

[51] Observation made in France by the Agence pour l'amélioration des conditions de travail about the hidden costs of poor working conditions. See for example: "L'évaluation économique des coûts des conditions de travail", in *Lettre d'information* (ANACT), No. 22, Sep. 1978. For a practical example, see Gordon Robertson: "Absenteeism and labour turnover in selected Ontario industries", in *Relations industrielles* (Quebec, Laval University), No. 1, 1979, pp. 86-107). The sample comprised 1,600 establishments, or 24 per cent of the undertakings in nine industry groups in Ontario, selected from all sectors of the economy. The author of this study, which was carried out under the auspices of the Ontario Department of Labour, notes, for example, that of the undertakings having problems in this field very few have done anything to try to solve them or to attempt to calculate costs; it is said that it is not uncommon for companies to overstaff by as much as 10 per cent, particularly in production areas, in order to avoid the disruptive effects of absenteeism.

[52] Pépin and Tonneau, op. cit. in note 31.

[53] National Board for Prices and Incomes: *Hours of work, overtime and shift-working*, Report No. 161, Cmnd. 4554 (London, HMSO, Dec. 1970), Appendix F, pp. 126-133.

[54] Joseph, op. cit. in note 46, p. II-355.

[55] A. Doyelle: "Réduction du temps de travail et durée d'utilisation des équipements", in *Travail et emploi* (Paris), Jan. 1980, p. 75.

[56] The German Economic Institute, a body controlled by the employers in the Federal Republic of Germany, stated in 1979 that the comparison of hourly wage costs in the manufacturing industries in that country with those in other countries was unfavourable, but that wage costs were only one factor in production and competition; if other factors were taken into account (productivity, imported raw materials, social benefits), the country was in a better competitive

position than appeared when only wage costs were compared. *UIMM — Documentation étrangère*, No. 364, June 1979, p. 9 (including references in German). See E. A. Doggett and J. C. Cresswell: "Aspects of United Kingdom trade competitiveness", in *Economic Trends* (London, Government Statistical Service, Central Statistical Office), No. 304, Feb. 1979, p. 79.

[57] In the United States, for example, while falls in productivity were still recorded in certain sectors in the third quarter of 1979, there was an increase of 3.3 per cent in manufacturing industries, with 8.7 per cent for non-durable goods alone. Lawrence J. Fulco: "Productivity declines continue into third quarter 1979", in *Monthly Labor Review* (Washington, DC), Feb. 1980, pp. 46-48.

[58] Joseph, op. cit. in note 46, pp. II-335-343.

[59] Wassily Leontief: "Observations on some of the worldwide economic issues of the coming years', in *Strategy for the 'eighties*, Discussion Paper No. 2 for the 24th World Congress of the International Metalworkers' Federation, Munich, 24-28 October 1977, pp. 53-61. The writer asks: "By how much would the wages of long-distance telephone operators have to be cut in order to prevent the installation of modern, automatic switching equipment?" In his view, even if the wage rate fell by 10 per cent and total employment increased as a result of this by 5 per cent, there would still be a net 5 per cent loss in total labour income (p. 60). Thus, if wages were cut, it would have to be a very considerable cut to make the same savings as would result from mechanisation. See also "Leontief sull'orario", in *Economia* (Confederazione Italiana Sindacati Lavoratori), 14 May 1979, pp. 4-5. Also Gus Edgren: "Employment adjustment to trade under conditions of stagnating growth", in *International Labour Review*, May-June 1978, pp. 289-303.

[60] Inquiry by correspondence at the end of 1978, to which 526 replies were received. The inquiry covered production workers in establishments of which 87 per cent were industrial; of these, 45 per cent were metalworking undertakings. "Les industriels: Oui, mais ... la réduction du temps de travail", in *L'usine nouvelle* (Paris), 22 Feb. 1979, pp. 102-108.

[61] Study by the IFO Institute of Munich covering 2,000 metallurgical undertakings, at the request of the employers' confederation of the Federal Republic of Germany. "La réduction de la durée du travail en Europe", in *Intersocial*, Apr. 1979, pp. 12-13.

[62] Mertens, op. cit., p. 10.

[63] Yves Lasfargue: "Réduction du temps de travail des cadres et créations d'emplois", in *Cadres CFDT* (Paris), Nov.-Dec. 1979, pp. 46-56.

[64] *Intersocial*, Apr. 1979, pp. 15-17.

[65] For France see in particular the study (already quoted in part) of the Centre de gestion scientifique of the Ecole nationale supérieure des mines de Paris carried out by M. Pépin and D. Tonneau: "Etude des conséquences des mesures de la réduction de la durée du travail (I)", in *Travail et emploi*, No. 1, June 1979, pp. 7-22; "Le comportement des entreprises face la réduction des horaires de travail (IIe partie)", ibid., No. 2, Sep. 1979, pp. 53-74; and "La réduction des horaires dans le travail continu (IIIe partie)", ibid., No. 4, Apr. 1980, pp. 41-68. See also Doyelle, op. cit. in note 55, pp. 65-84; and J.C. Gergoat: "La réduction de la durée hebdomadaire du travail dans l'entreprise. Etude de 241 accords ou décisions unilatérales récents", ibid., No. 3, Jan. 1980, pp. 31-64. Studies of work-sharing in France, the Federal Republic of Germany, Italy and the United Kingdom have also been carried out under the research programme on labour market trends by the Commission of the European Communities.

[66] Pépin and Tonneau: "Etude des conséquences des mesures de réduction de la durée du travail", op. cit. in note 65. The sectors studied were chemicals, printing, construction and furniture. The study was made in 1977 and covered small and medium-sized undertakings as well as some large industrial groups.

[67] ibid., pp. 15-16.

[68] Erich Staudt: "The significance of micro-economic analysis in assessing and implementing new ways of structuring working time", in *Mitteilungen aus der Arbeitsmarkt- und Berufsforschung*, 1979, No. 3, pp. 328-339 (in German with summary in English on p. 455).

[69] Gergoat, op. cit. in note 65. The undertakings belonged to the following sectors: energy (1), industry, excluding food processing, construction and public works (164), food processing (24), construction and public works (7), transport (8), commerce (25), services (10) and others (2). The reductions in working time currently being made are mostly adjustments of the undertaking's productive capacity to its market share; this kind of reduction is very rarely accompanied by wage compensation and is not usually covered by collective agreements or formal decisions; they are therefore omitted from the sample covered.

[70] The fact that this figure is only approximate is due to the lack of sufficiently precise information to enable us to determine whether there is full compensation, or whether the latter relates only to some reductions in working time in the undertaking and not to others.

[71] David Wainwright: "Shrinking the week and sharing the work: A practical response to the pressures of the times", in *Personnel Management* (London), Oct. 1979, pp. 48-52.

[72] See, among ILO publications, Marc Maurice: *Shift work* (Geneva, ILO, 1971); and J. Carpentier and P. Cazamian: *Night work: Its effects on the health and welfare of the worker* (Geneva, ILO, 1977). See also J. B. Sloane: "Economic aspects of shift and night work in industrialised market economies", in *International Labour Review*, Mar.-Apr. 1978, pp. 129-142.

[73] "A debate on shiftworking: GMW Research Department prepares contribution", in *General and Municipal Workers' Union Journal* (Esher, Surrey), Nov. 1979, pp. 10-11.

[74] "La création de la cinquième équipe se généralise en Suède", in *Intersocial*, Feb. 1979, pp. 31-32.

[75] "Netherlands experimenting with a 5-shift system", in *European Industrial Relations Review* (London), Mar. 1980, pp. 22-23.

[76] Doyelle: "Réduction du temps de travail et durée d'utilisation des équipements", op. cit. in note 55.

[77] This is confirmed by a number of other case studies, from which it appears that undertakings are not necessarily interested in extending shift work. It should also be noted that production technology is moving towards a breakage of the link between the worker and the machine. The end result ought to be that the machine would operate on its own for most of the time, while the majority of the tasks performed by human beings could be accomplished during the normal day shift. See Stefan Agurén and Jan Edgen: *New factories. Job design through factory planning in Sweden* (Stockholm, Swedish Employers' Confederation, 1980), p. 106.

[78] Doyelle: "Réduction du temps de travail et durée d'utilisation des équipements", op. cit., Annex III: "Etude de quelques cas concrets", pp. 80-83. These cases relate to: a photographic undertaking, a factory making vegetable sponges, a factory making bottles and other glass products, a tyre-manufacturing plant, two motor-car plants, one undertaking making jewellery and parts for household electric equipment and motor cars, an electrical construction plant, a plant making aluminium containers, a brick and tile works and a small furniture factory. The author explains in Annex II that manufacturing costs taken into account consist solely of those of a unit of output leaving the workshop — capital and labour costs, and nothing else. A margin has to be added, varying according to products, to bring the manufacturing cost up to the sales price. Capital intensiveness is regarded as average when capital cost represents 40 per cent of production cost and as high when it reaches 60 per cent.

[79] For example introduction of a system of unequal rotation between semi-continuous and continuous processes, with shifts of 9 hours in the morning (5 a.m. to 2 p.m.) and the afternoon (2 p.m. to 11 p.m.) and a night shift of 6 hours (11 p.m. to 5 a.m.); or in a continuous five-shift system, rotation of three shifts during the week on a semi-continuous basis with eight-hour shifts, and two weekend shifts of 12 hours each, which would completely liberate three weekends out of five.

[80] Pépin and Tonneau: "La réduction des horaires dans le travail continu (IIIe partie)", op. cit. in note 65 (transition to 38 hours in a glass factory).

[81] In France the Cour de Cassation (which is the highest court of appeal) has stated, with reference to annual working time, that it is lawful to calculate overtime on an annual basis, though previous decisions were to the contrary. However, an undertaking paying overtime on a weekly basis will find it difficult to change the practice, because of acquired rights (Pépin and Tonneau: "Etude des conséquences des mesures de réduction de la durée du travail", op. cit. in note 65, pp. 13-14).

[82] Brendan M. Walsh: *Worksharing and the unemployment problem in Ireland*, Report to the Federated Union of Employers (Dublin, Economic and Social Research Institute, Sep. 1979), pp. 16-17.

[83] European Trade Union Institute: *Overtime and the position of trade unions with regard to proposals for the restriction of overtime at European Community level* (Brussels, Euro-Inst., Aug. 1979).

[84] Franco Marziale: "Resolution of the Council of Europe on social security measures to be taken in favour of pensioners and persons remaining in activity after pensionable age", in *International Social Security Review* (Geneva, International Social Security Association), 1976, No. 3, pp. 319-320.

[85] Survey by the IFO Institute of Munich in 1977. See Mertens, op. cit. in note 5, p. 32, and *Intersocial*, Apr. 1979, p. 13.

[86] "Les conventions et les accords de préretraite", in *Revue française des affaires sociales* (Paris), Apr.-June 1979, pp. 151-162.

[87] Göran Crona: *Partial retirement in Sweden: Developments and experiences*, Document presented to the Ninth World Congress of Sociology, Upsala, Sweden, 14-19 August 1978.

POTENTIAL IMPLICATIONS FOR
THE COMMUNITY AS A WHOLE

7

Much wider issues come to the fore at the level of the community as a whole. Specific factors at this level throw new light on the problems involved in reducing working time. These factors include demographic trends, the situation in the labour market, national economic problems, the existence of fiscal or social transfers and the possibility of adopting policies and measures to mitigate the effects of a reduction. In the following sections, these various aspects will be dealt with under four headings: the potential redistribution of work, which is important because it enables an evaluation to be made of the effect of any reduction in working time on unemployment; the reactions of individual undertakings, which in combination have a general effect on the economy and on employment; the importance of increased leisure time, which is another, and neglected, aspect of any reduction in working time; and transfer payments, which play a major role in the cost-benefit analysis of any reductions in working time as it affects the community as a whole.

SCOPE FOR REDISTRIBUTION OF WORK

One factor covered in studies of the possible effects of reductions in working time has been the potential number of hours or days of employment that might be made available, at the national level, to provide jobs for those who are out of work and seeking employment. The theoretical potential amount is adjusted to take account of "slippages" which may in practice limit any possible positive effects of such reductions. Certain general trends in these ideas are set out below, followed by examples of retrospective analysis, and others concerning the present and the future.

General assumptions

The kind of approach examined here generally consists of calculating the number of jobs that may be created out of the time made available by reductions in working time, on the one hand, and of trying to determine the extent to which unemployment would be reduced as a result, on the other hand. With regard to the latter point, various assumptions are put forward concerning the manner in which these reductions may influence labour supply and demand. Assumptions concerning attitudinal changes affecting the demand for jobs are of special significance in this connection. In the following paragraphs certain deductions made in this study at an earlier stage are recalled, because they are not always identical with some of the assumptions about trends that are currently made. Assessments based on the calculation of theoretical "job equivalents", with suitable adjustments, result in various conclusions which take account of the demographic context and, in some cases, of foreseeable changes in the economically active population and in the labour market. This is important, because the effects of any reduction in working time on unemployment can be properly considered only in relation to what the level of unemployment would be if there were no redistribution of work.

From the point of view of the demand for jobs, the situation is one of rapid growth in the economically active population for a number of reasons, including the entry of young people into the labour market, an increased propensity on the part of married women to seek gainful employment, and a fall in the number of persons reaching retirement age. These trends are subject to variations from one country to another. The idea that a reduction in working time would increase the number of people looking for jobs does not appear to be based on any statistical evaluation. From our own research, it would seem that as far as non-employed women are concerned this risk is rather small. Moreover, lowering the retirement age without reduction of pension would apparently encourage many people to abandon employment altogether. However, account must also be taken of some rebounds: people who had become discouraged by jobseeking and had left the labour market might come back to it again. Another uncertainty that is often mentioned is that of a possible rise in demand for work on the part of persons already in employment. Estimates are made about overtime, however controversial such estimates may be, as we have seen. With regard to work on the sly and multiple jobholding, firm figures are scarcely possible. Our research shows that the risk of an extension of such practices is likely to remain low. In any event, it may well be that in such cases the supply is partly demand-induced. Finally, as a result of qualitative mismatches between labour supply and demand, such factors would not necessarily deprive unemployed persons of jobs that they might wish to occupy. It is quite likely that the need for money would have more effect in many cases than mere availability of free time.

From the point of view of the supply of jobs, it is assumed that measures for reducing working time would be introduced in the context of a recession, with a decline of employment greater than the decline in output, particularly as a result of technological advances. Management reactions to such a situation have shown that there are various possible uncertainties as far as any conversion of reductions in working time into new jobs is concerned: they include gains in productivity, reduced scale of output, absorption of potential unemployment and various practical problems. Moreover, if unemployed persons do not have the right qualifications, their chances of obtaining any jobs that become available are thereby restricted. In general, therefore, it would seem that any improvement in the employment situation as a result of this factor is likely to remain rather limited, at least in the short run, which is the usual context in which such arguments are put forward. A deliberate policy of maximising job opportunities (for example by limiting overtime or the reorganisation of work or production) may give positive results, to judge from past experience. However, this requires far-seeing management of working time and jobs; and such management does not seem to be very widespread.

One factor that may throw a more favourable light on this question is the fact that there is no hard-and-fast amount of employment, fixed once and for all time, to be divided and there is not necessarily a linear relationship between work and jobs, particularly in advanced industrial societies. At the level of the community as a whole, compensatory factors come into play. A mixture of these may bring about a real redistribution of work in the medium and long term. Experience of this kind has been evaluated in the past: some examples will be given before we look at the interpretations that are being made of the current situation.

Assessment of past experience

The contribution made in the past by reduced working time to the expansion of employment has been assessed in some cases. Such assessments have used, in particular, a number of correcting factors relating to gains in productivity or to the relative importance of economic growth or fluctuations on the one hand and reduced working time on the other. Exercises of this kind are difficult in themselves and made even more uncertain by the limitations of available statistics.[1] However, the results of some of these assessments are set out here for purposes of illustration.

In the Federal Republic of Germany[2] it is estimated that in spite of gains in productivity, reductions in normal weekly working hours made it possible to provide the equivalent of 200,000 jobs, with almost the same number coming as a result of lengthening annual leave. In addition, flexible retirement at 63 or 64 brought in almost 70,000 jobs. The number of jobs made available by other rearrangements of working time is estimated to be at least 80,000 from extension of part-time work, 80,000 from leave for training and retraining, nearly 70,000 from raising the duration of compulsory schooling to ten years, nearly 60,000 from partial unemployment and 20,000 from early retirement of severely handicapped persons and from maternity leave. Together, all these measures are said to have made available 800,000 jobs. The effect on unemployment figures is estimated at two-thirds of this total, part of the new jobs theoretically made available having been absorbed by hidden manpower reserves. In Austria the Council for Economic and Social Affairs estimated that reductions in working time brought about a 60 per cent increase in employment between 1959 and 1975, after allowing for gains in productivity and leaving economic fluctuations out of account. During this period weekly working hours fell to 40 from between 45 and 48 and annual leave increased first to three weeks and then to four.[3] In France an annual fall of 30 minutes in average weekly working hours between 1967 and 1976 is said to have resulted in the creation of 50,000 jobs a year, despite gains in productivity and leaving out of account the effects of economic growth.[4] According to another estimate, any jobs that were created in France in the 1970s were due entirely to reduction in average working time, since productivity and output have risen only very slowly since 1973.[5]

Assessment of prospects

Considerable research has been carried out to try to determine what effects the various means of reducing working time would have on employment and unemployment. Some studies have concentrated on specific measures for shortening working hours, such as overtime. For example in Spain it was calculated that 25,000 jobs would be created if the 100 major undertakings in the country reduced overtime by half. In the United States[6] the theoretical equivalent of overtime performed by production workers in manufacturing industry was estimated in 1978 at 1.2 million jobs, by converting the 2,400 million hours of overtime into jobs at the rate of 2,000 hours per year for each. It was thought that employment would grow by a little more than 8 per cent if this theoretical figure were translated into fact. In practice, however, it is believed that the effect would be much less, and the assumption could not be extrapolated to the whole working population because overtime is much less frequent or is even non-existent in other economic sectors or occupations. For various reasons of the kind already mentioned, employment would rise by only 2 per cent at the most for production workers in manufacturing industry.

Other estimates relate to the possible effect of reductions in weekly working hours. Thus, in the United States it was calculated that a 3 per cent reduction in average weekly hours -- amounting to about 1.2 hours -- would be enough to bring unemployment down to a level of 5 per cent, on the basis of 1976 labour statistics. Realistically, however, this theoretical percentage has to be revised downwards. In practice, the real effect would depend on the policies pursued by the Government.[7] In Switzerland it has been estimated that reducing weekly working hours of the Geneva state administration to 40 would make it necessary to recruit 1,000 new civil servants.[8]

In the United Kingdom the Department of Employment tried to determine the effect of various methods of reducing working time and came to the conclusion that reduction of overtime was the best way of optimising effects on employment without harm to the economy.[9] According to the Department, if all overtime worked in manufacturing industry could be converted into full-time jobs, there would be enough for all the unemployed in that sector, and if half of the overtime performed by male workers beyond 48 hours per week was replaced by full-time jobs, 100,000 unemployed would disappear from the register. In practice, however, there would be difficulties, particularly resistance from low-paid workers, who comprise a large proportion of those doing overtime, and the benefit to employment would be lower. Reduction of the normal working week to 35 hours might give employment to between 100,000 and 500,000 registered unemployed (between 40,000 and 200,000 for a 38-hour week), on various assumptions concerning the number of jobs created, increases in overtime and productivity per hour and per worker, and possible variations in the level of output. On the same hypotheses, there would be a fall in registered unemployment of between 25,000 and over 100,000 if annual leave were prolonged by one week, though these figures are likely to be over-estimates.

The Trade Union Research Unit[10] criticised these estimates for under-estimating the employment effects, and particularly for over-estimating the loss due to overtime. It pointed out that a 38-hour week would mainly affect manual workers, while a reduction to 35 hours would also affect non-manual employees, many of them women, who were often already working a week of 37 or 38 hours. If 48 per cent of the effect of shortening the working week to 35 hours were converted into increased employment, this would mean a rise of 890,000 in available jobs, and if the resulting fall in registered unemployment were 65 per cent (the Department of Employment's hypothesis), there would be 580,000 fewer unemployed.

Estimates concerning the possibility of reducing unemployment by lowering the retirement age depend on the assumptions made with regard to the proportion of workers who will actually retire in relation to the age group as a whole and the proportion of jobs vacated that will actually be filled: these assumptions have a strong influence on the results put forward. In Denmark it was estimated at the end of 1979 that nearly one-sixth of the working population aged 60 years or more had taken advantage of the lower retirement age of 60. Half of them were older unemployed or partially disabled persons, and according to some estimates only a quarter of the jobs thus released were filled by young workers.[11] A more recent estimate indicated that a third of the total number of potential retirees had applied under the new early retirement scheme in the first six months of its existence: the rate of job replacement was said to be 100 per cent.[12]

In the United Kingdom, according to estimates concerning a general lowering of retirement age under the national insurance scheme,[13] if the retirement age for men were lowered to 60, as for women, the level of registered unemployed would fall by 600,000 once firms and workers had become fully adjusted to the change. If the retirement age were 64, this figure would be reduced by four-fifths. In these calculations it was assumed that men aged between 60 and 65 would behave like those aged between 65 and 69, that there would be no serious shortage of workers to replace them and that the rate of replacement in the jobs vacated would be two-thirds.

The idea that measures might be taken to encourage employers to fill the vacancies left by workers who retire does not seem to have been considered when calculations of theoretical equivalents were made. In Belgium, where it was made obligatory to appoint workers under the age of 30 to the jobs of workers retiring, the actual replacement rate was estimated as being about 90 per cent.[14] In the United Kingdom the Job Release Scheme has apparently had only limited success, but it provides no more than a lump-sum payment to workers who voluntarily leave a job that might be filled by an unemployed person. According to some sources[15] it is said to have led to a reduction in unemployment by 70,000 between 1977 and the beginning of 1980, and 105,000 according to other sources, which also mention a replacement rate of 96 per cent.[16]

Some studies have analysed a wide range of methods of reducing working time. Thus, in the Federal Republic of Germany[17] the theoretical job equivalents were estimated as follows: 600,000 jobs for one hour less per week; 500,000 for an extra week's annual leave; 300,000 for lowering the age of voluntary retirement to 60 for men and 58 for women; 300,000 for the introduction of the tenth year of schooling; 300,000 for a year's maternity leave or sabbatical leave; and 300,000 to 400,000 for a 20 per cent increase in part-time employment. These figures would vary from one sector of the economy to another or from one occupation to another and, it was believed, would no doubt be cancelled out to a considerable extent by the fact that there was scope for increasing productivity in undertakings and by the likelihood that rationalisation measures already being considered would be put into operation sooner. Almost half the theoretical job equivalents would probably be lost in this way. Other specialists tried to correct the figures of job equivalents.[18] Their conclusion was that even without limitation of overtime a reduction of the working week to 35 hours would make available about 1,075,000 jobs. A reduction of one hour would produce 215,000 jobs, and one extra day's leave 50,000; lowering the normal retirement age to 60 would free 150,000 jobs, and to 58, 200,000. Other estimates[19] made by the Labour Market and Employment Research Institute were based on two different assumptions for the years 1979 to 1985: first that current trends in the reduction of working time would continue (particularly with regard to part-time working, annual leave and the extension of compulsory schooling), and secondly that they would accelerate. At the end of this period, on the first assumption and on the basis of rate of real growth of 3.5 per cent and an annual increase of labour productivity per hour of 3.4 per cent, 2.6 million persons would be unemployed. On the second assumption, of a constant rate of growth and a higher productivity rate, the number of unemployed would fall to 250,000; in 1985, among other reductions forming part of this range of estimates, the working week would be shortened from 40 to 38 hours and all workers would have six-and-a-half weeks of annual leave.

The inclusion of very diverse methods of reducing working time in evaluations of their effects reflects the current approach, which is to widen the range of choice in this field. But it also raises the problem of possible interactions among the various methods of reduction and also the question whether their effects would be cumulative or would partially neutralise one another. We may also ask what would be the potential for development of other ways of reducing working time which are not dealt with in the present study. For example, this potential would probably be quite large in the case of paid educational leave, which remains marginal in the countries under consideration, in spite of efforts to encourage its extension.[20] It will be noted in passing that, in principle, paid educational leave does not involve an increase in leisure, but merely a different utilisation of time which may be regarded as working time.

Some analysts believe that part-time employment provides a real possibility of making work-sharing a reality, but its development would also involve certain risks, particularly that of provoking a flood of new jobseekers (all those who have little interest in full-time employment). Besides, persons who are now normally employed and who go into part-time jobs might well feel entitled to return to full-time employment later. Opinions differ about the prospects of expanding the supply of part-time jobs. Opposition to part-time employment is losing strength among employers, in spite of the specific problems it involves. Some writers believe that the chances of expansion of part-time working among core workers are rather doubtful and that its effects at the macro-economic level would probably be insignificant, but that that is no reason not to encourage it.[21]

The Commission of the European Communities has devoted particular attention to the possible relation between the spread of part-time working and reduced working time[22] and has underlined the need to take account of part-time working in readjusting working time, and to redefine this problem in future reductions of weekly working hours. It has pointed to the danger of an increase in the total number of persons seeking employment and of legal or illegal multiple jobholding if part-time employment develops. On this view, employment can be increased only by the creation of new part-time jobs which would not be merely the result of an arbitrary subdivision of existing full-time jobs. Innovations must be made, for example by systematic reduction of overtime or the creation of part-time shift work. Even on the most favourable assumption, an increase in part-time employment would make only a modest contribution to solving urgent employment problems.

THE ECONOMY AND EMPLOYMENT

Other studies relate more directly to the possible consequences of reductions in working time on the economy and, through the multiple reactions between the measures for reducing working time and various economic parameters, on employment and unemployment. They deal in the main with effects on industrial and commercial firms and take the reactions of their managers (treated as an aggregate) as the starting-point for various sequences of more general effects; these reactions are seen as occurring within the framework of economic mechanisms which may vary, depending on the economic theories supported by the writers concerned. Some of the economic studies are of a classical type, while others are macro-economic studies, in some cases using econometric models. Various examples are given below. A final section will deal with the objections and reservations that have been put forward concerning macro-economic and econometrical approaches in a field such as that being examined here.

A reduction in wages in parallel with a reduction in working time is accepted as a possibility in many studies: in that event the expected effects on employment are sometimes more favourable, sometimes less. In view of the specific terms of reference of the present study, we shall concentrate on analyses of the effects of reductions in working time without a reduction in wages. It should be noted, however, that when the studies talk about maintaining wages, they seem to mean actual real earnings and do not make the distinction implied by the social aim, namely that there shall be no diminution in the wages or living standards corresponding to the previous normal working hours.

General studies

The possible consequences of reductions in working time are dealt with in certain general economic studies that do not necessarily concentrate on such reductions. Sometimes they draw the conclusion that it is impossible to assess the consequences. Thus, in an OECD study of economic prospects it was stated towards the end of 1978 that available indicators showed a probable continuation of moderation in increases in nominal wages in many countries and that no one knew what influence a reduction in working time might have on productivity and unit labour costs.[23]

Other analyses relate specifically to the possible consequences of reductions in working time and arrive at their forecasts on the basis of the general situation in the economy and in the field of employment. Thus, according to the Austrian study already mentioned, it was to be expected that the trend towards underemployment and a slow-down in growth would affect developments in that country; the possible effects of a reduction in working time on employment would then become evident more rapidly and be more marked.[24] It is to be noted that there was very little unemployment in Austria. On the other hand, in the view of certain Belgian economists[25] it was doubtful whether a rapid reduction in working time would bring about a major diminution of unemployment in Belgium because of the tendency of undertakings in that country to retain manpower, particularly core workers; the surplus employees would be reabsorbed and hourly productivity would grow automatically. These economists believed that shortening working hours, like other methods of reducing working time, would have a significant effect only if there were an upsurge in economic growth accompanied by other basic measures.

Certain analyses stress the need to take the specific characteristics of the various sectors of the economy into account. In the Netherlands the economic experts of the Economic and Social Council pointed out that different effects were to be foreseen, as far as employment was concerned, from one sector to another. A reduction in working time would have varying effects depending on capital intensiveness, the degree of utilisation of productive capacity, the extent to which production was directed to the domestic market and existing reserves of labour. Shift work might help to maintain output, but it was not very common in the Netherlands and, since it was unpleasant, it was unlikely to be widely accepted. In public offices and services it would be possible to increase employment by means of systems of appropriate rotation of personnel, but it would be necessary to increase capital spending, particularly on buildings, with the result that the services would become more costly and perhaps of lower quality. According to the experts' report, a reduction in working time ought to be generally applied and be accompanied by a proportionate reduction in earnings.[26] According to an estimate from another source, the introduction of a fifth shift with reduced working hours for the 30,000 workers on four shifts would theoretically create 5,500 new jobs. However, the real effect would doubtless be much less, since the undertakings concerned were not located in areas with high unemployment, hourly labour costs would increase and there would be a contagious effect among other workers that would be damaging to the economy.[27]

Another study mentions a number of factors which may contribute to overcoming excessive pessimism: the burden of unemployment payments would be reduced, which would partly compensate for any increases in the total wage bill; reduced profits might not be reflected in reduced investments if the undertaking's financial situation were healthy; the volume of production might increase because of an expansion of consumption due to the extension of leisure and the stimulus to investment caused by the reduction in working time. The author concluded that the most realistic approach, at least in the short run, would appear to be to consider a reduction of working time as an aim in itself, irrespective of employment problems, and to seek ways of implementing it at the lowest cost.[28]

The idea that a reduction in working time remains a valid social objective in itself has also been expressed in other analyses which, however, have expressed grave reservations about the effects of such a measure on employment.

In other analyses it is assumed that specific efforts will be made to reduce working time. One author[29] has drawn attention to the elasticity of employment in relation to wages, and to the need to take delayed reactions into account. In his view, an upturn in employment due to a fall in real wages (or any other method of bringing down prices) would have little chance of success in the short term, but might have some chance in the medium term. He believes that small reductions in working time would have almost no effect on employment or the quality of life, and has proposed an average reduction of six hours a week (15 per cent), with 10 per cent compensatory hiring of new workers. He suggests that claims for wage increases should be abandoned, but does not rule out the possibility of discussions about the wages of the lowest-paid. In his view, the wage costs of undertakings ought not to be allowed to increase by more than 5 per cent in real terms, namely at the same average rate as modernisation of equipment. About a third of the reduction in working time (the 5 per cent difference between the reduction of hours and the compensatory hiring of new workers) would be financed from gains in productivity and a sixth from employment of unemployed persons (each of whom costs in benefits paid and social security contributions unpaid roughly half the wage of an employed person). To finance the remaining half of the reduction, three methods are possible: a less unequal distribution of income, which would require a degree of solidarity that it is perhaps utopian to expect; limitation of increases in wage costs, on the average, to half of the reduction in working hours, with a ceiling of 7.5 per cent a year; or state intervention to finance temporarily about half the cost of the compensatory hiring of new workers.

One of the questions raised in some of these studies is: what is the most favourable economic situation for reducing working time? While many analysts seem implicitly to accept the principle that it is only in periods of prosperity that such a measure can be implemented, others claim on the contrary that it would be desirable to go "against the current".[30] A reduction in working time should be avoided in a period of full employment when the labour market is already over-extended; one should rather choose periods of underemployment when there are jobseekers who can be absorbed without risk of further tension. Moreover, if the reduction in working time is seen as a wage gain to be included among all the costs that undertakings can accept or have already accepted, taking their productivity increases and prices into account, then the disadvantages connected with the reduction (loss of competitiveness, fall in growth, etc.) may be less evident. A reduction in working time then becomes merely a means for workers to participate in economic progress, chosen in preference to higher wage increases. A progressive reduction in working time would thus be one of the usual ways of achieving this participation.

According to certain estimates, if it is assumed that the choice between higher wages and more spare time falls almost entirely in favour of increased leisure, and if working time can be reduced by 4 per cent a year without loss of output, it would require about three years, without increase in real wages, to bring average weekly working hours down to 35.[31] Other writers, basing themselves on similar assumptions, have attempted to determine the margin of manoeuvre that would be available if part of the wage increases made possible by moderate economic growth were exchanged for more free time. One of them, the United States, came to the conclusion that there would be a reduction in annual working time, which would fall from 1,911 hours in 1976 to 1,598 hours in the year 2000. This reduction might take one or more of a variety of forms (a 33-hour week, 11 weeks of paid annual leave, paid sabbatical leave of 13 months every seven years, retirement at the age of 56). On the basis of a survey showing that 65.7 per cent of workers questioned would be ready to give up 10 per cent of their future wage increases to have more leisure, he considers that in this case annual working time could be brought down from about 1,900 hours in 1978 to about 1,500 in 1990 for workers in the OECD countries. This would assume that the workers would make the same choice three times in the course of the next ten years. The author believes that part of the work time that would be made available in this way could probably enable jobs to be found for unemployed persons, but he suggests no figures.[32]

One point that seems to be generally accepted is that in any event reductions in working time within the limits made possible by increases in productivity would not raise any particular problems. The report prepared by the ILO for a tripartite technical conference on employment held in 1963, which led to the adoption of the Employment Policy Recommendation (No. 122), 1964, of which certain provisions relating to reduction of working time were quoted in the introduction to the present report, pointed out:

> While sporadic short-time working is unsatisfactory, it is perfectly reasonable that a community benefiting from technical progress should choose to take out part of the benefit of higher productivity in the form of shorter regular hours. This has happened over the course of history and will no doubt continue to happen. Annual hours of work may of course be shortened by lengthening paid holidays as well as by shortening weekly hours. Shortening regular hours at times when technical change is especially rapid may reduce dislocation and displacement.[33]

At the time of writing, productivity was continuing to increase in industrialised countries, if not always throughout the whole economy, where a slow-down had been noted and sometimes a fall in absolute figures, at least in some sectors. In 1979 some gains in productivity were recorded in the economy as a whole in all the countries covered by the statistics of the Economic Commission for Europe[34] except two. The recorded gains were consistently higher, and sometimes much higher, in the manufacturing sector. Compared with gains recorded for the economy as a whole, given below in parentheses, those for manufacturing were 8.5 per cent (2.5) in Sweden, 6.5 per cent (4.5) in

Austria, 5.5 per cent (3) in the Federal Republic of Germany and France, 4.5 per cent (4) in Finland and 4 per cent (3) in the Netherlands. In Canada and the United States, where productivity per worker fell by 1 per cent and 0.5 per cent respectively in the economy as a whole, there was an increase in the manufacturing sector of 0.5 per cent in Canada and 2 per cent in the United States.

Macro-economic studies

Working time

A number of macro-economic studies, some using econometric models, have been carried out on reduction of average working time. Most of them come to negative or rather pessimistic conclusions about the effects of such a measure on employment, output, inflation and the balance of payments. Normally, they assume that reductions in working time will be imposed unilaterally, without supporting or accompanying measures, with no change in general policies relating to the economy or to employment and no co-ordination with other countries; usually make no distinction between different sectors of the economy. It is scarcely possible to draw generally valid conclusions from them, because the assumptions on which they are based vary enormously as regards the scale and timing of the reductions and their expected direct effects on employment, productivity and the degree of utilisation of productive capacity; the presumed secondary effects derive from the particular model applied. In general, most of the analyses assume productivity gains much lower than in the past.

Some examples will suffice to show the kind of assumptions and reasoning that are used.[35] In the Netherlands the models of the Central Planning Bureau assumed a reduction in weekly working hours from 40 to 35 between 1979 and 1983, and the resulting estimates showed unfavourable effects on output, employment and the balance of payments if wage levels were maintained. The effects predicted were more favourable on the assumption that wage levels were not maintained, although there would be falling production and capacity as a result of adjustments in private consumption and investment in the latter case; after ten years, 100,000 to 115,000 additional jobs would have been created, depending on whether losses in productive capacity were made up or not.[36] Other estimates[37] were made on the basis of somewhat different assumptions (for example, a drop in production of 4 or 5 points instead of 9 points as in the exercise just described, with wage adjustments of 7 or 8 per cent). They produced positive conclusions: on the basis of a model of labour supply and demand distributed by sectors, sex, and full-time and part-time employment, they predicted that between 210,000 and 320,000 new jobs would be created, depending on the input chosen.

Models used by the Treasury in the United Kingdom include variables relating to interest rates and money supply.[38] Those used in France in 1979 made it possible to compare two series of effects corresponding to two different schools of thought, particularly as regards the development of productive investments.[39] One model (DMS) linked investment with profits. It foresaw a rise in wages leading to a fall in profits only partly compensated by higher prices, a reduction in investments and in hiring of new employees and a fall in household consumption and in exports. The other model (METRIC) assumed that investment was more likely to be determined by expectations about demand. The sequence was different: rise in wages, growth of consumption, therefore growth in economic activity, which caused undertakings to invest and take on more workers; the increase in output made it possible to reduce very considerably the effect of higher wages on profits. With an average reduction of one hour in actual working time added to current trends towards shorter working hours, and with maintenance of wage levels, there would have been 143,000 fewer unemployed according to METRIC and 84,000 fewer according to DMS, after a period of three years. The deficit in the balance of payments would have been lower under the DMS model, and would have continued to fall, but consumer prices would have risen much more rapidly. On the assumption that undertakings would have reacted by restructuring their work processes, the effects on employment would have become more favourable.[40]

In Belgium the models used to study the effects of rapid reductions in working time were gradually improved, particularly to take into account a possible slow-down in the rise of purchasing power agreed upon by the trade unions in exchange for increased leisure, and to avoid over-estimating the possible effect that a fall in unemployment might have on wage increases. The estimates did not usually show any notable positive effects on employment. However, if it was assumed that overtime was eliminated, with a consequent slight reduction in unit wage costs due to the disappearance of hours paid at premium rates, this gave much more positive results for employment. A run through a more recent version of model RENA(V), with a possible fall in working hours from 40 to 36 per week between 1977 and 1980, predicted a slow-down in private consumption and positive effects on growth, some investments and export opportunities; unemployment would fall considerably in the first five years but very little afterwards because of lack of stimulus to overall demand. New models incorporating working time among their parameters were designed, and were expected to provide better indications of the effects of the various possible ways of reducing working time.[41]

In Belgium, also, the trade unions criticised the kinds of economic theorising embodied in macro-economic analyses and econometric models.[42] The following objections were put forward against version "RENA III": mechanistic link between higher costs and reduction of weekly working hours without taking account of resulting productivity gains; arbitrary additional increase in wage costs linked with the Phillips curve,[43] while even after a reduction in weekly working hours there would still be considerable unemployment, in view of the then current level of 500,000 unemployed; the assumption that exports were extremely sensitive to wage costs, which were themselves supposed to rise with excessive speed, thus exaggerating their effect on the country's ability to compete, the whole sequence then arriving logically at negative conclusions. These criticisms stressed one particular argument: while reduced working time was in fact being put forward as a substitute for wage increases, the models assumed that both would occur simultaneously.

The Belgian General Federation of Trade Unions (FGTB) put forward a "counter-model" based on giving priority to the reduction of weekly working hours to 36 over two or three years; wage claims would be marginal over this period, except for such problems as those relating to lower wages and to certain specific undertakings. The following sequence of effects was assumed: relative stability of gross income (increase in leisure); fall of approximately 150,000 in potential unemployment; diminution in expenditure on unemployment, lower tax burdens and therefore stability in net incomes and relaxation of pressure for further wage increases; a rise in domestic consumption (reduction in the number of the unemployed and fall in precautionary savings by individuals). It was also estimated that public expenditure would fall by 30,000 million Belgian francs and receipts would increase by 15,000 million. According to this analysis, wage and other labour costs would increase by 5 or 6 per cent; over two or three years, such an increase would enable undertakings to remain competitive, with the result that any jobs that would be saved or created would be permanent. In addition, there would be no increase in inflation.

An analysis published in the Netherlands provides an example of the different results obtained with, and without, the Phillips curve. It compares the results of the Central Planning Bureau model with those of the other models mentioned above for that country. One of the most striking differences relates to wage and price trends. With the Phillips curve, no additional jobs are created in the first three years; the result becomes slightly positive (61,000 jobs) in the tenth year, but falls again to stabilise at 4,000 jobs in the 15th year. On the other hand without the Phillips curve, after a period of negative results the trend changes, and 237,000 new jobs appear for the tenth year and 314,000 for the 15th.[44]

Other models testing hypotheses based on different economic policies produce different consequences as far as employment is concerned. One Belgian study[45] compared two different economic policies for the years 1978 to 1983, involving concrete measures: one was a continuation of the relatively non-expansionist policies of the past; the other was expansionist and conceived as part of an international drive to promote economic recovery. The model was complex: for example, expenditure under unemployment insurance was "endogenised". In the scenario reflecting slow growth, and with persistent unemployment, the reduction in working time was speeded up to 1.5 per cent a year instead of the 1 per cent that appeared to be the long-term trend. In the absence of appropriate instruments it was not possible to integrate into the model the reactions to a general atmosphere of recession, such as precautionary measures, resistance to technological progress and protectionism. In the second scenario domestic demand was stimulated by budgetary measures, and the volume of international trade was assumed to be expanding. Working time was reduced by only 1 per cent a year.

In the first scenario employment grew, but not enough to compensate for the rise in unemployment, and the latter also increased. Rises in real wages remained moderate, but there was also no significant increase in profits. The deficit in the balance of payments worsened, as did the budgetary situation. In the recovery scenario there were increases in income of all kinds (wages, incomes of the self-employed, gross profits of undertakings). Public finances improved considerably after one year of unfavourable results. The balance of payments improved. Intermediate projections based either on domestic expansion with the international context unchanged, or on an upturn in international activity generating a return to growth but with no positive domestic policy, gave less favourable results. The second scenario produced much more favourable results, except with respect to inflation, but there was still no return to full employment. In the authors' view, this was probably due to the fact that the proposed measures were relatively modest in scale, as compared with the severity of the slump and the need to consider a more complex programme providing in particular for a co-ordinated reduction of all costs, subsidies to support employment, deliberate manipulation of exchange rates and interest rates, and greater selectivity in the policies applied. All these measures would have required elaboration of the model so as to produce more refined results. In the results obtained from the second scenario the authors found a justification for the idea that there should be a co-ordinated drive by a majority of countries to promote economic recovery.

In France forecasts relating to 1985 made in 1980[46] took into account 27 different scenarios of the possible development of the economy. The basic forecasts, the main aim of which was to maintain the balance of trade and keep the value of the franc stable, gave a total of 2.2 million unemployed in 1985. At the request of the national planning agency and of employers' and workers' organisations, additional forecasts were made, employment being included as a priority objective and no longer as an accessory passive result. One of the possibilities put to the test involved a big reduction in weekly working time, to 35½ hours in 1985 instead of 38½ as in the basic scenario. Subject to acceptance of only a moderate increase in purchasing power (+ 0.36 per cent or + 0.7 per cent on average per year, depending on the scenario used, instead of 2.3 per cent in the initial assumption) and a smaller increase in consumption by households, the positive effects on employment were very significant (1,613,000 unemployed in 1985 in one case, and 1,588,000 in the other, instead of the 2.2 million mentioned above). In the two cases investment by undertakings and gross national product increased more than in the basic scenario, and the rise in consumer prices was lower. In certain scenarios the national budget might be balanced and the national debt reduced.

Age of retirement

The possible macro-economic consequences of reducing the entire span of working life by lowering the age of retirement do not appear to have been the subject of research to the same extent as the reduction of average working time during working life. It seems to be agreed that if the retirement age were lower, there would be no diminution of potential output; but various theories may be put forward concerning the comparative productivity of the workers who leave employment and those who take their place, and the wage costs represented by the latter. The financial effects at the level of the undertaking are believed to vary depending on whether the measure would be financed by an increase in employers' or workers' contributions or both, and the possible sequences of results are worked out by analogy with different hypotheses about the maintenance or non-maintenance of existing wage levels. The possibility considered in the few macro-economic analyses available during the preparation of the present study seems to be that of a general lowering of the retirement age, and not that of selective measures.

In France, according to a model established some years ago, which assumed that increased social security contributions would be paid, on equal terms, by workers and employers and that there would be a subsidy from the State to the National Solidarity Fund, the increase in the number of retirees would exercise pressure on the labour market, and this would tend to raise nominal earnings, and thus diminish competitiveness; growth would slow down, inflation would worsen, and the balance of payments would deteriorate together with public finances.

Macro-economic effects were subsequently calculated by analogy with the variants used for the projections made for the Seventh Plan.[47] The age of retirement was assumed to be lowered to 62, producing about 325,000 additional retirements. The increase in employers' contributions was treated as having the same consequence as a reduction in working time without loss of wages,[48] and the increase in workers' contributions as corresponding to the variant which assumed a reduction in working time without maintenance of existing wage levels, and without loss of productive capacity.

In the Netherlands the Central Planning Bureau prepared projections for the plan published in 1979, based on the possibility of a lowering of the retirement age from 65 to 60. The effects of this measure on employment and on diminishing unemployment were found to be slight, because of the assumption that only half of the eligible retirees would actually retire, and that only half of the jobs thus vacated would be filled, since employers would seek to increase productivity rather than fill vacant jobs. Moreover, an aggravation of unemployment was expected in the medium term, if the measure were to be financed by employers' contributions to the pension fund rather than by extra payments from workers, because of the resulting increase in labour costs.[49] The experts of the Economic and Social Council of the Netherlands thought it likely that productivity would increase and labour costs fall if the retirement age were lowered, since young workers are supposed to be more productive than older workers and are paid relatively less.[50]

Reservations

This brief review of assessments of macro-economic effects and of calculations using econometric models reveals how impossible it is to arrive at unchallenged conclusions of general validity. The analyses are conditioned by the logic of the theories built into them, and these theoretical assumptions may be determinant. In fact, these analytic instruments cannot be used without making specific options concerning economic policy and employment. There is a recognised need for refining these models to make them a more complete reflection of the real situation, particularly by taking account of differences between economic sectors and the context of economic fluctuations. It is impossible to avoid some degree of uncertainty, and it is important to recognise that this is so; this is the case particularly with assumptions about the international background and the possibility that workers and their organisations will accept a fall in nominal wages. Furthermore, assessments of effects leave out of account a factor of great importance, namely the effect of an increase in leisure.

Models of this kind present the great advantage of showing the interdependence between the major economic parameters. But they also have a number of general inadequacies that are being remedied only very gradually.[51] The actual experience described in the previous chapter also shows that in dealing with a question such as the reduction of working time, there is a whole area which has as yet not been investigated by micro-economic research. For example, working time is not necessarily a decisive variable in some major decisions. It should therefore be given its "proper place" in appropriate fashion in the models to correspond with the diversity of actual situations.

The use of econometric approaches to deal with work-sharing has aroused a certain amount of criticism.[52] One particular objection made is the lack of refined analysis of conditions of substitution between factors of production, the failure to separate overtime from the total amount of working time and the neglect of relations between work-sharing and trends in income distribution and national savings. The Belgian planning bureau has itself acknowledged that it has oversimplified in certain respects[53] and that this limits the value of the traditional models used; it is gradually improving its models. In France the Giraudet report also pointed out that the models ignored the major importance of the methods of adjusting working time. Such methods were necessarily based on weekly working hours and did not take account of the essential factor, which was the number of hours actually worked in the year. Moreover the models could not be based on actual human, management and market behaviour, since there was no means of analysing such factors.[54]

The fact that these models only take account of overall developments in average working time makes it impossible to use them for working out selective policies for reducing working hours. As the Giraudet report also pointed out, the transition from a measure or set of measures adopted by regulation, legislation or collective agreement to an actual medium-term result lies outside the scope of existing models, in the absence of sufficient micro-economic data, which are in any event too diverse and complex to be integrated into an overall approach.[55] In practice such a macro-economic model apparently proved to be unsuitable for forecasting the consequences of measures laid down in the French law of 1 July 1978, which grants entitlement to compensatory time off in respect of 20 per cent of overtime in excess of 42 hours. Contrary to the forecasts made on a theoretical and macro-economic basis about its effects, this law has played a significant role in recent trends towards a reduction in weekly working hours. It may provide an explanation for the concentration of actual working time noted in a wide sample of undertakings around two figures, 42 hours and 40 hours, which is a target in relation to which the law plays a decisive psychological and sociological role.[56]

EFFECTS OF INCREASED SPARE TIME

Increased spare time has aroused much less attention than reduced working time, despite the fact that it is the obverse of the same coin and has its own repercussions. This is no doubt due to habits of thought, but this neglect may also be due to certain difficulties and to the fact that any consideration of the question of spare time must begin by putting a number of accepted ideas into question. Leisure generates deep changes in the economy and in human behaviour. These changes make it necessary to examine what is really at stake, such as people's way of living in times to come, the content of growth, and the capacity of economic systems to adapt to new economic and social challenges. Study of the problems involved in reducing working time has to include such questions, because the proposals being made in this field seem likely to tip the balance between work and leisure towards the latter.

It obviously cannot be the intention here to deal fully with such far-reaching questions; this study will restrict itself to sketching some of the possible consequences of increased leisure for the quality of life, to outlining the theoretical problems involved in trying to take account of the economic value of spare time, and to referring to some existing studies of economic effects.

Quality of life

The possible effects at the level of the individual on ways of living ought to be reflected, at the level of the community, in the form of general trends. In fact the gaps in available information already noted in Chapter 5 are even wider here. On the basis of various observations, there seems to be a general consensus on certain points. First, past increases in spare time have changed people's ways of living, and further increases in leisure seem to be required to improve the quality of life in view of the growing difficulties of daily life today. Secondly, small reductions in working time would probably have only a very slight effect in that regard. Thirdly, large reductions would have a much greater effect; however, in the absence of appropriate policies to improve the framework in which we live (housing, transport, and a variety of other facilities) they may well provoke a number of difficulties in practice.

Thus the Swedish Commission of Inquiry on Employment, which considered that the six-hour day or the 30-hour week would be premature in the 1980s, raised the problem of town planning that would arise if these measures were applied in a city like Stockholm, because a large number of new inhabitants would be needed to meet the need for additional personnel in the service sector. The Commission came down in favour of selective reductions for the most vulnerable categories and in particular for parents of small children.[57] The likelihood of changes in the geographical distribution of the population, who would endeavour to get away from towns for half of the time, thus creating problems with regard to the safeguarding of the rural environment, has been mentioned in a number of other countries.

An increase in leisure would probably also have an influence on human and social relationships, in private, professional and social life. The Danish Institute for Social Research, in past studies of the foreseeable evolution of the needs of older people, mentioned the possibility that a reduction in working time would enable young people in employment to give more help to their parents.[58] A recent Swedish report submitted to the Nordic Council of Ministers[59] on the consequences of a large reduction in working time mentions, in addition to probable effects on economic development and private consumption, the effect that shorter working time might have on relations between parents and children and the possibility that it might contribute to greater equality between the sexes. Mention has already been made of the fact that many writers regard a reduction in working time as important for improving the status of women. It may suffice here to recall the observation made by an ILO consultant in connection with possible ways of doing away with discrimination on the basis of sex in social security schemes, who said:

> The best solution has been indicated in this paper: a general shortening of working hours; possibilities of employment for all women ...; assimilation of periods of leave for family duties to periods of employment for social security purposes. ... .[60]

One possible effect of a major reduction in working time mentioned is the development of group activities and so-called "non-market"production of a voluntary or self-governing character. The concept of "non-market" production is not always clearly defined and seems to be used in a number of different senses. However, what is important here is the conclusions that are drawn. According to one writer, participation in non-market activities might reduce wage claims and make possible a limited reduction in wages in the event of a reduction in working time.[61] Other writers stress the economic value of services initiated "from the grass roots"; these are said to be cheaper and better adapted to people's needs than those provided by large institutions or agencies, which are unsuitable for dealing with individual cases, local circumstances and the specific problems of poor people and of social outcasts.[62] In any event, it appears to be generally agreed that various legislative, administrative, financial and other incentives are necessary to help to develop such non-market activities.

Finally, it is important to consider a possible increase in free time in the context of other major trends in the improvement of the quality of life. These include, first, the tendency to relax time constraints over workers without necessarily changing the duration of working time. This is a matter of rearranging working time in a variety of ways. One essential factor in current policies for improving the quality of life seems to be the attempt "to give men and women the opportunity of exercising a free and responsible choice about the use of their time". In a number of countries social policy is already moving in this direction, as may be seen, for example, from the introduction of flexitime, the possibility of taking "parental" leave, the concern to develop part-time working, and the opportunities provided to enable workers to choose when they shall retire.[63] A combination of reductions and flexible arrangements of working time would probably produce visible effects. On this point, however, as on many others, we have to be content with guesswork.

In the second place, there is a growing movement in favour of improving the quality of work itself, setting off a series of possible consequences in connection with the quality of leisure, economic structures and employment. In Sweden the relation between leisure and the quality of work has aroused interest, particularly from the point of view of the degree of freedom at work. It has been noted that participation in socially active leisure pursuits is strongly conditioned by experiences at work; it would be encouraged by the adoption of measures to make work more creative. The result would be an increased consumption of leisure services, changes in the structure of such services and the creation of jobs in the sectors concerned. In Sweden as in other economically advanced countries, services employ a growing proportion of the workforce and provide jobs involving a degree of "active" initiative higher than the average. It is considered that an increase in "active" jobs and in the demand for leisure services would therefore have a good chance of starting a self-perpetuating movement.[64] But we are already touching on the questions dealt with in the following sections.

Problems of theory

There is little doubt that an increase in free time would be very important for the economy; yet its only acknowledged effect is the consumption of goods and services connected with leisure, because time that is not devoted to production for the market is normally regarded as "unproductive". This concept has been the subject of criticism. It is pointed out that, as a result of the assumption that leisure is "unproductive", the balance of opinion as between working time and leisure is biased towards the former.[65] In itself, the manner in which certain uses of free time are reflected in figures reveals theoretical preconceptions and distortions. Some people claim, for example, that there is no justification for including commuting time as a factor of enrichment because of the consumption of petrol it causes and because the motor car has to be changed more often as a result of being used more. Similarly, criticisms have been levelled against the tendency to consider time spent on training as no more than a cost to the undertaking, when qualified personnel are an essential factor in productivity and in raising the level of employment.[66]

The theoretical problems of economic accounting raised by activities occurring during spare time are aggravated by the kind of consumption that leisure brings with it in advanced industrial societies. It comprises a large proportion of services which are defined as unproductive or only marginally productive. An observation to this effect was made during a round table meeting convened under the auspices of the International Social Security Association concerning consumption by retired persons. The general report raised the following question about the money spent by non-employed persons:

> ... Who can say, *a priori*, that this kind of consumption is of lesser economic "value", and particularly of lesser human importance, than the kind of consumption we see today? Here we return to the observation made by certain participants about the existence of a labour market which is very important both quantitatively and qualitatively, and which is short of staff. These are the social, health and education sectors, sectors which are today called (for whatever reasons!) non-productive, though their direct, immediate function is to improve the human situation.[67]

In fact, there are a number of technical difficulties about measurement which have so far not been resolved. But consideration is being given to these problems. Some research workers are trying to establish the interdependence between leisure activities and almost all sectors of economic activity, and have demonstrated how leisure generates a considerable demand in all those sectors. The field that has been the subject of most attention is tourism.[68] But there are others, for example sport (about which an attempt has been made to establish subsidiary accounts in national accounts),[69] recreation, culture and "do-it-yourself". It would be interesting to find out, by breaking down and reclassifying the consumption and production involved, how the development of activities connected with spare time has already affected the demand for certain traditional industrial products, including textiles and clothing, furniture, sports and games equipment, and machinery.

It would also be useful to work out analytical systems that would enable us to know how the demand generated by spare time activities affects imports and exports. Here again international tourism comes to mind as a cause of important foreign exchange transactions. But this relates only to holidays of some length. It seems to be agreed that extended weekends (and longer holidays in periods of recession) [70] are more likely to promote tourism in the home country; this would be an incentive to regional development and would strengthen the demand for local products and services. The demand for services due to a general increase in free time would need to be studied in relation to the fact that on the whole the proportion of imported factors of production is apparently much lower in this sector than in industry and industrial investment. The same point may well arise in connection with "do-it-yourself" and other "non-market" activities.

It may well be that some of the difficulties relating to measurement are insurmountable. We know, for example, that recreational activities are important for personal well-being and health. We suspect that there is a relationship between opportunities for recreation and personal self-expression on the one hand and social stability on the other. But the strong probability that measures to increase leisure would make a favourable contribution, through an appropriate policy to promote recreational activities, cannot be statistically established.

Studies of economic effects

To our knowledge, no studies of the economic effects of increased leisure exist that can be compared with those concerned with reducing working time. Generally speaking it is recognised that time is a necessary dimension in consumption as it is in production, and that a fair amount of spare time is required to consume certain goods and services (for example, through listening to music, going sailing, keeping oneself informed by reading or tuning in to broadcasts, or looking after the home and the garden). However, no one seems to have given much thought to the practical consequences. For example tourism is usually considered from the point of view of its international aspect, which assumes that people in other countries will have increased leisure, and the development of tourist facilities is very often linked with the trend towards increased leisure, as though that trend will continue as a matter of course. The Economic and Social Committee of the European Economic Communities has expressed the view that a new strategy for growth is needed, directed particularly towards satisfying needs corresponding to the new requirements of the quality of life in such fields as preventive medicine, community culture, people's housing and leisure. [71]

A few available studies deal with the possible economic effects of increased leisure. One of them, already some ten years old [72] and based on the previous 15 years' experience in Western Europe, forecast an increased demand for goods and services required for productive spare-time activities, travel, sport and purely recreational purposes. The estimated increase was higher for the first two types of goods and services, while the last was the most difficult to assess. Such increases would lead to changes in the structure and geographical distribution of production, with a new balance being established between towns and recreation areas as periods of leisure were extended. The construction and public works sector would be most affected. Enormous public investments would be required to satisfy the demands of leisure. It would also be desirable to rearrange working hours so as to avoid worsening some of the problems arising from the way they are organised at present: traffic jams at the start and end of the day, crowds in the shops at certain peak times of the day or week, particularly in food shops, congestion at holiday times (at weekends or in summer), alternation of busy periods and dead periods in towns, seasonal fluctuations in production.

According to an analysis based on developments in the Federal Republic of Germany and in Switzerland, there is likely to be an extension of free time at weekends in the 1980s: flexitime will accentuate this trend by starting the transition towards the four-and-a-half-day week. Yet the ways in which leisure is used change very slowly, because in this field the scale of values and standards of behaviour are socially determined. In the 1980s we should expect a predominance of "living" over "having" — greater individualism, greater need for knowledge, changes in eating habits and increased demand for goods and services connected with health, more concern about the environment and energy, a redefinition of the relation between work and leisure and a more marked division between material and non-material values.[73]

The same study goes on to say that consumption would not reach saturation point because human needs are flexible and grow as a result of competition. The goods and services for which demand would fall are those corresponding to elementary needs, since these do not readily respond to elasticity of incomes and may be replaced by services whose price is falling. This decline would be compensated by a demand for more expensive products of higher quality. Expenditure on leisure would increasingly go on the accumulation of a wider range of experience. Consumption of services should increase, with more than half of private demand being directed to services by about the middle of the 1980s. The markets of the future will be those that satisfy the demand for specific leisure services (travel, sport, hobbies, mass communications, culture and entertainment) and that relating to comfort in the home, health, safety, transport and communications. Because of the growing individualisation of tastes and preferences, there would no longer be surges of consumption of goods such as motor cars, colour television sets and hi-fi systems. The author of this analysis concludes that these changes in structure, which together will have a positive effect, provide an opportunity for future economic development which should not be missed.

In the United Kingdom the trend towards longer holidays led to a forecast of a 30 per cent increase in the number of jobs in the tourist sector within ten years. The Chairman of the English Tourist Board believed that the total would exceed 2 million in 1990 and would continue to grow until the end of the century, by which time he believed that everybody should have seven or even eight weeks' holiday a year. Any new agreement to make holidays longer would help tourist activities to develop.[74] A study of the leisure market in the United Kingdom[75] forecasts total expenditure of more than £54,000 million in this field in 1985, with more than £26,000 million going on social activities and £12,000 million on homes and gardens; travel within the country comes next, but rather far behind, followed by holidays abroad, also far behind. According to these forecasts, weekly working hours in 1985 for male manual workers will be 42 (38 for women) and 37 for male non-manual employees ($35^1/_2$ for women). A significant proportion of increased expenditure would come from non-manual employees, who would have more money to spend. In the author's opinion, the development of leisure activities is being slowed down by the inability of management to adjust to a changing market. Leisure industries are also at a disadvantage because they are fragmented, subject to harsh competition and unable to put forward collective views in dealing with governments. Nevertheless, they can contribute to neutralising actual and potential social problems arising from the utilisation of increased leisure time.

In analyses of the economic effects of a reduction in working time an important role is usually attributed to variations in the income of workers and households; these have certain consequences on their propensity to consume and to save, with effects in turn on output and investment. For the purpose of the present study we have to take the case in which leisure would increase without change of income, but with consequences for the composition of the demand for goods and services. This is a hypothesis that goes beyond normal patterns of economic thought. One analysis made a long time ago already considered this possibility, assuming a reduction in working time limited to the equivalent of the gains in productivity.[76] Its conclusions are summarised below.

Since the reduction in the amount of work would be proportionate to the gains in productivity, the basic situation would remain unchanged: the same production, the same wages. In principle, therefore, there would be no need for any particular modification in the economic system. In practice, however, the author believes that the increase in spare time would change the behaviour of workers in their role as consumers, at least in economically advanced countries where the various possible uses of income are not subject to vital or urgent needs. Increased leisure is a stimulus to a variety of expenditure on such objects as home improvements, "do-it-yourself", travel for pleasure and entertainment. The propensity to save would probably diminish. With the increase in demand directed towards certain sectors, the result would be a tendency for the economy to expand. In the last analysis the consequences would depend on the state of business and the structure of the economy in general. If the limits of elasticity of supply have already been reached when demand is stimulated, an inflationary movement may be set off. If the economic situation is slack, an expansionary trend in the economy would obviously do no harm; it might even, in favourable psychological conditions, help to bring about an upturn in the economy in a slump. In the long run, however, a choice in favour of increasing leisure instead of increasing income would result in lower output, while capital accumulation would be reduced and the rate of economic growth affected.

Nowadays our understanding of micro-economic situations has improved and it would be necessary to supplement or modify this analysis in a number of points. For instance, we need to take account of the fact that many workers on low wages cannot make savings anyway. Therefore in any event their savings cannot be diminished; but production by oneself for one's own needs, which increased leisure makes possible, may generate new savings opportunities. Changes in the propensity to consume may also occur under the influence of factors other than variations in income. According to one recent study, if people have more free time, private consumption is stimulated by advertising, fashion, the urge to imitate other people. If a reduction in working time occurs on the basis of productivity gains an increase in the demand for labour would develop as a result of a growth in the propensity to consume irrespective of any possible expansion in other elements of demand.[77] An increase in leisure will lead to changes in the structure of production corresponding to changes in demand even if total output does not increase. These changes would be at the expense of industries whose products would no longer be in demand. In this case there would be a time lapse between the establishment of new structures and the adaptation of old ones. Special measures might be necessary to ensure a smooth transition. To assume that the demand for goods and services is fixed is to lock oneself into a system in which capital formation, growth and employment might automatically slow down, and this is not necessarily so.

There is therefore every likelihood that a reduction in working time, by increasing spare time, would provide new incentives to growth and employment. There may be a threshold to be passed, but merely to accept that past trends will continue,[78] to refuse to envisage the possibility of breaks or steps in development trends, or to fail to distinguish between different ways of increasing spare time, may lead to quite mistaken conclusions. The risk is particularly great if we make no attempt to imagine new forms of development and limit our thinking to the existing production of goods and services. The operation of the market exerts such an influence, because the market achieves an equilibrium applying to current conditions, not future ones. To prepare for the future, we need to go beyond the workings of the market, and seek new ways of thinking and new initiatives.[79]

An increase in free time obliges us in any case to go beyond the restricted framework of leisure and related activities such as art, culture and sport, and to enter into much wider fields such as those of the management of human and natural resources, regional planning, town planning and environmental questions. Thus according to the Commission of the European Communities the fostering of leisure activities of all kinds in rural areas is a way of improving the environment and, as one of the more important stimuli to economic growth, can create new employment opportunities on a major scale in all the countries of which the Communities are composed.[80] The many-sided nature of the possible effects of increasing leisure time caused the leader of the British Labour Party to propose the establishment of a new government department for the co-ordination of policies and the promotion of research concerning the arts, sport, entertainment and leisure activities. In his view, the silicon chip revolution made it necessary to work out a new national policy for leisure and to plan systematically in this field. Another Member of Parliament from the same party stated that keeping people mobile, active and interested saved money. Vandalism and hooliganism were the products of boredom.[81]

Thus there already seems to be agreement in principle that the authorities should adjust national policy with a view to ensuring a balance between the increasing commercialisation of leisure, on the one hand, and a contrary trend towards leisure that will educate, bring people into contact with nature, extend personal horizons and cause people to participate in activities in the public interest. It may be that this new development will have a favourable influence on the quality of employment and therefore on the efficiency of the economy, although there is no way of quantifying this possible correlation.

TRANSFER PAYMENTS

Measures to shorten working time would have effects on social and fiscal transfer payments (receipt of social security contributions and provision of benefits and other social services, public revenue and expenditure). This is a very important aspect of the question in advanced industrialised societies, where the community takes on an increasingly wide range of responsibilities in the interests of national solidarity. Would reductions in working time reduce these burdens? Or would they make them heavier? These questions will be answered in relation first to lowering the age of retirement and then to other methods of shortening working time. The contribution which policies relating to such transfers can make in connection with reduction of working time will be examined afterwards.

Effects of lowering the retirement age

Lowering the age of retirement is of direct concern to the community, in relation to the solidarity of the active population with those who are no longer employed, at a time when demographic trends are soon going to increase the ratio of older inactive persons to employed persons almost everywhere, though on different time-scales from one country to another. Lowering the retirement age would bring increased financial burdens, varying according to the success the measure would have among potential beneficiaries. We have seen that early retirement schemes, even with actuarial reduction of pension, have been very favourably received up to now, although the atmosphere of inflation and insecurity may modify this trend.

The Council of Europe attempted to evaluate the cost of lowering the normal retirement age by five years in ten countries, despite the difficulties involved in such an operation.[82] Account had to be taken of the great diversity of pension schemes, and their different systems of accumulating entitlement; guesses had to be made about the kinds of reform that may be introduced. The study was based on ten-year projections, and assumed that legislation would not be changed; it was restricted to long-term benefits (old-age and survivors' pensions). The estimates were published in 1977 and forecast for the following ten years a relatively modest increase in expenditure under many schemes, as a result of the expected fall in the number of older people in the 1975-85 period. Subsequently, this number would grow rapidly in most countries up to the end of the century, and this would bring with it much heavier financial burdens in most cases, depending on the degree of maturity of the schemes.

The Council suggested a less costly and more readily applicable system. It would consist of allowing individuals to reduce their employment by stages, starting some years before the age of entitlement to pension and going on with reduced employment beyond that age, for some years more.[83] Starting from the assumption of retirement age at 63 and of a worker having been fully employed till then and therefore entitled to a pension equal to 60 per cent of his or her wage, employment is assumed to be reduced by 10 per cent each year from the age of 59 to reach a minimum of two days a week at the age of 68. Wages are proportionately reduced but this reduction is made up for by a growing proportion of the worker's pension, reaching 115 per cent in the last year. The system is said to be actuarily neutral. Measures of this kind would certainly raise administrative difficulties. Moreover, sufficient part-time jobs would have to be found for the workers concerned.

The possible financial consequences for the community of lowering the retirement age would have to be evaluated in the light of a number of factors: loss of social security contributions (since the contribution period would be shorter), fall in tax receipts (due to the fall in income corresponding to retirement),[84] but also taxes and contributions paid by the workers taking over from the retirees and the financial effects of a possible drop in unemployment.

In the United Kingdom the Department of Employment has estimated the total cost of a possible reduction of the age of retirement to 60, from the point of view of pensions to be paid and loss of taxes and contributions. In spite of expected supplementary tax receipts and savings to be made in the payment of unemployment benefit, the financial cost would still amount to more than £1,000 million. In the Department's view, selective measures would be preferable, because a generalised lowering of the retirement age would have several disadvantages: irreversibility, aggravation of qualitative shortages, and concentration on occupational pension schemes, which would increase employers' charges by 2 to 4 per cent, depending on the schemes concerned, with probable inflationary effects and threats to competitiveness and employment in the long run. It also considered that progressive retirement would not only be difficult to implement for many undertakings, but would also cost more than a pure and simple early retirement scheme, because two people working part-time pay less taxes than one full-time worker. For the same amount of expenditure a generalised early retirement scheme would provide between one-and-half times and twice as many jobs.[85]

In the Federal Republic of Germany savings to be achieved by substituting unemployed persons for workers taking retirement at 63 were estimated in theory at DM79.2 million in 1976.[86] The assumption underlying this evaluation was that 165,000 workers benefiting from a lower retirement age would vacate jobs for 99,000 of the unemployed, a replacement rate of 60 per cent. As a result of the above-mentioned savings (consisting of amounts not paid in unemployment benefit), the average cost of pensions, which would otherwise have been DM1,100 per month per pensioner, would be brought down to a maximum of DM620. With a replacement rate of 75 per cent, the real monthly cost per pensioner would fall to DM500. More detailed calculations would also take account of the loss in taxes and social security contributions which the pensioners would have paid for two more years if they had not retired early (loss partly compensated by deductions made to pensions) and the receipts of taxes and social security contributions paid by persons occupying the jobs vacated.

In the United States, where the question has been vigorously debated, older workers are encouraged to go on working longer because it is feared that the cost of maintaining inactive older persons may constitute a heavy burden. According to some estimates, from the year 2020 onwards the burden will be severely felt, and older workers are therefore likely to receive attractive offers of employment.[87] The interest shown by these workers in more gradual retirement and in part-time employment is thought to provide good prospects that the burden can be lightened. However, some writers believe that the emergence of this trend, which seems to be more marked among self-employed persons, is being hindered by systems which penalise people who cumulate earnings from employment with a pension, or one pension with other pensions, and the slow development of part-time employment.[88]

Lowering the age of retirement would no doubt rapidly reduce labour supply and therefore, subject to "seepage", reduce the number of unemployed. From this point of view the effects would be greater if the opportunities offered to retired persons to carry on in gainful employment were restricted. However, there is a contradiction between what is logical to expect and the movement of public opinion, which favours voluntary retirement at the choice of the individual together with the free pursuit of activity that is considered to be good for older people. Society will no doubt have to weigh the financial costs and benefits involved; but here again, no attempt at quantification seems to have been made. In any event, considerations relating to demographic trends would seem to counsel caution with regard to any irreversible "cut-off" age for retirement.

The rise in the rate of women's employment has already contributed to lightening the burden imposed by the inactive on the employed. This trend seems to be irreversible and from the point of view of unemployment is the source of some anxiety, but it may in future become a favourable factor for public finances and social security finances. (It has also been noted that a second breadwinner in the family may reduce pressure for higher wages for men and strengthen their preference for more leisure, which may also help to keep inflation in check.) The entry into gainful employment of married women who were previously not economically active increases receipts from social security contributions and taxation, with little risk of increasing existing charges, since the women concerned were already receiving benefits and services financed by others. From this point of view too, a reduction in working time would be valuable in itself if it contributed to developing women's work.

In France, in 1975, owing to this development, the "economically active" (gainfully employed) population was growing at a faster rate than the total population, and the burden of non-earners on the employed was decreasing; the cost of older inactive persons was rising, but more slowly. In this respect France was in a favourable situation, similar to that of the Federal Republic of Germany, but less favourable than those of Denmark and the United Kingdom.[89] According to more recent estimates, the number of non-earners per employed person, which was 1.4 in France in 1975, will fall to 1.2 in 1985, and remain stable until the year 2000. This fall is said to be due to the reduction in the number of adult women who are not gainfully employed, and to the smaller number of children (lower birth rate). The proportion of economically inactive older people to the total economically active population, including the unemployed, would show little change throughout the period.[90]

In establishing the ratio of all persons not economically active, or of older persons in that cateogory, to the economically active population as a whole, we need to know whether the unemployed are included in the latter or not.[91] If the answer is yes, then the ratio is misleading because the unemployed are themselves a charge on the community. In any case, if lowering the retirement age contributed to placing unemployed people in jobs, the gainfully employed population would increase and not just the number of older inactive persons. On the other hand, if unemployment continued to grow, the cost of unemployed jobseekers would be added to that of inactive persons and would go on increasing, thus discouraging measures for lowering the age of retirement. There would thus be a serious risk of setting up a vicious circle that would itself be all the more serious because the growth of unemployment has already seriously weakened the financial basis of social security schemes.

Effects of reducing working time in other ways

A reduction in working time or an extension of paid annual leave (or both) would probably contribute to the solution of various social problems. Fatigue, stress, insecurity, physical and mental deterioration, and non-satisfaction of the need for family life, social contacts and creativity have a high cost in more ways than one: alcoholism, various kinds of disability, illnesses, invalidity, all kinds of accidents, family troubles, social maladjustment, violence, loss of output and charges on family income. Large reductions in working time for people most exposed to such risks would perhaps be particularly advantageous from this point of view. These possible favourable consequences might well be extended into the future, when it would be desirable to increase the proportion of the population having some kind of gainful occupation. Since workers today already have time to live better lives, later they would probably be in a better condition to go on working longer, if so required, and would also be more productive and perhaps cost society less than older people do today. This might be a source of considerable savings for the community. However, this approach assumes that people accept the idea that the solution to the problems of older workers lies in a policy of improvement of working conditions and the working environment from the outset and throughout all phases of working life; and this idea is relatively new.[92]

On all the points mentioned, there is almost no possibility of quantification. Perhaps absenteeism, provides a reference point from which to try to assess costs for society, and not merely for the undertaking involved, in workers' negative reactions to poor working conditions; but, as we have seen, it is difficult, if not impossible, to establish a clear connection between absenteeism and working time in the strict sense of the term. However, we can say that as a result of absenteeism production is actually the outcome of working time considerably shorter than is reflected in statistics about hours of work made available or paid for; consequently a reduction in working time, to the extent that it would mop up absenteeism that already exists, would have much less effect on production than formal statistics might lead us to believe. Moreover, since the community bears a large part of the costs of absenteeism in the form of payment of allowances, provision of medical care and shortfall in receipts from taxation and social security contributions, there would be a reduction of such costs if a reduction in working time without loss of earnings were in fact to succeed in reducing absenteeism. It should also be added that certain costs may ultimately pay for themselves, in respect both of the undertaking and of the community: as has been pointed out[93] workers may stay away from work simply to recuperate, and certain work processes or practices (automated or assembly-line production, acceleration of work pace, monotony or unpleasant nature of the job) may make workers feel that brief periods of absence from work are necessary to avoid even longer absences or more extended deleterious effects.

There remains a wide area to be explored in connection with the possible consequences of a reduction in working time in a number of other fields such as the utilisation of space and facilities and the reduction of idle time in daily life. Some estimates that have been made relate to possible reductions in unemployment, but in a limited context. Today, the cost of unemployment tends to be evaluated from the point of view of the damage it does to the structure of society, and not merely from that of its direct financial cost. For example it tends to increase people's need to seek medical advice, which imposes a heavier burden on health insurance schemes; but this is only one example among many, some of which are even less quantifiable than this.

Cost-benefit evaluations have been made about possible decreases in unemployment due to reductions in working time. The bases of evaluation are the same as those mentioned before. They take as their starting-point the fact that unemployment has a high cost (allowances, loss of social security contributions and fiscal revenue, public expenditure on various programmes to promote employment or on anti-unemployment measures), whereas a fall in unemployment brings savings and increased revenue and contributions. We have seen, in connection with certain macro-economic research in Belgium, that recognition of the financial effects in this field of an expected fall in unemployment may be regarded as a positive factor. In the United Kingdom, in connection with the idea of reducing weekly working hours to 35, the Department of Employment was less sanguine in this regard. It calculated that as unemployment fell, there would be net savings in public expenditure because the lower total of unemployment benefits and the higher receipts from taxation would exceed increased labour costs in the public service, but that this advantage would be counterbalanced by increased labour costs in the economy as a whole, with negative long-term consequences, including effects on employment. The Trade Union Research Unit, however, pointed out that net public savings would amount to several million pounds per year. If the Government tried to promote employment by specific measures, at the same time as reducing working time, it would be reasonable to provide financial assistance for these purposes, for example by reducing or abolishing employers' national insurance contributions in respect of new employees.

A study by the Commission of the European Communities, which is already some years old,[94] came to positive conclusions for some of its member States concerning net receipts by the State (including taxes on consumption) if unemployed persons were to find employment; according to these estimates, the receipts would exceed the total remuneration those workers would obtain. Moreover, if the public funds thus obtained were used to promote employment (for example, by subsidising employment in industry or creating jobs in the public sector) instead of paying unemployment benefit, budgetary deficits would get no worse and there would be an upturn in demand without inflationary effect, because the workers concerned would be producing goods and services.

Complete analyses of the costs and benefits for the community resulting from reduction in working time have not yet been carried out. For example we do not know what the direct and indirect effects of such measures would be on expenditure relating to health and accidents at work and elsewhere; enormous sums are at stake here. If shorter working hours were accompanied by an increase in shift work or night work, the community would no doubt have to bear specific social costs. But how should they be calculated? How can we quantify the benefits that may derive from such measures, in terms, for instance, of employment, production, removal of traffic jams, increased consumption and leisure activities and extension of use of certain services by consumers?[95] While we cannot be sure about this, it may be that transitional measures that reveal themselves to be necessary in practice will swallow up any short-term savings that are made on certain factors.

Some writers introduce into their estimates the consequences of "non-adoption" of measures for the reduction of working time in periods of growing unemployment. These include, for example, not only the direct costs borne by undertakings as a result of absenteeism and labour instability, but also the effects of social conflicts and the need to increase taxation to ensure the continuation of essential public services and for the repair of the damage caused by the deterioration of the social structure (rise in delinquency, crime and vandalism). One trade union analysis puts forward two kinds of claims: one gives priority to reducing working time and the other to wage increases where these are feasible; namely, in economically well-protected sectors with strong union organisation. In the second case, in view of the continuing growth in productivity in some sectors, the wage increases might be quite considerable. The following sequence of effects is foreseen if this policy is followed: increased inequalities in gross earnings between economic sectors; failing measures to slow down the rise in unemployment, an aggravation of the tax burden, bringing down net wages; a breakdown of solidarity among workers and between workers and the unemployed; agitation against taxation and threats against maintenance of social security and the role of the State. The author adds that partial unemployment changes people's attitudes towards leisure; this will be the subject of more spontaneous demands in the future, even if there are no unemployment problems. Moreover, if satisfactory decisions are not taken in connection with reducing working time, technical progress and productivity may well be totally rejected by workers, which could inflict enormous damage on society.[96]

Adjustment role of transfer policy

The influence which policies concerning fiscal and social transfers may exercise in the event of a reduction in working time is mentioned in a number of studies. As was already indicated in Chapter 6, wages, the basis of social security contributions, may encourage undertakings to operate long working hours, which may even nullify the dissuasive effect expected from the obligation to pay overtime at premium rates. Furthermore, some writers suggest that the fresh financial resources that would become available as a result of any reductions in unemployment might be used to promote employment in various ways (such as through job creation programmes and aid to undertakings taking on new workers in the event of shorter working hours), or to help the most vulnerable undertakings to absorb the first effects of shorter working time on their costs. Thus, in the debate on reducing working time, fiscal and social transfers are brought forward not only as factors which, in the present state of affairs, may modify some of the effects, but also as instruments that may be used deliberately to try to maximise the positive effects and limit to the minimum any possible negative effects of reductions in working time on unemployment.

In this field of assistance intended to promote employment and to combat unemployment valuable experience has been gained, from which one should be able to draw useful lessons. However, with regard to the reduction of working time further thought may well be required. Many existing studies deal with the effects of subsidies to maintain employment and compensate for short-time working, which are quite different situations. In these cases judgements about the practical effects are not always favourable: some people fear that such assistance encourages less scrupulous employers to accept subsidies for filling jobs which they would have filled in any case to meet their own needs, or for pursuing staffing policies which are normal in times of economic difficulties, or that compensation for short-time working will discourage the creation of new jobs, delay the adoption of new technology, oust non-subsidised labour in favour of workers in respect of whom subsidies are payable, and aggravate the employment difficulties of young people. Other research finds more positive results.[97]

In the continuing discussion about possible assistance by the State to try to ensure that reductions in working time take place in the most favourable conditions, attention is frequently given to means of reducing labour costs. In practice, in Belgium payments are made to undertakings which introduce the 38-hour week and take on more workers, subject to certain conditions relating to the total number of employees.[98] In Finland subsidies are paid to undertakings which engage an unemployed person under 25 years of age for a job previously held by a worker taking early retirement; to prevent purely ephemeral hirings, the system provides that if the new young worker is dismissed and his job is not filled by recruitment of the same kind within the following month, the subsidy comes to an end.[99] This policy of alleviating labour costs is often the result of concern to protect the competitivity of the undertaking and, in this connection, some people propose that policies for reducing working time should be applied differently in different economic sectors, depending on whether or not the sector is protected against competition.

The effects which reductions in working time accompanied by such supporting measures may have do not appear to have been tested. As regards competitivity in international markets, their practical effects would depend on the role which labour costs play in this regard. Mention has already been made of the extreme complexity of factors affecting success in competition for markets. We may perhaps recall the relevant passages from the report prepared by the ILO for the tripartite technical conference on employment held in 1963. The observations made therein about disparities in wages may be extended to disparities in labour costs in general. They concern the relativity of the benefits that may result from lower labour costs and, conversely, of the disadvantages resulting from higher labour costs:

> The degree of dislocation that imports [of manufactured products from low-wage countries] may cause seems to depend much more upon how rapidly the imports in question increase and how narrowly they are concentrated over a particular range of types and styles than upon the level of wages paid in the exporting establishments. ... Producers in high-wage countries usually have compensating advantages enabling them to meet competition from low-wage countries, not in all lines of production but over a wide enough range of products to enable the high-wage countries to balance their international accounts — without such compensating advantages they could not have become high-wage countries.[100]

More recently, an article published under ILO auspices stressed that the survival of Western industries in a competitive world market rested on the ability to adjust (i.e. on versatility of management, technology and a skilled labour force) rather than on absolute advantages in terms of production costs.[101]

Lowering social charges for undertakings is one possible way of reducing labour costs. It is recalled that these may increase if, when shorter working hours are introduced, new workers are taken on to make up for the lost working hours. A lower retirement age does not impose supplementary charges on the undertaking, to the extent that pensions are the responsibility of social security schemes or special pension schemes; however, there may be indirect financial consequences if the undertaking is obliged to pay more to the pension schemes. It is often claimed that the usual methods of financing social security schemes, by increasing labour costs, penalise labour-intensive sectors and thus impede the growth of employment. Where there is a ceiling on the amount of earnings serving as the basis for contributions, the burden is relatively greater for workers earning low wages; an employer would be less at a disadvantage by employing a higher proportion of workers paid higher wages. Some writers believe that the chances for women and young workers to benefit from any work-sharing measures are lessened by the fact that they are usually less well paid. Removal of the ceiling on earnings serving as the basis for contributions penalises occupations involving a high proportion of brain-work and commanding higher salaries (the very activities it is desired to encourage in the industrially advanced countries). Another problem is frequently mentioned in the same context: while labour costs are increased by social charges, capital costs are artificially lowered by various forms of assistance from the State.[102] Thus the chances of increasing employment when working time is reduced would be distorted in favour of capital. Labour-intensive undertakings are particularly heavily penalised in this respect. Yet many sectors to which an

133

increase in spare time might give a boost are those particularly affected by the above-mentioned anomalies. These problems are currently under discussion, irrespective of the likelihood of a reduction in working time. In particular the question arises whether "true" prices should not be fixed in relation to the two production factors, including co-ordinated action in a number of countries, and whether the methods of financing social benefits should be changed.[103]

Another form of policy concerning transfers which arises in connection with problems of reducing working time is incomes policy. We have seen that wage maintenance plays a major role in many theories and that the idea of varying future increases in purchasing power is accepted by several trade union movements. At present governments resort increasingly to taxation and social transfers to bring about redistribution in favour of the lowest-paid, and by their policies with regard to inflation they have the possibility of helping to maintain the purchasing power of earnings. It is in this much wider context than that of merely maintaining wages (whether completely, partly or not at all) that we should look at the real effects on incomes of measures for reducing working time.

The range of measures available to the State for the purpose of co-ordinating fiscal and social transfers with the reduction of working time is wide enough to deserve a study of its own. Approaches different from those considered here may also be envisaged, such as those which rely on organising the solidarity of members of the community on as wide a basis as possible, to reduce inequalities. A far-reaching view of solidarity at the level of the community is expressed, for example, in the idea put forward some years ago that the cost of overtime should be heavily increased and that a large part of the resulting amounts should be paid into an unemployment fund.[104] Other proposals, based on the fact that the whole community contributes to improvements in productivity, may oblige us to look beyond the context of the undertaking or of a particular sector of the economy, and to link the question of possible reductions in working time with the progress of productivity in general.

Notes

[1] On this subject see, for example, Arielle Beyaert: "Influence de la réduction de la durée du travail dans les industries manufacturières belges", in *Cahiers économiques de Bruxelles* (Brussels, Université libre, 1976), No. 71, pp. 387-410.

[2] Dieter Mertens: "L'aménagement du temps de travail", in *Emploi et nouveaux modes de vie*, International conference, 29-30 November 1979, The Hague (Paris, Institut d'éducation, Fondation européenne de la culture), pp. 21-22. According to estimates made by the Institute for Labour Market and Occupational Research of Nuremberg, 824,000 jobs would have been vacated since 1973, which would have meant 900,000 unemployed instead of 1,720,000.

[3] See "Adaptation of working time: Impact of a reduction in the annual duration of work", in *European Economy* (Luxembourg, Commission of the European Economic Communities, Directorate-General for Economic and Financial Affairs), Mar. 1980, p. 96 (and also the references to Austria mentioned therein).

[4] Commission de l'emploi et des relations du travail: *L'aménagement et la réduction du temps de travail dans le contexte des années 80*, préparation du VIIIᵉ Plan, note pour la Commission, document de travail, 5 May 1980, p. 10.

[5] Lionel Stoleru: "Deux atouts contre le chômage", in *L'expansion* (Paris), No. 134, 5-18 Oct. 1979, pp. 136-139.

[6] Joyce M. Nussbaum and Donald E. Wise: "The overtime pay premium and employment", in *Worktime and employment*, Special report of the National Commission for Manpower Policy (Washington, DC, Special Report No. 28, Oct. 1978).

[7] Robert Clarke: *Adjusting hours to increase jobs*, Analysis of the options, Special report of the National Commission for Manpower Policy (Washington, DC, Special Report No. 15, Sep. 1977).

[8] *La Tribune de Genève*, 1 Oct. 1980. Estimate by the Council of State, which reckoned the supplementary expenditure resulting from these new appointments at 70 or 80 million Swiss francs.

[9] "Measures to alleviate unemployment in the medium term: Work-sharing", in *Department of Employment Gazette* (London), Apr. 1978, pp. 400-402.

[10] John Hughes: "A shorter working week: How the Department of Employment got it wrong", in *Workers' Control Bulletin* (Nottingham, Institute for Workers' Control), 1978, No. 6.

[11] Economic Commission for Europe: *Economic survey of Europe in 1979, Part I: The European economy in 1979* (New York, United Nations, 1980; Sales No. E.80.II.E.1).

[12] Commission of the European Communities: *Community guidelines on flexible retirement*, doc. COM (80) 393 final, 14 July 1980, Appendix I, p. 1.

[13] "Measures to alleviate unemployment in the medium term: Early retirement", in *Department of Employment Gazette* (London), Mar. 1978, pp. 283-285.

[14] Guy Spitaels: "The unemployment absorption programme in Belgium", in *International Labour Review* (Geneva, ILO), Mar.-Apr. 1979, pp. 149-164; *The European economy in 1979*, op. cit. in note 11, p. 38.

[15] "Adaptation of working time: Impact of a reduction in the annual duration of work", op. cit. in note 3, p. 110.

[16] *Community guidelines on flexible retirement*, op. cit. in note 12, Appendix I, p. 3.

[17] Mertens, op. cit. in note 2, pp. 8-9.

[18] Memorandum '79: *Vorrang für Vollbeschäftigung: Alternativen des Wirtschaftspolitik* (Cologne), Pahl-Rugenstein, Klein-Bibliothek 162, Politik-Wissenschaft-Zukunft, 1979), p. 79.

[19] "Adaptation of working time: Impact of a reduction in the annual duration of work", op. cit. in note 3, p. 104.

[20] Jean-Marie Luttringer and Bernard Pasquier: "Paid educational leave in five European countries", in *International Labour Review* (Geneva, ILO), July-Aug. 1980, pp. 407-423. See also Claude Dumont: *L'OIT et le congé-éducation payé*, Communication aux journées d'études sur le congé de formation en France et en Europe, Paris, 4-6 avril 1979, organisé par le Centre français pour le développement de l'information sur la formation permanente et le Centre européen pour le développement de la formation professionnelle (Geneva, ILO; doc. CONDIT/1980/3).

[21] *L'économie demain: marché, plan et concertation, ou anarchie, rigidité et corporatisme?*, Troisième Congrès des économistes belges de langue française, Centre universitaire de formation permanente, Namur, 17-18 novembre 1978, Commission 2: "Le travail", président Jef Rens, p. 126. Core workers in this context are those within the employing organisation who perform the functions that are necessary for its regular operation; their jobs are usually skilled, difficult to obtain, but stable and providing certain advantages (such as security, training, seniority benefits and career opportunities).

[22] Commission of the European Communities: *Voluntary part-time work*, Communication from the Commission, doc. COM (80) 405 final (Brussels, 17 July 1980), and especially the Annex to Document V/179-4/80-EN, 15 June 1980 appended thereto, pp. 16-18.

[23] *OECD Economic Outlook* (Paris), Dec. 1978, p. 34.

[24] "Adaptation of working time: Impact of a reduction in the annual duration of work", op. cit. in note 3, p. 96.

[25] *L'économie demain: marché, plan et concertation ou anarchie, rigidité et corporatisme?*, op. cit. in note 21, pp. 125-126.

[26] Sociaal-Economische Raad: *Rapport van de Commissie Economische Deskungiden Inzake Arbeidstijdverkorting* (The Hague, Uitgave van de Sociaal-Economische Raad, 1979), 28 Apr. 1979, summarised in *Social and Labour Bulletin* (Geneva, ILO), 4/79, pp. 393-394.

[27] L. Voogd: "Shift work in the Netherlands", in ILO: *Management of working time in industrialised countries* (Geneva, 1978), pp. 72-75.

[28] François Eymard-Duvernay: "Les 40 heures: 1936 ou ... 1980?", in *Economie et statistique* (Paris, Institut national de la statistique et des études économiques), June 1977, pp. 21-22.

[29] Jacques H. Drèze: *Salaires, emploi et durée du travail*, conférence pour le Colloque "Inflation, emploi et change", marquant le cinquième anniversaire de l'Institut de recherches économiques et

sociales de l'Université catholique de Louvain sur la base d'une étude de l'auteur et de Franco Modigliani (1979, mimeographed), pp. 16-18.

[30] *L'économie demain: marché, plan et concertation ...*, op. cit. in note 21, p. 125; and Mertens, op. cit. in note 2, pp. 1-2.

[31] Francis Blanchard: "More leisure — More work?", in *ILO Information* (Geneva, ILO), Oct. 1979, pp. 1-2.

[32] Fred Best: "The time of our lives: The parameters of lifetime distribution of education, work and leisure", in *Society and Leisure* (Prague, European Centre for Leisure and Education), May 1978, pp. 95-124; and idem: "Work time reforms in the future: Some long-range implications of expanded part-time jobs and flexitime in the Federal Government", in *Flexitime and part-time legislation*, Hearings before the Committee on Government Affairs, United States Senate, 95th Congress, Second Session, 29 June 1978, pp. 91-105. With updating of earlier calculations by Juanita Kreps and Joseph Spenger, the survey mentioned is the subject of the publication by Fred Best: *Exchanging earnings for leisure: Findings of an exploratory national survey on work time preferences*, Research and Development Monograph 79 (Washington, DC, United States Department of Labor, 1980), pp. 68-77.

[33] ILO: *Employment objectives and policies*, Report I, Preparatory Technical Conference on Employment, Geneva, 30 September-15 October 1963, p. 198.

[34] *The European economy in 1979*, op. cit. in note 11, table 1.11, provisional data. This refers to output per person employed, which is called "in short, labour productivity", in the text.

[35] For a recent account of this research, see "Adaptation of working time: Impact of a reduction in the annual duration of work", op. cit. in note 3, pp. 87-111.

[36] *Social and Labour Bulletin* (Geneva, ILO), 3/79, p. 292; and "Adaptation of working time: Impact of a reduction in the annual duration of work", op. cit.

[37] W. Driehuis and M. Bruyn-Hundt: "Einige effecten van arbeitstijdverkorting", in *Economisch Statistische Berichten* (Rotterdam), 21 Mar. 1979, pp. 289-300; and "Adapatation of working time: Impact of a reduction in the annual duration of work", op. cit., pp. 99-100.

[38] ibid., pp. 102-103.

[39] According to the specialists of the national institute of statistics and economic research, the models correspond to two plausible possible developments. A choice between them cannot be made on the basis of observation of the past, and their relevance can be judged only on the basis of an evaluation of economic trends at the time when the wage increases take effect.

[40] Gilles Oudiz, Emmanuel Raoul and Henri Sterdyniak: "Réduire la durée du travail, quelles conséquences?", in *Economie et statistique*, May 1979, pp. 3-16. The analyses relate to about 13 million out of a total of about 22 million gainfully employed persons. The gain in productivity was assumed to be zero in the medium term. The increase in the number of employed persons was expected to create greater tension in the labour market and cause pressure for rises in hourly wages. The rise in wages was assumed to be 72 per cent, to be added to expected normal wage increases.

[41] Mimeographed documents of the planning agency concerning the reduction of working time.

[42] L. Hujoel: "La réduction de la durée du travail", in *Socialisme* (Brussels), Feb. 1979, pp. 13-18.

[43] The Phillips curve assumes that partial absorption of unemployment, by strengthening the negotiating power of trade unions, will enable them to obtain greater wage increases. Objections have been raised against it, for structural and institutional reasons; see for example Economic Commission for Europe: *Economic survey of Europe in 1978*, Part I: *The European economy in 1978* (New York, United Nations; Sales No. E.79.II.E.1).

[44] A.B.T.M. Vanschaik: "Maken wij er werkelijk meer werk van?", in *Economische Statistische Berichten*, 16 May 1979, pp. 484-489, particularly table 6, p. 488, concerning the cumulative effects for each year; also "Adaptation of working time: Impact of a reduction in the annual duration of work", op. cit. in note 3, p. 100.

[45] Thérèse Debois-Pere and Richard de Falleur: "La croissance lente ne résout rien", in *Cahiers économique de Bruxelles* (Brussels, Université libre), 1979, No. 83, pp. 285-304. In the version of the model used, an exogenous reduction in average working time is supposed to reduce total production capacity proportionately, so that employment increases as a result of a rise in the rate of capacity utilisation. Thus no positive result of the reduction on labour productivity is assumed. The reduction is also reproduced in total wage costs, in the absence of an exogenous correction of hourly wages.

[46] Jean-Pierre Dumont: "La réduction du chômage nécessite une forte croissance des investissements et un freinage des salaires et de la consommation", in *Le Monde* (Paris), 14 June 1980, p. 41; Gilbert Mathieu: "Quelle politique sociale", ibid., 28 June 1980, p. 12; and "Le VIIIe plan: les scénarios de l'emploi", in *L'Express* (Paris), 14-20 June 1980, p. 116.

[47] Oudiz, Raoul and Sterdyniak, op. cit. in note 40. See also Commissariat général du plan: *Rapport du Comité emploi et travail*, préparation du VIIᵉ plan (Paris, La Documentation française, 1976), pp. 332-334.

[48] The compensating increase in wages was assumed to be 72 per cent on average, but it was combined with expected normal wage increases, bringing the total close to maintenance of the full wage.

[49] *Social and Labour Bulletin* (Geneva, ILO), 3/79, p. 292.

[50] "Adaptation of working time: Impact of a reduction in the annual duration of work", op. cit. in note 3.

[51] On the inadequacies noted, such as over-simplification, too high a level of aggregation, lack of flexibility, lack of internal coherence and ignorance of micro-economic situations and of sociological conditions, see for example Commissariat général du plan: *Rapport du Comité emploi et travail*, op. cit. in note 47, Ch. III, pp. 62-65. See also Pierre Boisard: *Bilan de recherches sur la réduction de la durée de travail* (Paris, Ministère du Travail et de la Participation, Centre d'études de l'emploi, Apr. 1979), pp. 23 and 23*bis*; and observations in "Adaptation of working time: Impact of a reduction in the annual duration of work", op. cit.

[52] See for example Denis Piet and André Zylberberg: "Le partage du travail: un enjeu économique", in *Droit social* (Paris), Jan. 1980 (issue devoted particularly to a symposium on work-sharing), pp. 67-74.

[53] For example, no distinction between nominal working time and time actually worked, definition of production capacity and labour demand in man-years (and not in number of hours), assimilation of labour cost to wage per worker (instead of hourly wage), failure to take account of the effects of changes in the number of hours paid on total wages and disposable income.

[54] Pierre Giraudet: *Rapport de mission* (on adjustment and reduction of working time), 22 Apr. 1980, mimeographed document, p. 10.

[55] ibid., p. 9.

[56] J. C. Gergoat: "La réduction de la durée hebdomadaire du travail dans l'entreprise: étude de 241 accords ou décisions unilatérales récentes", in *Travail et emploi* (Paris), Jan. 1980.

[57] *Intersocial*, Apr. 1979, p. 2.

[58] Frede Østergaard: "Methodology of long-term study in needs of the aged", in United Nations Economic Commission for Europe: *Approaches and methods used in long-term social planning and policy-making* (New York, United Nations document ECE/EC.AD/3; Sales No. E.73.II.E.7), p. 154.

[59] Second report of the Swedish delegation on questions of working time (SOU 1979:48), 28th Session of the Nordic Council, 1980.

[60] M. Grounin: *Social security issues affecting women*, Committee of Social Security Experts, Geneva, 26 November-3 December 1975, document CSSE/D.3 1975 (Geneva, ILO, 1975; mimeographed), p. 23.

[61] Pierre Boisard: "Enjeux d'une réduction de la durée du travail", in *Bulletin d'information* (Paris, Centre d'études de l'emploi), Apr. 1979, pp. 1-14.

[62] "On devrait être libre de gérer son temps", Interview with Mr. Jacques Delors, in *Le Nouvel Observateur* (Paris), 8 Jan. 1979, pp. 38-39. See also Xavier Greffe and Jocelyne Gaudin: "Partage du travail et mode de développement", in *Droit social*, Jan. 1980, pp. 86-99.

[63] J. de Givry: "Time to live -- Time to work", in *ILO Information*, May 1979, p. 10; see also Georges Spyropoulos: "New patterns of working time in industrialised countries: An international overview", in *Rivista di diritto internazionale e comparato del lavoro* (Padua), Jan.-Dec. 1978, pp. 187-200.

[64] Torkel Alfthan: "Level of living surveys in Sweden: Some issues and findings", in *International Labour Review*, Sep.-Oct. 1978, pp. 597-609.

[65] See the proceedings of the symposium on work-sharing in *Droit social*, Jan. 1980, and in particular Greffe and Gaudin, op. cit. in note 62, p. 39.

[66] Gabriel Ducray: "Vocational training today: The changing relationship between training and employment", in *International Labour Review* (Geneva, ILO), May-June 1979, pp. 265-281.

[67] Clément Michel: "General report on the round table meeting", in *Implications for social security of research on aging and retirement* (Geneva, International Social Security Association, 1977), Studies and Research, No. 9, pp. 67-74, especially pp. 70-71 (report of round table meeting, The Hague, 27-29 april 1976).

[68] See Economic Commission for Europe: *Planning and development of the tourist industry in the ECE Region* (New York, United Nations, 1976; Sales No. E.76.II.E.4), Ch. 2, pp. 26-30, and the references given in the footnotes to that chapter.

[69] See in particular Chantal Malenfant-Dauriac: *L'économie du sport en France*, TEM Analyse, Centre d'études des techniques économiques modernes, 1977, No. 7 (Paris, Cujas). In connection with the importance of a single sport in a national economy, see Gérard Albouy: "L'industrie du tennis: 1,5 milliard de chiffre d'affaires", in *Le Monde*, 17 June 1980, p. 25, and Annick Baumann: *Le tennis, monographie d'un secteur économique* (Montrouge, 1980) quoted therein.

[70] See, for France: "Les agents de voyage touchés par la crise pour la première fois", in *Le Monde*, 14 June 1980, p. 23.

[71] See the record of the 176th Plenary Session of the Economic and Social Committee of the European Communities, Brussels, 27-28 February 1980.

[72] Jacqueline Poelmans: "La société industrialisée actuelle, génératrice d'une diminution progressive du travail et d'une augmentation des loisirs", in *Les loisirs dans la société industrielle*, Congrès international "Les loisirs dans la société industrielle" organisé par la Fondation Van Clé, Brussels, 5-7 April 1973 (Antwerp, Fondation Van Clé, 1974), pp. 41-60.

[73] Klaus Schrape: "L'accroissement des loisirs et son incidence sur la demande des consommateurs", in *Le mois économique et financier* (Basle), 1980/3, pp. 4-9.

[74] Jonathan Hunt: "More play, more work", in *The Observer* (London), 27 Apr. 1980, p. 26.

[75] Francis Kinsman. "Profiting from a problem: Leisure in the eighties", in *The Times* (London), 28 Jan. 1980, p. 16; idem: *UK leisure markets: Survey and forecasts to 1985* (London, Staniland Hall Associates, Economic Advisers and Business Forecasters, 1979), pp. 14, 24-25, 49-52, 75 and 78.

[76] "Sharing the benefits of productivity", in *International Labour Review* (Geneva, ILO), July 1960, especially pp. 22-24.

[77] Dieter Kunz and Wolfgang G. Müller: "Productivity-oriented reduction of working-time as an instrument of employment policy", in *Mitteilungen aus der Arbeitsmarkt- und Berufsforschung* (Stuttgart, Berlin, Cologne, Mainz), 1977, No. 4, pp. 494-505 (in German with summary in English on p. 557).

[78] In France, for the Seventh Plan, for example, it was assumed that current trends would continue in the field of leisure.

[79] Henri Tezenas du Montcel: "Rénover la politique industrielle", in *Le Monde* (Paris), 13 Nov. 1979, pp. 21-22.

[80] See in this connection "La protection du cadre de vie des Européens", in *Trente jours d'Europe* (Paris, Commission des Communautés européennes), June-July 1979.

[81] "Filling in leisure time created by the silicon chip revolution", in *The Times* (London), 26 Jan. 1980, p. 5.

[82] Conseil de l'Europe, Comité directeur pour la sécurité sociale, Comité d'experts en matière de sécurité sociale dans sa composition d'actuaires: *Projet de rapport sur les effets combinés de l'abaissement de l'âge de la retraite et du vieillissement de la population sur le financement des régimes de sécurité sociale relatifs aux prestations long terme* (Strasbourg, 22 Feb. 1977; doc. CD/SS(77)1).

[83] Franco Marziale: "Resolution of the Council of Europe on social security measures to be taken in favour of pensioners and persons remaining in activity after pensionable age", in *International Social Security Review* (Geneva, International Social Security Association), 1976, No. 3, pp. 286-288.

[84] For the possible effects on taxes and social security contributions payable by retired persons, see Leif Haanes-Olsen: "Taxation and pensions", Ch. V of International Social Security Association: *Social security and taxation*, Studies and Research, No. 13 (Geneva, 1979). This study covers five industrialised countries. It seems that there are usually quite a significant number of older people below the tax threshold.

[85] "Measures to alleviate unemployment in the medium term: Early retirement", op. cit. in note 9, pp. 283-285.

[86] Joint authorship: "The labour market in the Federal Republic of Germany in 1979. Development, structural problems and employment policy measures", in *Mitteilungen aus der Arbeitsmarkt- und Berufsforschung*, 1979, No. 1, p. 24 (in German with summary in English on p. 59); see also *Community guidelines on flexible retirement*, op. cit. in note 12, Appendix II.

[87] Leonore Epstein Bixby: "Retirement age policy and employment", in *Work time and employment*, Special report of the National Commission for Manpower Policy (Washington, DC, Special Report No. 28, Oct. 1978), p. 396.

[88] Comment by Joseph Quinn (on the article by Leonore Epstein Bixby), ibid., pp. 397-409.

[89] Maryse Huet: "Emploi et activité entre 1968 et 1975", in *Economie et statistique*, Nov. 1977, pp. 59-63. The inter-country comparisons are based on the Community labour force survey of 1975. For a longer-term forecast (year 2000 and beyond) see Hervé Le Bras and Georges Tapinos: "Perspectives long terme de la population française et leurs implications économiques", in

Population (Paris, Institut national d'études démographiques), special issue, Dec. 1979, pp. 1391-1449.

[90] François Eymard-Duvernay: "Combien d'actifs d'ici l'an 2000?", in Economie et statistique, Oct. 1979 (Dossier Horizon 1985), pp. 33-46.

[91] i.e. whether the reference is to the proportion of the population that is "currently" or "usually" "economically active". This terminology is explained in ILO: *Report of the Conference*, 13th International Conference of Labour Statisticians, Geneva, 18-29 October 1982, Resolution concerning statistics of the economically active population, employment, unemployment and underemployment (in Appendix I, pp. 2-6).

[92] See ILO: *Older workers: Work and retirement*, Report VI (1), International Labour Conference, 65th Session, Geneva, 1979.

[93] David A. Bunnage: "Current research into work absence at the Danish National Institute of Social Research", in *Absenteeism and social security* (Geneva, International Social Security Association, 1981), Studies and Research, No. 16, pp. 53-57.

[94] Commission des Communautés Européennes: *Analyse comparative des instruments de la politique de l'emploi dans certains pays membres*, Etudes, Série politique sociale, No. 37 (Brussels, 1979), pp. 151-161. Taxes on consumption are included in receipts.

[95] See on this subject P.J. Sloane: "Economic aspects of shift and night work in industrialised market economies", in *International Labour Review* (Geneva, ILO), Mar.-Apr. 1976, pp. 129-142.

[96] L. Hujoel: "La réduction de la durée du travail", in *Socialisme* (Brussels), Feb. 1979, pp. 15-18.

[97] For a general view of this discussion, see the following contributions in OECD: *Collective bargaining and government policies* (Paris, 1979): R.A. Hart and P.J. Sloane: "Working hours and the distribution of work", pp. 247-263; and Harao Shimada: "Comment on paper by Hart and Sloane", pp. 265-272. See also Sar A. Levitan and Richard S. Belous: "Reduced worktime: Tool to fight unemployment", in *Worklife* (Washington, DC, United States Department of Labor, Employment and Training Administration), Apr. 1978, pp. 22-26; idem: "Work-sharing initiatives at home and abroad", in *Monthly Labor Review* (Washington, DC), Sep. 1977, pp. 16-20; Peter Sadlier-Brown: "Work-sharing in Canada: Problems and possibilities", in *HRI Observations* (Montreal, C.D. Howe Research Institute), June 1978; J.F. Colin and J.M. Espinasse: "Les subventions l'emploi, un essai d'analyse", in *Travail et emploi* (Paris), June 1979, pp. 37-49; R.W. Crowley: "Work-sharing and layoffs", in *Relations industrielles* (Quebec, Laval University), 1979, No. 2, pp. 329-334; "Canada: Experimental projects in work-sharing prove successful", in *Social and Labour Bulletin* (Geneva, ILO), 3/78, pp. 250-251; A. Calame: *Impact and costs of wage subsidy programmes: Experiences in Great Britain, Sweden and USA*, IIM Papers, IIM/80-1a (Berlin, International Institute of Management, July 1980); Robert Clark: *Adjusting hours to increase jobs, Analysis of the options*, Special report of the National Commission for Manpower Policy (Washington, DC, Special Report No. 15, Sep. 1977), pp. 48-50; *Work time and employment*, op. cit. in note 6, in particular Ch. III: "Work sharing, unemployment and the rate of economic growth", by Jeffrey M. Perloff and Michael L. Wachter, and "Comments" by Howard Young, Wassily Leontief and Courtenay M. Slater, pp. 101-141; and two mimeographed World Employment Programme research working papers with restricted distribution: Laurence Massenet: *Alleviating unemployment: The special programmes adopted in Great Britain* (Dec. 1977); and N. Phan-Thuy: *Controversies on marginal employment premiums as an anti-inflationary job promotion measure in industrialised countries*, a preliminary view (Mar. 1979).

[98] A plan for subsidies providing for higher payments was condemned by the Commission of the European Communities as being in violation of the principle of price competition among member States, as laid down in the Treaty of Rome. See *Bulletin of the European Communities* (Luxembourg, Office for Official Publications of the European Communities), 1979, No. 10, p. 28; and *European Industrial Relations Review* (London), Oct. 1979, p. 4.

[99] *Social and Labour Bulletin* (Geneva, ILO), 4/79, p. 409.

[100] ILO: *Employment objectives and policies*, op. cit. in note 33, p. 227.

[101] Gus Edgren: "Employment adjustment to trade under conditions of stagnating growth", in *International Labour Review* (Geneva, ILO), May-June 1978, p. 292.

[102] See in particular: *L'économie demain: marché, plan et concertation, ou anarchie, rigidité et corporatisme?*, rapport de la Commission 2: "Le travail", op. cit., pp. 122-126. Also Commission of the European Communities, Directorate-General for Social Affairs: *Outlook for employment in the European Community to 1980*, Report on the first phase of the work of the Group of Independent Experts, document V/409/76-E (Brussels, July 1976), particularly pp. 49-51.

[103] See for example International Social Security Association: *Methods of financing social security: Their economic and social effects*, Studies and Research, No. 15 (Geneva, 1979).

[104] Jean-Jacques Dupeyroux: "Un autre partage du travail", in *Le Monde*, 17 May 1977, p. 44. This idea was taken up by the French Minister of Labour and Participation ("La réduction de la durée du travail", in *Lettre d'information de l'ANACT*, Oct. 1979).

CONCLUSIONS: DESIDERATA

8

Having reached this point, we should normally ask ourselves questions such as these: Are there any reasons for taking specific action with regard to working time, or is the continuing trend towards shorter working time enough in itself? If it is necessary to foster or hasten this trend, to what extent should we do so and how? What difficulties would arise if we were to respond to the current proposals made about shortening working time? What advantages would be gained? Is it necessary to shorten working time in order to reduce unemployment? Is reduction essential to bring about an improvement in the quality of life? While a great deal has been written about all these questions, the results of that research do not put forward very convincing answers. They are very limited in scope, unbalanced and usually far too theoretical. Moreover, they leave unanswered a number of prior questions facing parliaments and governments, which would have to introduce the necessary incentives and regulations to diminish the negative effects of shorter working time and strengthen its positive effects. Would they be willing to do so, and if so how? What priorities should they follow?

A COMPREHENSIVE POLICY

One point comes out constantly in the present study: the need to avoid considering a reduction in working time as an isolated, exogenous measure, to be taken without consideration of its side-effects. Reductions that are part of the long-term trend towards shorter working hours meet this condition; that is why they are generally accepted as raising few problems. It is when an attempt is made to hasten the trend that risks may arise in the economic field, particularly as regards inflation and the balance of payments, with the added danger that unemployment will be not reduced but aggravated. However, this kind of thinking rests on the assumption that economic and employment policies are unchanging. If those policies were changed, the pessimistic forecasts just mentioned might also change.

It seems to be generally accepted that the effects of reductions in working time would depend on the policies applied to bring them about, on other measures accompanying and supporting them, and on the political, economic and social context in which those measures were applied. In the earlier chapters of this study an attempt was made, wherever possible, to describe the role of the general context and of such accompanying and supporting measures, but it was, of course, not possible to analyse in detail the wide areas in which new approaches should be sought: economic policy, employment policy, development of human resources, income transfers and redistribution, protection of the physical environment and use of leisure time, to mention only a few.

However, as regards policies for reducing working time as such, we are obliged to conclude that the assumptions made in the studies reviewed in the present book generally exclude the possibility of a coherent approach relying on flexible recourse to a variety of measures with a view to attaining selected objectives. They seem to ignore the experience obtained during several decades of steady reduction of working time and the multiplicity of methods that have been developed, both in the day-to-day operation of undertakings and in the fields of industrial relations and social policy. There is no reason why those measures should not play their part in the future as they have done in the past.

Current thinking about reduction of working time, as expressed in official reports or in statements by workers' and employers' organisations, is directed towards gradual, flexible approaches taking maximum account of economic constraints and individual preferences with regard to work, leisure and income. Such approaches must be imaginative, and often call for innovation. A case in point is the choice in favour of more leisure and less income, which implies that workers are willing to exchange future increases in purchasing power against a qualitative improvement in their standard of living and that employers are prepared to grant benefits that raise difficult management problems, instead of wage increases that are more or less automatically reflected in prices. This is also the case with regard to a reduction in annual working time, which requires complex adjustments of existing arrangements for compensatory rest and guaranteed leave if the existing spirit of social protection is to be respected, misunderstandings avoided and adequate supervision exercised. It is equally true of the difficult problem of reducing overtime, which is given priority in many countries. Here there may be scope for a combination of practical arrangements, restrictive provisions together with complex combinations of wage increases, compensatory rest periods and redistribution of income in favour of the lower paid. Analyses of the effects of a reduction in working time do not assess the possible effects of such diverse measures; it may indeed be an impossible task.

We have also seen that except in some evaluations of theoretical job equivalents, very little has been written about the consequences of a combination of several separate measures for reducing working time, yet in practice in preparation for the adoption of policies in this field a number of measures might be considered, such as raising the school leaving age and introducing paid educational leave. The latter, which has been excluded from the present study because it is not mentioned in most of the analyses of effects that have been made, might in fact play a central role. It not only represents free time away from work; it may also contribute to correcting qualitative and quantitative imbalances in labour supply and demand, increase productivity and improve competitiveness. Against the background of the far-reaching changes taking place in advanced industrial societies, paid educational leave has a specific role to play in connection with increased leisure time: it is an exceptionally useful way of enabling people to acquire the new knowledge required for a better understanding of the world in which they live and for better utilisation of their leisure time.

The analyses which have been reviewed here also did not attempt to test the possible effects of a combination of several methods of reducing working time to achieve selective objectives. For example, a reduction in working time combined with a lowering of the age of retirement may aggravate shortages in certain skilled occupations, but this danger can be overcome by developing paid educational leave and, while awaiting newly trained skilled workers, by postponing shorter working hours or lower retirement age for employees with skills in short supply or by encouraging them to cumulate gainful employment with their retirement pension. The idea of programming reductions in working time so as to avoid bottlenecks does not seem to have been explored in any depth.

We also need to ascertain the possible effects of reductions in working time by placing them in the wider context of an overall policy comprising all aspects of working time. The policy to be followed with regard to part-time employment, for example, may modify some of these effects. It is now clear that several countries are interested in this form of employment, but it is not always possible to discover whether it is intended to be a substitute or a complement for reduced normal working time. For people who are opposed to shorter working time without loss of earnings, part-time employment offers the advantage that it corresponds to a large-scale reduction in working time, but without maintenance of earnings. If its development is given priority, unemployed persons seeking full-time work might be obliged to accept part-time employment, in other words to accept lower wages if they have no other means of subsistence. The fear has been expressed that concentration on part-time employment may disturb a negotiated reduction of working time, or even put it in jeopardy.

The combination of reduced working time with the development of voluntary part-time work might open up new horizons for the community as a whole. The costs resulting from shorter working time with maintenance of previous earnings might in fact be counterbalanced by savings and receipts from the extension of part-time working, while benefits might also accrue from a fall in unemployment. Similarly, the risk of contraction in the demand for goods and services which part-time working might engender might be counterbalanced by the support for demand resulting from the maintenance of previous earnings accompanying reductions in working time, and from any increase in employment. Such arguments, which might be correct at the level of the economy as a whole if compensation between advantages and disadvantages were fully operative, would not necessarily also be correct at the level of particular undertakings. Appropriate transfer measures might restore the balance in such cases. It would be worth testing a strategy of this kind, if that were feasible; it would be of benefit to undertakings, in enabling them to exercise greater flexibility in their management of the workforce, and also to employees who want more humane conditions and more individual treatment in their conditions of work. However, there are obstacles to the development of demand for voluntary part-time employment. It is sometimes impeded by uncertainty about the status of part-time work. Removal of this uncertainty is therefore essential; moreover, this would contribute to eliminating misunderstandings that seem to exist among many people about the connection between reduced working time and part-time employment, and might also render discussion of these questions less acrimonious.

The need for comprehensive policies must also be considered at another level: that of co-ordinated action among nations. Many people believe that this is essential if we are to avoid a situation in which a country reducing working time on its own finds itself at a competitive disadvantage internationally. We have seen that this argument, which relates more specifically to the part played by labour costs as a factor in winning and retaining markets, is a matter of controversy. However, whether or not it has any basis in fact, it has always slowed down or even paralysed social progress, particularly during slumps, when it becomes a real obsession. This was recognised long ago by the ILO, which as early as 1931 observed that it was realistic to acknowledge that "even if the conditions governing international competition are less incompatible than has often been thought with an improvement in working conditions in any one country, the fear inspired by such competition is clearly an obstacle to improvements of a social nature".[1] Parallel improvement of conditions of work in a number of countries simultaneously may help to overcome this obstacle.

At present the principle of co-ordinated action with regard to arrangement of working time is accepted at the level of the European Communities. This action, which would include some measures for reducing working time, raises complex problems. International competition exists among all industrialised countries and between the latter and the economically less developed countries. However, industrialised countries have the advantage of being able to benefit from rapidly developing new technologies. The question is whether they will be able to ensure that these new technologies serve social progress. According to the Commission of the European Communities, the large increases in productivity made possible by new micro-electronic technology constitute one of the essential prerequisites for reducing annual working time and overtime, while safeguarding ability to compete.[2]

APPROPRIATE MEASURES

An essential feature of current discussions on reduction of working time is the role played by evaluations of the practical steps to be taken. Yet the proliferation of studies, particularly macro-economic ones, increasingly gives the impression that there is a gap between abstract reasoning, which sometimes makes it appear that a theoretical impossibility exists, and economic and social reality. One of the most important changes that has occurred in the analysis of effects is the progress made in micro-economic and sociological understanding. The previous chapters have presented a number of examples. They provide information that may help to define the most suitable measures to be taken in practice. Generally speaking, it seems that the problems to be faced will be more complex than abstract reasoning would lead us to expect. They may therefore appear to be harder to overcome; but they are practical, technical problems, and the case studies that are beginning to pile up reveal a great wealth of capacity for adjustment and a lively imagination in the search for fresh solutions for these problems.

The measures that can be taken to introduce or promote reductions in working time are many and various. The research devoted to the consequences they may have usually neglect this fact. We will restrict ourselves here to emphasising two particularly important aspects. The first, which is of capital importance if any reductions in working time are going to succeed in industrialised, market economy countries, is the machinery of industrial relations. As has been pointed out, labour-management relations and the nature of collective bargaining exercise an influence on the efficacy of policies and the performance of the economy.[3] The existence and participation of employers' and workers' organisations and the practice of collective bargaining are essential if reduced working time is to become a feasible proposition; but the reduction of working time brings yet other interests into play. Some United States economists believe that the essential issues of the controversy about working time and employment are of a normative, political rather than economic character. To be sure, economic principles are involved but, on this view, their role is in the nature of an incantation: we must keep up the appearance of economic discourse although the real issues depend upon the power relationships between unions and management and different political groups.[4] Observations of this kind introduce a dimension into the debate that is largely absent from previous studies.

The second aspect, closely linked with the first, is that in practice replies have to be found to specific questions not only about the role of collective bargaining in any process of reducing working time but also about the possible usefulness of legislative or regulatory action. Does collective bargaining render such action pointless? Or should collective bargaining lead the way toward such action? Would such action be useful in promoting or supplementing collective bargaining? The questions arise mainly in connection with the reduction of daily, weekly or yearly working time, whereas a lowering of the retirement age essentially concerns social security schemes. For the time being, reduction of working time is being left to the processes of collective bargaining, whereas government action tends to concentrate on lowering maximum working hours, and in some cases on promoting collective bargaining through various inducements.

The role to be played by any legislative or regulatory action will obviously depend upon the traditions of each country. It may be deemed necessary, for example, to ensure that all employed persons have the same chance of enjoying the benefits of social progress; it makes it possible to correct the result of action by pressure groups, and thus tip the balance in favour of the underprivileged, or to create deliberate inequalities in compensation for such factors as the harshness of certain kinds of work, or for the special vulnerability of certain categories of workers such as those who are young or ageing, as well as pregnant women and parents of young children. Without necessarily laying down strict standards to be applied immediately, laws or regulations may establish a framework accompanied by a variable time-scale corresponding to various economic and social constraints, while leaving maximum leeway to collective bargaining. If the central role is left to negotiations, there still remains the question of the extent, depending on the objective, to which such negotiations may need to be co-ordinated, given generalised application or supplemented to fill the gaps that they will obviously leave in relation to some sections of the community. These various possible courses of action are not assessed in the studies reviewed in earlier chapters; it would seem that it is impossible to do so with the analytical tools currently available.

The most controversial issue of all is one of principle, namely whether a standard lower than 40 hours a week should be established. In some cases the existence of the standard of the 40-hour week seems to set up a psychological blockage that is harmful to further progress in reducing working time. The dominant attitude in official circles is in favour of new regulations based on a diminution of annual working time. This approach is viewed favourably at the level of the European Communities because it has the advantage of leaving the choice open between reduction of weekly working hours and prolongation of annual holidays; it is also considered that it makes possible a more coherent approach to national situations from the points of view of economic conditions, costs and social progress. There is very little practical experience on which to draw for judging what the chances are of reducing working time satisfactorily on a yearly basis. While such a course may appear theoretically attractive, many trade unions fear that it will cause them to lose many of the social guarantees they have so hardly won in past social conflicts. To help to overcome this kind of suspicion, it would be useful to specify without delay whatever new social guarantees are to be provided.

If we consider possible reduction in working time from the point of view of the objectives it is hoped to achieve, we may find that this has consequences for the kind of measures to be adopted. As has been seen, reductions in working time may be proposed for a variety of reasons (improvement in the quality of life, at work and away from work; sharing the fruits of improvements in productivity; a contribution to bringing down unemployment). As these reductions are carried out, a large number of factors may play a role (organisation of work, remuneration, nature of jobs, personnel and human resources management, productivity, profitability). Among the objectives proposed, there is no doubt that it is the contribution to improving the employment situation that gives rise to the most complicated problems in practice. Collective bargaining seems to be the most suitable means of dealing, within specific production sectors, with ways of avoiding dismissals through reductions in working time combined with work-sharing, and with filling the jobs of workers who retire, though the main general decisions about the number of workers to be employed remain the prerogative of management. The redistribution of work proposed by some people who want to reduce unemployment by this means goes beyond work-sharing: it calls for a co-ordinated approach on the two fronts of reduction of working time and active employment policies, the latter being supported by appropriate policies with regard to the economy and to transfer payments. This raises the question of the fundamental political options in each country.

If it is limited to the objective of participation in the benefits of improved productivity, a reduction of working time ought not to raise any new problems. It was an integral part of past developments. Nevertheless, although the upward trend in productivity is continuing, it would appear that there are impediments to the reduction of working time which should accompany it. This is hard to explain. Many of the studies of the possible effects of reductions in working time even give the impression that the situation has become frozen, and take into consideration no productivity gains other than those resulting from the reductions themselves. These ideas are difficult to reconcile not only with the trends mentioned above but also with the spectacular advances to be foreseen from the development of micro-computers and telecommunications.

It may be that there is a misunderstanding due to the different connotations associated with standards laid down in laws or regulations. These lay down minimum protection (in this particular case a level of working time not to be exceeded except in clearly defined conditions, or a minimum amount of paid annual leave). This protection is merely a minimum, yet there is a tendency to regard it as a ceiling. Perhaps this is due to the fact that for an employer the theoretical choice between giving the workers more free time or more earnings is not as open as the theory of sharing the benefits of improved productivity supposes. If the undertaking hopes to market an increased output, it has no interest in trying to maintain its output at the existing level while reducing working time; if it does reduce working time, it can increase output only by overcoming problems relating to investment, recruitment, training and organisation. If it does not feel itself constrained to reduce working time by the existence of a statutory standard, it will naturally choose the option of raising wages. If these arguments are correct, two conclusions have to be drawn. First, the role played by appropriate social standards as incentives to action is irreplaceable in this situation. Secondly, we should not underestimate the technical problems that a reduction in working time involves for management even when the reduction does no more than reflect improvements in productivity. Costs are not the only determining factor, and for technical reasons it is important that management should be given reasonable time to adjust, particularly in periods of economic difficulty.

A DYNAMIC APPROACH

Because of the rapidity of change in the industrialised countries, a reduction of working time requires a dynamic approach. The analyses made of effects of such reduction do not always meet this requirement, and their conclusions are therefore bound to inspire serious reservations. It is particularly important that certain changes should be borne in mind. They relate to the structure of economic activities, the characteristics of the economically active population, work and employment. In the countries under consideration here, production comprises a growing proportion of items that are not tangible and not quantifiable; this relates both to the inputs of material production and to social or even artistic activities the aim of which is to improve the welfare and raise the cultural level of the people. However, the most detailed analyses made have concentrated on material production and, within those limits, on forms of work where the product can be quantified by outside observers: in other words manual labour above all, or to be more precise repetitive manual labour. They make extrapolations from this basis, closely examining the possible evolution of a form of production that is only a small part of actual production in advanced industrial societies. If there were an extension of free time, non-quantifiable production ("do-it-yourself", voluntary work) would also grow. Moreover, advanced economies rely increasingly on employing people with high qualifications. Analyses made hitherto assume that capital and labour are mutually exclusive, whereas in the activities with a high "knowledge content" that carry the seeds of the future an essential part of capital is in fact incorporated in the workforce.

Current changes in the nature of production in advanced industrialised societies therefore reopen the question of the productivity concept. In much of the discussion, the growth of productivity is considered as imposing an upper limit to be respected lest shorter working time endanger the economy. Thus a vital social issue depends on a questionable concept. In the economies considered here, actual production comprises a rapidly growing proportion of activities of a social nature or activities which contribute only indirectly to material production and which for purely conventional reasons bear the stigma of being "unproductive". Yet, as one productivity expert said in epigramatic terms about some of these activities: "It is by writing that one produces the best potatoes." He was alluding to all those activities which do not have a direct physical effect on production but which nevertheless contribute to it in decisive fashion: in general, such non-manual activities as forecasting, lengthy intellectual analysis, management, accountancy, legal services and research and development.[5] For the purposes of the present study, we need to know whether currently employed systems of measurement of productivity give a satisfactory picture of economic results.[6] Logically, the latter are likely to be underestimated at the level of the community if the methodology used does not change while there is an increasing proportion of activities the real product of which is underestimated.

Work and employment are also undergoing deep changes. Reduction of working time, which is the variable linking work and employment, would therefore come to pass in a shifting environment. The concept of employment ought itself to be more flexibly defined, particularly since the relationship between employment and end-product is becoming increasingly indirect; moreover, "people in employment should not be added together, they supplement one another".[7] Jobs interact, and the dynamism that shorter working time might set off might lead to some unexpected results. Ways of calculating working time ought therefore to be as flexible as possible. Some writers go so far as to say "if we do not think of the volume of labour supply in terms of hours per year rather than of persons ... it will be an illusion to expect to be able to cope with present and future employment problems in the industrialised countries".[8]

Scientific and technical progress promises spectacular increases in productivity and should make it possible to reduce working time considerably in the future and to restructure jobs in relation to the reduced working time. This operation should be facilitated by the fact that in advanced industrialised economies it is less and less possible, in an increasing number of functions, to establish a linear relation between a given "quantity" of work to be performed and a strictly determinable period of time, and hence volume and length of employment, which is itself determined by the problematical number of hours of work required. Numerous factors outside the individual worker's control exercise an increasing influence on final results, and their connection with a period of physical presence at the workplace is becoming increasingly tenuous. This trend may accelerate in future, and may even reopen the traditional question of separation of home and workplace. Futurists talk of the possibilities that computer terminals offer in that respect in numerous occupations. Work would be done at home, an arrangement which would bring with it such advantages as flexible work schedules, better work environment, facilitated care of children, decongestion of urban centres and of the highway network and savings in energy. The notion of working time, which is still closely linked with physical presence at a specific place, may lose part of its justification as a means of supervision of the work performed by the employee and as a criterion for setting rates of remuneration.

An increase in free time (which is the corollary of reduced working time) would probably hasten this change. The few analysts who have considered this aspect of the question forecast expansion in service activities if this happens. The balance between time at work and away from work has already been upset, and further reductions in working time would probably raise problems that would constitute real challenges to our society. Even if it is no longer necessary for production, in its present form and as it is now measured, to continue to grow, the likelihood is that its structure will have to change to meet new economic and social demands resulting from a preference for more leisure rather than more income. Difficult decisions will have to be made not only as to a shift in economic activities but also with a view to overcoming the resistance of established group interests which have developed on the basis of the existing organisation of production. To mention only problems affecting employees, what is spare time for one set of persons tends to be working time for others in all services requiring direct contact with the public or with customers, and this situation raises problems that are far from being resolved.

As to the possible effects of any reduction in working time, it would be useful to have analyses reaching further into the future and taking into consideration different possible models for advanced industrial societies. The brief section on the effects of increased spare time shows how few tools we have to do this, while the developments just outlined show how necessary it is. Such analyses would provide useful indications for deciding whether, for example, an attempt should already be made at this stage to focus the movements towards a reduction in working time so as to keep future developments under control, perhaps in co-ordination with measures to promote a shift in economic activities. Would such action open up new prospects of solving the serious unemployment problems we can foresee in the future? This is a question that must be answered as a matter of urgency.

From the analyses reviewed here, it appears that large-scale reductions in working time would be required to split up the work to be done into a larger number of jobs and to bring about changes in ways of living that would be sufficiently marked to give a spurt to industrial economies in difficulty. But it also appears that the larger the reductions and the faster they are carried out, the greater the danger of bottlenecks, and thus of arriving at results quite contrary to what was hoped for, if we accept the hypothesis of an otherwise static situation. Gradual reductions under determinedly forward-looking overall policies would help to overcome the difficulty. It should be an aim of the continuing research in this rapidly developing area to provide us with answers to this problem.

Notes

[1] *The International Labour Organisation: The first decade*, Preface by Albert Thomas (London, Allen and Unwin, 1931), p. 31.

[2] Commission of the European Communities: *Employment and the new micro-electronic technology* (communication from the Commission), session of the Standing Employment Committee on 26 February 1980, doc. COM (80) 16 final (Brussels, 5 Feb. 1980), p. 4.

[3] Haruo Shimada: "Comment on paper by Hart and Sloane", in Organisation for Economic Co-operation and Development: *Collective bargaining and government policies*, Papers presented and report of general rapporteur, Conference held at Washington, DC, 10-13 July 1978 (Paris, 1979), pp. 270 and 272.

[4] Jeffrey M. Perloff and Michael L. Wachter: "Work sharing, unemployment and the rate of economic growth", in *Work time and employment*, Special report of the National Commission for Manpower Policy (Washington, DC, Special Report No. 28, Oct. 1978), p. 88.

[5] Jean Fourastié: *La productivité* (Paris, Presses universitaires de France, 1980), pp. 86-87.

[6] See in particular Albert Rees: "Improving the concepts and techniques of productivity measurement" (recommendations of the Panel to Review Productivity Statistics, funded by the National Center for Productivity and Quality of Working Life), in *Monthly Labor Review* (Washington, DC), Sep. 1979, pp. 23-27. One of the conclusions was that no new source of error in measurement had appeared, and that there was therefore no underestimate of productivity gains.

[7] Alfred Sauvy: *La machine et le chômage: le progrès technique et l'emploi* (Paris, Dunod, 1980), p. 303.

[8] Luigi Frey: "L'impact des changements structurels dans l'offre de travail sur le chômage et le sous-emploi", in the publication of the European Cultural Foundation: *Emploi et nouveaux modes de vie*, International conference, The Hague, 29-30 November 1979 (Paris, Institut d'éducation, Fondation européenne de la culture), p. 35.